GALEN ON FOOD
AND DIET

D0165581

The modern world is fascinated by diet and the effect it can have on health, with advice abounding on what we should or should not eat. This pre-occupation was also very much a feature of the ancient world, at least among those who could afford the time and money to listen to the advice of a doctor.

At the apogee of ancient medical advances stood Galen (AD 129–c. AD 210), once the personal physician to the emperor Marcus Aurelius. A prolific writer, among his surviving works is what he believed to be the definitive guide to a healthy diet, based on the theory of the four humours. In these treatises Galen sets out this theory, which was to be profoundly influential on medicine for many centuries, and describes in fascinating detail the effects on health of a vast range of foods, from lettuce, lard and fish to peaches, pickles and hyacinths.

Galen on Food and Diet makes all these texts available in English for the first time, and provides many captivating insights into the ancient under-standing of food and health. With clear, elegant translations, supported by a lucid introduction, helpful notes, and an extensive bibliography, this volume is an invaluable resource for classicists, ancient historians and all those interested in the history of food.

Mark Grant is a Classics teacher at Haileybury College in Hertford. He has worked as a cook and trained in catering management, and has researched into Roman food and diet for more than twenty years. His previous publi-cations include *Anthimus: On the Observance of Foods* (1996), *Dieting for an Emperor* (1997) and *Roman Cookery: Ancient Recipes for Modern Kitchens* (1999).

GALEN ON FOOD AND DIET

Mark Grant

London and New York

First published 2000
by Routledge
11 New Fetter Lane, London EC4P 4EE

Simultaneously published in the USA and Canada
by Routledge
29 West 35th Street, New York, NY 10001

Routledge is an imprint of the Taylor & Francis Group

© 2000 Mark Grant

Typeset in Sabon by
Curran Publishing Services Ltd
Printed and bound in Great Britain by
Biddles Ltd, Guildford and King's Lynn

British Library Cataloguing in Publication Data
A catalogue record for this book is available
from the British Library.

Library of Congress Cataloging-in-Publication Data
Galen
[Selection. English. 2000]
Galen on food and diet / [Translation and notes by] Mark Grant.
224 pp. 15.6 x 23.4 cm.
Includes biographical references and index.
1. Nutrition – Early works to 1800.
2. Diet therapy – Early works to 1800.
I. Title: On food and diet. II. Grant, Mark. III. Title.
QP 141.G25213 2000
613.2–dc21   00-036628

ISBN 0-415-23232-5 (hbk)

ISBN 0-415-23233-3 (pbk)

In memory of Fred Luck
1909–1993
and Maria Luck (née Szántó)
1899–1988
for their humanity and generosity

CONTENTS

ACKNOWLEDGEMENTS

In that remarkable novel *The French Lieutenant's Woman* by John Fowles there is a scene where a doctor has a discussion with a geologist. This is not a notable event in itself: the twist is that they both have common scientific ground. The nineteenth century witnessed the twilight of that general unity of arts and sciences which stretched back to the philosophers of the sixth century BC living on the Aegean coast of what is now Turkey. Then medicine was so closely linked with philosophy that later scientific progress was virtually strangled by the desire to force logical perfection on to nature.

There are few today who can claim to be as conversant in one discipline as the other, for the sum of knowledge has expanded multifariously. Galen could write on anything from linguistic problems to the intrigues in the imperial palace, but he was an intellectual giant even in his own age. Any errors in this book must therefore be ascribed to my lay conceptions of medicine, although my own fascination with things medical is surely the result of my being born into a family of physicians.

Many people have inspired me in my work, but at the cost of seeming invidious I would like to mention just two of them. Professor Elizabeth Craik has been my academic lodestone amidst the hurly-burly of school teaching, whilst Professor Ian Kidd afforded me the priceless opportunity to engage in postgraduate study at the lovely University of St Andrews where I first began reading Galen. My dear Alison, Anna and Toby have kindly shown their indulgence in my classical preoccupations without branding me as too eccentric a father and husband.

Mark Grant
Haileybury College,
January 2000

ix

1

INTRODUCTION

The life of Galen

Medicine occupies a central position in our lives today. We expect to be diagnosed correctly and to receive the latest treatment based on extensive scientific research. The media enthusiastically recount breakthroughs in our understanding of disease, or complex operations that can restore our quality of life. Alongside this progress psychologists have noted our increasing bewilderment and even anger in the face of death. Wonder at what medicine can achieve is disturbed by what it cannot. It is difficult then to envisage a world where medicine could offer only some comfort and where death, especially among the very young, was always lurking as a very real threat. Yet many historians concede that palliative care by Galen would have been far preferable to anything that was to be available until the closing years of the nineteenth century.

Galen was born in AD 129 at Pergamum, a large city on the Aegean seaboard of what is now Turkey.[1] As his father was an architect and interested in education, Galen was given lessons in mathematics and geometry. For a child from a wealthy background this was in some ways unusual, the emphasis in Roman schools being on the literature and rhetoric necessary for a career as a lawyer or a town councillor. On the other hand architecture, whilst an essential part of Roman civilisation, was not a profession that commanded a particularly high status. This liberal and in some ways radical background allowed Galen the scope to experiment: he was not bound by his family to enter into what was regarded as a traditionally safe career. Moreover, since Pergamum had long been an intellectual and cultural centre, Galen was able to attend the lectures of the Stoic and Platonist philosophers who were attracted to the city by its great library. It is an indication of his mental abilities that Galen was only fourteen when he began these studies.

In addition to its academic excellence, Pergamum was a religious centre with a large sanctuary dedicated to Asclepius. As the son of Apollo, Asclepius acted like a bridge between the divine and the human, for although he was a powerful deity, he was nevertheless concerned enough with mortals to try to combat death through his patronage of medicine. Healing by psychological means was conducted at temples around the Roman world, the sick sleeping in the precincts in the hope of dreaming about their own particular cures.[2] Even outside the temples, dreams were held to predict the future and advise on future courses of action. When Galen was seventeen his father received such a sign: he was to study medicine.

Hippocrates wrote in the fifth century BC that a good doctor should travel.[3] On the death of his father in AD 148 (or perhaps AD 149), Galen spent a number of years training with medical experts in Smyrna, Corinth and Alexandria.[4] There was no uniform medical curriculum or even a shared belief in how the body worked. Instead there were groups of adherents to several different theories, sometimes referred to as schools, based around opposing philosophical premises.[5] Now fully trained, Galen returned to Pergamum in AD 157 and became the doctor to the gladiatorial school in the city. Again, this was an unusual step for an educated person. Gladiators may have fascinated the Romans by their oath of submission to death, but they were still considered socially to be very low or even outside the accepted laws of normal society.[6]

What Galen presumably gained from this appointment was a detailed knowledge of anatomy. Contrary to modern popular belief, gladiators did not usually fight deliberately to the death, especially in a provincial city like Pergamum. Whilst Rome could afford mass slaughter, the expense of training and maintaining gladiators meant that any other city had to harbour its resources. Gladiators were taught to draw blood for the entertainment of the spectators, but once outside the arena doctors were at hand to stitch and bandage ready for the next show. That is not to say that death was avoided, yet it was not a foregone conclusion.[7] Working with gladiators also allowed Galen to experiment with regulating the diet for healing and building strength. In many instances diet was the only resource that could be applied, so its prominence in all ancient medical writings is understandable.

In the absence of a police force, except in Rome itself, ancient cities were prone to social unrest. The autumn of AD 161 saw Galen leaving Pergamum to avoid being caught up in such an event, perhaps provoked by the sort of food shortages that he mentions throughout his dietetic writings. He travelled around the eastern Mediterranean, researching the properties of various plants and minerals used medicinally in Lemnos, Cyprus and Palestinian Syria (modern Israel), before reaching Rome in the summer of the following year.[8]

Marcus Aurelius had just become emperor. Rome was at the height of its power and prosperity. Galen began to build up his reputation in the capital, giving public lectures and anatomical demonstrations and writing about anatomy. These endeavours came to a close in the summer of AD 166. A Roman army returning from a campaign in the Middle East brought with it the plague and Galen seems to have thought it wiser to return to Pergamum than to try to practise his medicine on those afflicted. In addition, his growing influence had made him numerous enemies among the medical profession and in the face of this violent jealousy he began to harbour doubts about his own physical safety. His efforts, however, had made him famous enough for Marcus Aurelius to invite in AD 168 him to join his military headquarters at Aquileia in northern Italy. Moving to Rome the next year with the imperial family because of another outbreak of the plague, Galen spent the rest of his life in the capital. He became so successful that he was appointed as personal physician to Marcus Aurelius himself. His voluminous writings he authenticated in his treatise *On My Own Books*.[9] It is now thought that he died in about AD 210, although earlier estimates put his death at about AD 200.

Galen the doctor

The name of Archagathus has been passed down as the first Greek doctor to have practised at Rome. According to Pliny (*Nat.*29.6.12–13) he set up his surgery in the capital in 219 BC.[10] Both he and his successors were very much engaged with the upper echelons of society that had developed a keen taste for all things Greek, following the wars of conquest that ended with the complete subjugation of that country by Aemilius Paullus in 168 BC. At the same time the lower classes were deeply suspicious of doctors, preferring home cures passed down through the family, magic and astrology, and the assistance of herbalists. Yet from the diverse evidence of writers such as Cicero, Seneca and Plutarch, a general picture can be constructed of what a Roman aristocrat demanded of a doctor, in particular the sort of friendship that could offer comfort throughout the duration of an illness.[11]

Educated Romans were for the most part conversant with current medical theories. For example Cicero (*Cic.ND* 2.137–8) describes in precise detail how the body was believed to process food, the disquisition only ending to avoid any possible offence over the nature of defaecation. Celsus, writing in the time of the emperor Tiberius (AD 14–37), wrote an encyclopaedia whose extant part discusses medicine in a tone that seems to reflect an educated person's view of the discipline.[12] Later in the first century AD Seneca makes frequent remarks in his letters about his illnesses and alludes to the sort of help that might be expected in such cases, whilst Pliny pays great attention in his *Natural History* to the broad scope of medicine as it stood in his day.[13] Petronius (*Petr*.42.5–6) even satirises medicine, focusing on the notion that an illness could be restrained by a starvation diet (Hp.*Nat.Hom*.9=6.54–6L). Not only that, but medical books were available from shops in the Argiletum, open lectures were presented by practising doctors, and surgeons would demonstrate their prowess with the knife in front of audiences.[14]

But how Galen fits into this picture is still open to debate. Modern consensus seems to suggest that the status of doctors in the eastern part of the empire was greater than that of their counterparts in the western part, although paucity of evidence must be held up as a strong caveat in this discussion.[15] Patronage is, however, almost certainly the answer to Galen's rapid rise to fame. His family was connected with the leading citizens of Pergamum, and these in turn had connections with the influential and powerful in Rome; so when he arrived in the capital in AD 161, he could quickly become friends with senators and others in the imperial court. Right from the start he was in a far higher position socially than most other doctors who similarly came from the eastern Mediterranean.[16] His private means are further demonstrated when he left Rome the following year, for he had to employ an auctioneer to sell off his house in Rome (*Prog*.9.2=14.648K) – he was no struggling tiro waiting on the largesse of others.

It has been pointed out that Galen was not the only doctor to have a strong showing in both medicine as well as other intellectual pursuits. Thrassippus of Corinth, for instance, was deemed pre-eminent in medicine and poetry.[17] Where Galen was different was in his combative style of rhetoric, his overwhelming sense of self worth and importance, his literary productivity that was enormous by any standard, and his blind assumption that he alone was graced with the ability to bring Hippocrates' work to completion. That he was able to write so much was, of course, due to his use of other medical works as a core outline.[18] Even if he did add further comments as he thought appropriate, his overall knowledge of medicine was by no means dissimilar from that of his contemporaries. He may have served as physician to the Roman elite, but his writings on food and diet can be used as a legitimate source of what generally counted for medicine in his time.

The Hippocratic background

Throughout Galen's writings the name of Hippocrates is invoked, either in support of a particular idea or to ridicule the views of an opponent. Sometimes Galen goes as far as to idealise Hippocrates almost as if he were a god (e.g. Gal.*Us.Part*.1.9=1.16K). There were several factors which seem to have contributed to this point of view. To begin with, writers of the second century AD were particularly fascinated with the classical past, whether its literary style or philosophical ideas. The former tendency is derided by Galen throughout his dietetic works, for he believed that current nomenclature and phraseology were far to be preferred over archaising sentences (e.g. Gal.*Alim.fac*.2.44.5=6.633K); the latter Galen believed in very strongly, because for him Hippocrates had discovered all that there was to know about medicine, and all that needed to be done was to interpret and explain his theories in more detail.

Even from the time of Hesiod (Hes.*Op*.109 ff) the ancient world had looked back to a mythological golden age when life was good, simple and healthy. Galen had no single philosophical basis for his science because there were so many competing theories about how the body functioned; his teachers had revered Hippocrates and had taught him to commit certain apothegms to memory. This procedure accorded well with rhetorical practice and its need for pithy statements by which arguments could be supported. Otherwise known as 'the pointed style', it was preferred by writers such as Seneca and Tacitus. It is easy to view Galen's adherence to this method with some cynicism, because he often could not remember where some Hippocratic quotes derived, and yet he was always certain that he knew exactly what an ambiguous statement in Hippocrates actually meant.[19] None the less the method behind this reasoning served as a sound support for his practice of medicine and for his place in Roman society.

Galen's teachers were certainly not unique in their reverence for Hippocrates. Even in the fourth century BC the legend of Hippocrates as the perfect doctor existed, saving patients from the plague, resisting the financial inducements of the Persian king, above all working strenuously as a Greek among fellow Greeks.[20] When the emperor Marcus Aurelius called Galen the finest doctor and a unique philosopher (Gal.*Praen*.11=14.660K), this was as a compliment to the image Galen had constructed of himself, an expert in classical ideas despite the decadence of the contemporary world.[21]

To carve a niche in Roman society meant fighting fierce competition. But claiming that all he was doing was to elucidate Hippocrates' ideas gave Galen the wherewithal to win this fight. If an opponent attacked him, then that opponent was attacking Hippocrates, and who could have prevailed against such a potent and hallowed legend?

Diet within medicine

Scribonius Largus, writing at the time of the emperor Claudius (AD 41–54), summed up the stages of medical care (*Scrib.Larg.intr.*6): first came diet, then drugs, and finally either cautery or surgery. Omitted from this list is venesection because not all the schools of medicine advocated this procedure. Diet was therefore not the only way by which disease could be treated, although it was perhaps the most important. As Scribonius Largus states elsewhere (Scrib.Larg.*intr.*2), most people were terrified of the knife or hot iron, but there were factors other than fear behind this emphasis on diet.[22] Plutarch (Plu.*Mor.*73D) held that a good doctor was someone who used sleep and diet rather than violent drugs to effect a cure.

Manual work denoted a low social status in the Roman world, yet surgery obviously depended wholly on the knowledge gained from actual experience. This awkwardness can perhaps be seen in the arguments promulgated by some doctors in support of this learning by trial and error.[23] To achieve greater prestige, a doctor had to avoid dirty hands. As Galen was only too well aware, philosophy was the key to this respectability. On the one hand a training in philosophy may have allowed a doctor to communicate more effectively with patients, whilst on the other hand it created the feeling of trust and friendship that Seneca stressed was so important for medical practice and technique.[24] Even so, medicine was considered, by the upper end of Roman society, a craft to be shared with slaves and freedmen, a prejudice that did not begin to dissipate until the later empire.[25]

It has been estimated that some 80 per cent of the patients Galen recorded in his works belonged to the elite, whereas only 46 per cent were sophists and 21 per cent were of the lower classes.[26] He himself said that he wrote for Greeks and for anyone who, whilst not actually Greek, at least made efforts to attain the qualities of the Greeks (Gal.*San.Tuend.*1.10=6.51K). If this statement referred to those educated in Greek literature and philosophy, then his focus was very much on the rich and powerful. Moreover, the intimacy demanded by dietetic medicine of the patient's way of life made for a pronounced concentration on the upper strata of society, for only they could afford the time and the expense such details naturally required.[27] Prescribing a diet backed by humoral science to these patients kept a doctor's hands clean and gave a definite intellectual cachet to the interaction.

That a good diet ensured health was a fundamental concept of ancient medicine, since food could cause disease or restore health through its effect on the balance of the humours. Thus prevention was in every way better than a cure. By contrast drugs, venesection, cautery and surgery were drastic, to be used only when diet could no longer help. But there was another idea behind this reliance on diet: everyone had it in their power to control their way of life and this gave to food a moral dimension that accorded well with contemporary Stoic views on life.[28] Moderation and balance were essential in the pursuit of truth and the ultimate good. Diet was therefore raised from mere eating for the sustenance of the body to a higher philosophical plane that bolstered its importance within medicine as a whole.

Some foods could also serve as drugs. For example, edder-wort had to be boiled two or three times before its medicinal quality was removed (Gal.*Alim.fac.*2.62.1=6.649-50K). What mattered was the manner and the circumstances under which a particular substance was applied, since the same substance could act as a food or as a drug.[29] From the evidence of Galen's dietetic works, a substance generally could be classified as a food if it did not have a pronounced effect on the body – whether that effect was diuretic, laxative, cathartic or the like – whilst a drug acted forcibly as a purge, vermifuge, emetic or similar. So through careful preparation, cooking and seasoning whatever was normally regarded as a drug could be rendered as a food.

Galen's view of the body

Cooking was a process that was believed, in Hippocratic medicine, to be applicable not only to the ripening of fruit and vegetables, but also to the process of digestion. Opposite, therefore, to the concept of raw and unripe were coction and ripeness. The innate heat of the body cooked foods. Thus Dioscorides (Dsc.2.110.1) could describe a stomach burning with an intense heat. By the same token, the more foods had been processed and cooked in the kitchen, the more easily they could be digested in the body.[30] Galen does not set out his ideas about the digestion as a coherent theory, but rather his views on the subject have to be drawn together from across the whole gamut of his writings.[31] In broad outline, he thought that food and drink were partly digested in the stomach. The resulting material then entered the liver through the first veins (which we now call the portal system) to be converted into blood. From the liver the veins carried the blood, now fortified with nourishment, to all the parts of the body. Air, however, was needed for the maintenance of this bodily warmth. This was drawn in through the lungs and the pores of the skin. As with a fire, smoke was produced during the creation of heat and the digestion of food and drink. So when discussing milk, Galen (Gal.*Simpl.Med.*2.13=11.491K) holds that in some people it is turned into a fatty smoke. Here the arteries acted as the vents for the burning process, at the same time as regulating the temperature of the body.

The circulation of the blood was never discovered by Galen, but there was posited instead the gradual ebb and flow of blood through the body. There is a focus on blood throughout ancient medical writings, primarily because it is so easy to see, whether in wounds or in menstruation. One of the main problems that doctors tried to combat was fever, always present in infectious conditions like the common cold and transmitted diseases such as malaria. Many ancient doctors thought that there was only one cause of fever. Galen, on the other hand, argued that there were three causes: first, overheating through exposure to the sun, particular foods and drinks, or problems with transpiration; second, inflammation (accompanied possibly by putrefaction) of excrementious matter, that is residues left in the body after digestion; and third, the flux of humours to a particular part of the body that subsequently putrefies. A carefully regulated diet could help avoid the production of anything excrementitious. If such matter did accumulate, then venesection was the best way to draw it off. But whereas the Methodics had argued that in venesection one rule applied to all, Galen was adamant that a doctor had to match a diet or the tapping of blood to the individual patient, because everyone was by temperament different.[32]

Dietetics according to Galen

Modern medicine can be divided into several discrete areas. At the forefront is western scientific medicine, explaining disease through the physical and chemical world. But even traditionalists acknowledge the potential effectiveness of alternative medicine, whether it is based on heavily diluted extracts of wild plants or the application of specially scented oils by massage. Then again there are eastern forms of medicine like acupuncture that can provide relief from a range of ailments. This wealth of ideas is mentioned because so often ancient medicine is criticised for its incoherence, yet the different schools of thought can in some ways be compared to the wide range of contemporary ideas regarding healing. The analogy is not of course complete, because in the ancient world there was no dominant mode of practice until Galen made his appearance. His great contribution was to try to systematise the various avenues earlier doctors had taken. Despite his own apparent misgivings about this systematisation, and his belief that further research should be conducted along the lines that he suggested, he was so successful that his writings eclipsed those of his contemporaries to the extent that few of these survive today.

Galen was uniquely equipped to make a mark on medicine. On a purely practical level, he was of independent means thanks to the legacy of his father. That meant he could write and work at his own leisure without having to look to a demanding patron.[33] As regards theory, he was extremely well educated, especially in philosophy and rhetoric. This enabled him to attack his rivals in a sharp and logical fashion. No doubt the audiences at his public lectures enjoyed his verbal thrusts and quirky humour.[34] Yet it was philosophy that Galen regarded as underpinning his ideas. Philosophy had always been held in great honour among both the Greeks and the Romans, while medicine suffered from poor esteem. It is true that the status of doctors had begun to rise under the empire, although the fact that the training of slaves into the profession had to be suppressed, indicates the underlying attitude of society.[35] Galen's emphasis on philosophy as a key to becoming a good doctor may be his attempt to link the honoured with the maligned disciplines. It certainly gave him the prestige to mingle with the upper echelons of society, if not as an equal, then certainly as someone to be admired.

While philosophy may have raised the status of medicine, it also hindered the substantiation of ideas. Stoicism, in particular, involved the use of the conditional to prove a hypothesis. So in Galen the admonition recurs frequently as to how a point that is about to be made is obvious from the subsequent inference.[36] There is, nevertheless, a certain logic to Galen's discussion of diet and food. To summarise this discussion very briefly, Galen asserted that health could be maintained only when the four humours were evenly balanced within the body. Comprising blood, phlegm, black bile and yellow bile, the humours could break with this symmetry if the body was abused, either through a faulty diet, unaccustomed exercise or a change of climate. Interacting with the humours were the four qualities to whose operation was attributed the birth and decay of all living things. The qualities consisted of hot, cold, wet and dry. Diseases were thought to occur when there was an imbalance of the humours or when there was an immoderate increase of one or more quality. Indigestion could be put down to an excess of phlegm brought on by excessive eating.

In order to counteract this complaint, a hot and drying remedy would be prescribed, consisting perhaps of pepper and wine. A good doctor had to apply reason and experience to obtain the necessary knowledge and understanding of how foods worked. Some might be suitable for the old, but not for the young, whilst others might benefit the majority, but harm those who suffered from a pathological peculiarity.[37]

The concept of logic in these writings on diet must, however, be qualified since there is some uncertainty about whether even Galen had a properly developed overview of what he was promulgating.[38] One of the difficulties lies in the dichotomy in ancient medicine that has already been raised, that is between a science founded on philosophical principles and a technique based on the observation of the body, the former being high in social status, the latter rather low. It is perhaps significant that *On the Powers of Foods* was published when Galen's medical and social position was not in question, for this work is very much a practical manual firmly rooted in the pathology of the body and the humours. On the other hand questions of orthography are raised not only just out of interest, but also because philology was considered a highly respectable pursuit. This is what makes these dietetic treatises so important, for they are both a record of medical practice and a commentary on the social mores of the Roman empire.

The treatises

Galen's most important dietary treatise is *On the Powers of Foods*. Written around AD 180, sometime after *On Hygiene* (Gal.*Alim.fac.*1.25.3= 6.539K), it gives an encyclopaedic view of how the inhabitants of the Roman empire ate. It generally follows earlier treatises on the subject by Diocles, Mnesitheus, Philotimus and the Hippocratic treatise *On Diet*, relating the foods that can be matched to the temperaments of particular patients.[39] In geographical scope it ranges from Rome itself to the cities on the Aegean coast of what is now Turkey, and in social observation from peasants on the brink of starvation to the fashionable delicacies of the rich.[40] These divides obviously fascinated Galen, since he writes of the contrast between city and country (e.g. Gal.*Alim.fac.*2.48 and 68=6.636 and 657K), although how they were supposed to assist in the practice of diet he does not explain. It may be that they are no more than rural facts designed to interest a reader, perhaps eliciting a brief moment of surprise from his educated audience that anyone could behave quite so boorishly in the countryside. Such an explanation would certainly dovetail with the amusing story of the leaden and drastically flatulent meal that Galen ate whilst out walking (Gal.*Alim.fac.*1.7.2-3=6.498-9K).

In this treatise foods are carefully classified according to their powers: salty or sweet, good or bad for the stomach, promoting one or other of the humours, sharp or bitter, sour or watery, easy or difficult to digest, slow or quick to pass through the body, costive or laxative, composed or fine or thick particles, cooling or heating. Often recipes are given, because Galen believed that a good doctor should also be a good cook.[41] The short treatise *On Barley Soup* complements this larger work and provides an interesting view of Galen's polemical style, although the absence of any internal references to outside events or other works makes any attempt at affixing a date rather problematic.

The medical background to these two dietary works is given by the other texts. *On the Humours* is probably not by Galen, but it is included as a succinct synopsis of humoralism. In general it does not misrepresent Galen's finely nuanced view by giving more emphasis to the qualities rather than the quantities of the humours. It may have been written within a century of Galen's death.

In the course of considering one particular humour, the treatise *On Black Bile* adds further details about the importance of balancing all the humours within the body. That this was written after *On the Natural Faculties* (Gal.*Atr.Bil.*7=5.136K) suggests a date of composition not before the period AD 169 to 175. What happened when the balance went awry is described in *On Uneven Bad Temperament*. The ensuing diseases are featured in *On the Causes of Disease*, categorised according to whether they are hot, dry, wet or cold. A *terminus ante quam* can be established since this treatise mentions (*Caus.Morb.*6=7.23K) *On Therapeutic Method*, a work written sometime between AD 169 and AD 180, so it is reasonable to assume that it was composed at about the same period as *On the Powers of Foods*.[42] A reference in *On Uneven Bad Temperament* (*Inaeq.Int.*7=7.748K) to *On the Causes of Disease* at least shows the temporal connection between these two works, although further precision is perhaps impossible.

A feature of these texts is the combative pose struck by Galen. Earlier writers like Erasistratus are derided, scorn is poured on those who cannot understand a seemingly simple idea and the impeccable logic of Galen's own arguments is stressed. As has been noted, medicine was not a uniform system, and publishing in antiquity meant reading aloud to a not always appreciative audience, so it was always necessary to buttress ideas with rhetoric. Whilst at times this style to a modern reader makes Galen seem on occasion egotistical, it is in fact no more than what his rivals were doing,

11

although on the whole he may – if we can trust his own account – have won his debates.

The texts

These works have not been translated before into English. The Latin translation that accompanies the edition of the Greek text by C. G. Kühn has therefore served as a useful companion when translating; it was, after all, designed for those studying medicine in the twilight of Galen's long period of predominance. Not wanting to stray far from Galen's words, I have tried to strike a balance between the literal and what can be read comfortably. Inherent in this approach is a danger of slippage. Yet I believe it far preferable, for example, to translate 'pepsis' as digestion, even this means simplifying the definite gap between the ancient and the modern concept of this bodily function. For the purist the original text is readily available for comparison and it would be a pity to obscure by continual reference to the original a translation designed for those not necessarily with any Greek.

For unlike many ancient works with their mythological and historical allusions, what Galen writes is surprisingly accessible to the modern reader. Apart from the occasional reference to another doctor – and many of these figures are in any case shadowy with the disappearance of the books they wrote – there is little that blocks a view of the Roman empire at its height as seen through the eyes of a highly educated but, at the same time, quite ordinary citizen. The size of the empire and the relative ease of travelling through it are emphasised by Galen's comments about his travels in (among other places) Egypt, Cyprus, Syria and Greece.[43] The range of foods – but alongside this the uncertainty of the harvests – is listed in precise detail. Conversations with teachers and students are recorded, alongside impromptu meals with peasants in the countryside, comments by farmers and the problems of pollution in the big cities. Medicine and food are combined with an observant eye for sociological details. There are few writers from the Roman world who allow us such a window on everyday life.

For *On the Humours*, *On Black Bile*, *On Uneven Bad Temperament*, and *On the Causes of Disease* I have used the text edited by C.G. Kühn (Claudii Galeni, *Omnia Opera*, Hildesheim (Georg Olms, reprint of 1823 Leipzig edition) 1965). This is the most recent omnibus edition of Galen's books and, despite the size of the task, mistakes in orthography and omissions are surprisingly few.[44] With *On Barley Soup* and *On the Powers of*

Foods I have had recourse to a more modern edition prepared by K. Koch, G. Helmreich, C. Karbfleisch and O. Hartlich (*De Ptisana, De Alimentorum Facultatibus*, Corpus Medicorum Graecorum 5.4.2, Teubner (Leipzig and Berlin) 1923). This contains the Greek text and details of important variations in manuscript readings, together with brief references to other ancient authors who describe similar ideas or points.

2

ON THE HUMOURS

Whatever the basic element of the world may be, among animals it is the humour, just as of course in the measurement of time it is the season. The humours do not possess a single identity or likeness: rather as regards their active and passive qualities, through which they both owe their existence and have constructed their origins in us, they differ from each other in many ways, and not least in their nomenclature. To begin at the beginning: the elements from which the world is made are air, fire, water and earth; the seasons from which the year is composed are spring, summer, winter and autumn; the humours from which animals and humans are composed are yellow bile, blood, phlegm and black bile.

The humours are all combined with moisture and heat, dryness and cold. Thus blood, air and spring are moist and hot (although some people might disagree with this statement regarding air); yellow bile, summer and fire are hot and dry, whilst black bile and earth and autumn are dry and cold; phlegm, water and winter are cold and moist. Humours, elements and seasons are both akin and divergent. For example, air and fire are not the same in dryness and moisture, but are united by their heat; fire and earth are not the same in coldness and heat, but are both very dry; similarly earth and water are cold, but they are set apart by their respective dryness and moisture; water and air are moist, but differ as to heat and coldness.

In the same way the humours and seasons agree and disagree with each other, thereby achieving what is called 'disharmonic' mixing. Yet regardless the elements never change and each remain in the same place, maintaining their permanence in any movement towards each other through nourishment that is provident and suitably proportioned; similarly the seasons occur and are named after the movements of the sun to the south and to the north.

The humours are not like the seasons because they differ amongst themselves in many ways: in place, colour, power, consistency and quality.

14

Moreover it is vital that the humours do change, just as the elements must change into one another, not always keeping to the same process of change or maintaining a balanced increase, although there is a certain pattern of mutation from what is earthy to what is watery, from what is watery to what is airy, and from what is airy to what is fiery. So there is an irregular change from phlegm to yellow bile, and from blood to black bile. The proof of this argument lies in earthy and melancholic blood, and salty phlegm which in many ways resembles blue bile and easily mutates into it. Phlegmatic bile and blood saturated with mucus present similar properties, as among people with a dropsical or cachetic condition, just as with unmixed yellow bile in people with a hotter and drier constitution. For those who suffer from indigestion, a green bile appears in vomiting and defaecation.

It is therefore in these sort of changes that what is dominant has precedence, whilst the opposite occurs when these changes occur through what is harmonious. A particular humour might on occasion metamorphose into one or another sort of humour according to temperature, time, place, age and diet: for all humours arise and increase at every moment and season. For example, in summer there is a predisposition towards bitter bile, especially among those people who have leanings towards this condition through age, constitution, diet or, above all, through external factors. The prime causes of yellow bile are stress, anger, emotional trauma, labour, physical exercise, insomnia, fasting and hunger. Phlegmatic bile comes about from sleep, drinking water, the consumption of sea food and moist diets in general, and viscous edibles that consist of thick particles. Blood is generated by meat, fowl, eggs and all those foods that are both wholesome and easy to cook, unless something special alters what is eaten. The same is true for black bile, but the surrounding circumstances are more complicated.

When we make proper use of foods in recipes, the attendant humours follow. The blood increases at puberty; hence teenagers are cheerful and enthusiastically disposed to games. But the yellow bile in adolescents makes for anger, sexual drive and bullying early in this stage of life; whilst later there is a surge of black bile, the worst sort of humour, since wherever it rushes it is hard to resist or divert, thus making this stage of life devious, revengeful and stubborn. In old age there is phlegm, when there reigns sluggishness, loss of memory and lethargy.[1] This is because old age is moist and cold, just as the prime of life is dry and cold. Puberty is hot and moist, whilst adolescence belongs to an analogous and superior humour.

The humours owe their origin, maintenance and movement as follows: for blood the liver, veins and both nostrils; for yellow bile the bladder, the area around the liver and the ears; for phlegm the stomach, loin muscles

15

and the mouth; for black bile the area below the liver, spleen and eyes, as has already been stated. As regards their colours, blood is red and phlegm is white; there are seven types of yellow bile (yellow, which people call basic, pale-yellow, red, leek-green, yolk-yellow, verdigris and woad); whilst the proper tint of black bile is of olive oil.

Blood is sweet to the taste; yellow bile is bitter; black bile is sharp; phlegm is ordinarily neutral, but it can also be salty, sharp and frequently sweet. There are four different types of black bile: one in the blood's sediment, another when yellow bile is overheated, another called 'tarry' because it has the shine of bitumen, and another by nature resembling blood. Further details can be added: blood and phlegm are by consistency thick, as is black bile. Yellow bile is thin, light and buoyant. The other two humours are heavy. Blood commands a central role in the distribution of heat.

It seems that health is characterised by the equality and symmetry of these humours. Diseases occur when the humours decrease or increase contrary to what is usual in terms of quantity, quality, shifting of position, irregular combination or putrefaction of whatever has rotted. Just as it can be said that diseases occur as a result of an excess of the humours, so health returns by means of the removal or of the addition of the humours, their thinness and thickness, and generally through their mildness and symmetry.

Hippocrates put this extremely neatly in the sixth book of his *Epidemics*: you should eject some humours by force, put some humours in, thin and temper the humours in one case, but not in another, for they furnish the sequence of remedies according to the cause of the disease.[2] The humours must be mixed precisely in quality and equal in quantity, so that health when prevalent may persevere, but when absent may be summoned. This is why they are called humours, because at the same time they aid humectation. It is clear that, if this is health, then such a condition is not disease, as has been shown. Since the types of disease are divided into different kinds, the differences in kind must be advanced from among the different causes. Humours are both causes and symptoms: the former is what occurs externally, the latter is what is meant by increase and decrease, that is, as has been stated before, according to age, time and the effect of diet, whenever these are radically changed.

This is what Hippocrates seems to be saying when he states that some humours flourish and prevail at one time, others at another time, adding that different complexions are due to the predominance of whatever humours are prevalent in a particular temperament, and that diseases arise according to the nature of the dominant humour in an individual. Moreover, in the introduction to his work *On Humours* he says: 'the colour of the humours, when they are not disturbed, is like that of the flowers'.[3]

16

The predominance of the humours generally changes according to the passing of the various stages of life, just as it it seems the characteristics of the soul change. Even that is delineated by the humours. Blood causes a cheerful nature; yellow bile a nature that is angry, insolent or fierce; phlegm a lazier and more stupid nature; black bile a nature that is more impetuous and angry. The character of the soul can be altered in diseases through the kind of humour that is dominant, as in the case of delirium. All diseases that come about because of blood are accompanied by singing and laughter, whilst all those that come about through yellow bile follow rashness and bitterness. This is why Hippocrates also said: 'Derangements of the mind with laughter are less dangerous, but when combined with seriousness they are more so.' He was referring to seriousness here as boldness. Again, all characters that are based on black bile are more silent, cultured and feature sad faces; conversely, all characters that have phlegm as their foundation are frivolous and unsettled.

Hippocrates stresses this elsewhere, for example in the first book of his *Epidemics*, when Silenus was deranged with singing and laughter. In the third book of his *Epidemics*, he mentions that a bold delirium occurred in the case of Philiscus: 'for he went mad around the middle of the day'.[4] Yellow bile was the cause of the disease. In Cyzicus he says that a woman who had given birth to twin daughters went mad, and that her delirium was characterised by a sullen and despondent face, since she fell silent and did not listen to anyone.[5] Black bile was the cause of her disease. He says that Pithion, who lived near the temple of the Earth, became delirious and went mad. In this case the cause of the disease was phlegm.

The person who administers care should know the multiple causes of these diseases. As Hippocrates says, if you know the cause of a disease, you can apply whatever is beneficial for the body from the remedies that will combat the disease. With diseases, whoever as regards healing wants to pose accurate questions, to reply correctly to anyone asking the same, and to contradict effectively must consider the following: first, what the causes are of diseases, which will allow for the promulgation of the reasons, so in the case of age, an adolescent falling ill will be particularly affected by the blood, as of course was shown earlier; second, the time of year, for in spring the blood is especially troublesome; third from diet, for one drink or food is productive of one humour, another of another humour, so for example blood follows on from drunkenness and gluttony. This is what Hippocrates determined when he learnt that Silenus had become ill after drinking. He mentions too the wife of a gardener who had suffered menopause as a consequence of her excessive eating. Fourth from place, if in fact a hot place effects hotter diseases; fifth from eruptions, for bloody pustules are red and round, phlegmatic pustules are flat, and other pustules otherwise, just as Hippocrates says in his *Aphorisms*, where heat spots are shown to come about in spring and summer, since they are the result of blood and bile; and finally from colour, where the cause of a disease may be diagnosed as from the predominance of a humour.[6] This is no less than the the most accurate way of reaching the best diagnosis, a system believed by Diogenes and his learned contemporaries to be akin to divination. These physicians discussed the colours at great length and divided the diseases according to their different appearances: the red, the bloody, and the flame, in which bitterness was excessive; and the black and the white, sufferers of which were called phlegmatics. The diseases resulting from these humours were called red, flame, black and white; but I do not understand how, by omitting so many pieces of evidence for the medical art and especially those which afford an accurate assessment of the diseases, they could assign the complete categorisation of the diseases to colours alone.

3

ON BLACK BILE

Black bile is a topic over which some have spent far longer than is needed for the art of medicine, whilst others instead have hesitated to promote any decent length of exposition, just as some have said nothing at all.[1] It is this last category of people that is more at fault than those who add useless information, because it is easier to cut out excess verbiage than to search for whatever has not been been mentioned. Following this line of thought, Hippocrates seems to me as a prime example of someone who includes all that is vital for the conduct of this art, just as conversely Erasistratus is a prime example of someone who leaves out everything.[2] I think that the pupils of Plistonicus, Praxagoras and Philotimus, who discussed the humours in the greatest detail, usefully define some of what was only sketchily described by Hippocrates, although over some of his other ideas they argued erroneously.[3] Of the more recent writers, the best books that have been written about black bile are by Rufus of Ephesus.[4] You could say with good reason that Rufus wants nothing more than an attentive audience, not those who contradict purely for the sake of an argument, a habit which is prevalent among quite a few modern doctors, particularly those who describe themselves as Methodics or Erasistrateans or Asclepiadeans.

Some of these doctors have devised captious arguments which try to prove that any discussion about the humours is useless for medical requirements. My intention is therefore to consider what exactly is useful, as I usually do, and then turn to whatever follows on logically from this. I shall not hesitate in my conclusion to do away with any of those arguments which have been propounded by people who hold that the theory of the humours is worthless. To avoid loss of clarity during my discussion, I shall take just one name for each humour and so try to describe them throughout in these terms. However, I cannot do this properly without delineating the outward appearance of the humours. I shall do

19

this immediately, starting with the humour that is the best known to everyone.

This humour can be seen, in the case of injuries of an artery or a vein, to pour at once from the cavities in which it is stored. It is redder when it comes from the veins, but generally yellower when it comes from the arteries. Each of these two types congeals immediately, not just when they exit the body, but when they are still inside too. So that is the case in both events. You can observe the process of coagulation culminating in a thrombus, which is the usual word that the Greeks use to describe congealed blood. It also seems to congeal not only in the cavities of the stomach and intestines, but also in the cavities of the bladder, where urine is collected, and in the lungs and the rough artery, or in other words in the artery that lies between the abdomen and the lungs, and for women in their wombs.

The colour red is generally predominant in this humour, so the best sort of blood is in fact exactly like this. However, on occasion it appears either yellower or blacker than this, just as of course it appears either thinner or thicker in consistency. Sometimes it is found that the blood of those who have had a vein opened is thin owing to the absorption of moisture, which during the process of congealing is separated and occupies a position above the blood.

It is quite reasonable to assume to something of what has been drunk should be carried through the body together with the blood that is produced in the liver, because later it is not only exuded through the urine, but also through the sweat and the exhalation which is designated as unseen to the perception. Phlegm too sometimes appears to float on the surface of the blood, whilst in contrast the blood as a whole can seem so thick and dark that it resembles raw pitch.

Therefore whatever pours out of the veins and the arteries, however it might look, is given just the single label of blood, since none of its different guises which I have just mentioned have been given separate names. All types of blood congeal immediately, even if they pour from a fleshy part that has been cut open by a deep wound.

There is another fluid that is similar to thick dark blood which can be seen when it is secreted either during vomiting or defaecation, but this fluid does not congeal, even if it is in contact for a long time with the surrounding air. Sometimes this fluid affords a sharp and sour sensation to those who are vomiting, whilst at other times it has no noticeable quality, since it contains no sweetness, which is what blood has, nor saltiness, which is what blood and phlegm have on occasion, nor bitterness, which is what yellow bile possesses. So salty blood and phlegm are clearly unhealthy.

Blood generally is sweet; but phlegm, just like water, has no quality. Yet if its quality is changed naturally, it not only becomes salty, but also sharp, although it then absorbs a certain amount of sweetness too. This humour, whatever its quality, is called phlegm, but only if it is white. It shares the property common to every other humour, and that is that it does not congeal. Descriptions of briny or salty coupled with a humour make no difference to the nomenclature, for both varieties signify the same thing.

There is another humour which always tastes bitter to those who are vomiting. It is not always yellow, since sometimes it is cream in colour, but when it stays consistently yellow it is thicker that when it is cream. Using these facts, anyone fully conversant with the humours can effectively judge that yellow bile will appear pale if a fine moisture and a watery consistency are combined. Some people call this moisture watery, others serous, since it can be bracketed with that which produces urine and sweat. Just as yellow bile grows paler in colour and softer in consistency after the addition of fine moisture, so it takes on the colour of raw egg-yolk when it has been reduced by evaporation over a length of time. Hence it is called 'yolk-coloured'. This bile, whether it is cream, yellow or yolk-coloured, has its generation in the vessels.

Another fluid is created in the stomach which is leek-green in colour. It is called 'leek-green' after the colour of leeks, in the same way as verdant is named from its similarity to the verdigris on bronze. One fluid is even called 'woad-like' from the colour of blue woad.

All these fluids share the same property of permanence. So some people call a fluid red if it is close to thin blood in consistency, but because it does not congeal they designate it a fluid. I have perhaps discussed these ideas at greater length than the proposed subject of my treatise warrants, although I find myself propelled into detail through the facts associated with my argument, the usefulness of my research and the brevity of my purpose. Let me return now to my discussion of black bile.

Black bile must be distinguished from dark blood because it does not congeal, but not of course from anything that is specifically labelled black. Such things often appear in vomit and faeces, although they are completely different from black bile, not just in strength, but also in perceptible power. They certainly do not have any sourness or sharpness, whilst black bile exhibits these qualities through two senses: taste, for those who vomit it up, and smell, for the same people and those around. But it does not react with the earth to produce effervescence, as black bile does.

Yet even if black bile appears similar to very sharp vinegar in this respect, it does contain something that is the complete opposite of the portion of its substance which consists of thick particles, and for this reason it first corrodes and then completely ulcerates those parts of the body with which it is in contact when neat. Since vinegar is composed of fine particles, it passes through the body, but because black bile is thick, it settles and causes corrosion.

Through what I have described, black bile can be seen as distinct from other black substances, whether they are humours, waste matter or nutriments. No fly or other creature would wish to have a taste of it, just as they would avoid saturated brine, for nothing living survives in saturated brine, as is shown by the Dead Sea. Its formation therefore appears to be destructive, the result of black bile being heated too much. You must remember, of course, that black bile which results from an excessive heating of yellow bile is more destructive than the black bile I mentioned before, just as one humour is more drastic in its action compared with another fluid, by which I mean yellow bile compared with a fluid that looks like the sediment in blood.

Those who research the working of medicine say that this has an appearance similar to the watery juice that flows when olives are pressed and to wine lees. But as is the case with many other things, names which are the same do not preclude an opposite nature, but shared names nevertheless do deceive some people, and so they are misled when two humours are being discussed and think it is for the good that black bile sometimes appears in vomit and faeces.

However, when I was about twenty I learnt from my teacher, who was called Pelops, the distinguishing features of these two fluids, and I have since observed them throughout my life up to the present moment. I have always noticed that the fluid of genuine black bile is fatal when excreted, but that the evacuation of black matter is quite often beneficial. This alone is enough to know when practising of medicine, especially if you learn both the distinguishing of the proper times for its evacuation as well the theory behind all of this, which I will now proceed to set out in detail.

For anyone who has not discovered through long experience what occurs in each of these evacuations, it is understandable for there to be wonder or disbelief if the body is hurt when an extremely bad humour is evacuated; the opposite might seem to be the case, that the body will be restored to the best of health once the harmful humour has been evacuated. According to this argument, this is what happens when black matter is evacuated. But, as I have said, anyone who has realised through long experience that this is the case will easily find the cause of the process, especially if there is a wish to discover what causes black bile.

The initial stages in the detection of black bile have now been stated, but it would be a good idea to include the whole of the explanation. Since this juice is distributed from the bowels and intestines to the liver, a certain amount of its consistency is composed of small particles, but some of it is composed of large particles, just as different foods have different consistencies. We know that nature controls the body and does everything to preserve life; we can also observe the passages which act towards the evacuation of whatever is useless in food and drink; it would therefore seem that none of this is surprising, so I shall again consider how the sediment in blood can be removed, how this sediment can be classified, and through which parts of the body it is produced.

First of all, however, since I am beginning an inquiry which will be solved by rational argument, I should say that I discovered this knowledge through testing, and that I have experienced all of this through experiment over a long period of time. The blood which comes from letting is seen to be thicker and darker in bodies with dry and hot constitutions; and similarly according to the particular time of the year, the locality, physical conditions, way of life and diet.[5] Regarding diet, there are foods consisting of thick particles which are dry, such as lentils, snails, ox and goat, especially if these have been preserved, and dark wine that is thick and rough. All diseases that stem from a bad temperament that is hot and dry, such as remittent fevers, produce thick dark blood. The present chronic infection, which has come about because of the long summer, also is the cause of blood which resembles that brought about by remittent fevers. Quite a few of the patients who were cured suffered an evacuation through the stomach – which can be included among whatever is labelled dark – for the most part on the ninth day of the illness, but sometimes on the seventh or the eleventh day.

There are lots of differences between these dark things: some are in nature close to black bile, some on being excreted cause no sting or unpleasant smell, but many lie midway between these attributes. Anyone who is ill does not have an evacuation of the stomach like this, but instead the whole body breaks out all over in black pustules. Sometimes these pustules fall off like scales, when they have dried and subsided, but only gradually and many days often the crisis. Everyone who excreted genuine black bile died, for such bile shows that the blood has undergone extreme digestion.

Other sorts of pustules also appeared on the skin of many people without any accompanying fever. In these cases the skin became swollen and dried as nature forced the excess of black bile to the surface. It is from this sort of condition that what people call elephantiasis stems. If such a condition occurs with a fever, then the eruption of black bile into the skin causes anthrax. Eruption without a fever, but when blood is visible, is usually the cause of elephantiasis.

When black bile is on its own, it immediately creates a dark tumour, and in time what is termed cancer, for the humour then is very harsh and malignant. When it is more moderate, it eats through the skin and causes a hidden cancer that has no visible wound. So it is evident that diseases like this, and particularly cancer, stem from black bile, whenever the veins can be clearly seen as reaching to the affected part of the body, since veins absorb thick black humour. This is because nature continually tries to cleanse the blood, separating from it whatever is bad and directing it away from the important parts of the body, sometimes to the stomach and bowels, at other times to the surface of the body.

Everything that possesses a substance made up of small particles passes through the skin, sometimes in a perceptible way, as in the instance of those who sweat, whilst whatever is thicker cannot pass through the thickness of the skin, but is trapped there, and anything that is hot causes anthrax, but anything that is not hot causes cancer. If black bile is moderate in its qualities, it produces red elephantiasis after it has been mixed with blood; the longer it stays, the darker it becomes.

Often nature opens a vein in the anus and secretes such a humour mixed with blood; to this condition is given the title of haemorrhoids. In such cases you should observe closely what sort of blood is being excreted: whether it is the blood that gymnasts and athletes have, or in other words the blood of people who are in excellent health and have good humours; or whether it is darker and thicker than this. Nature often moves this sort of blood to the veins in the legs, which is how stretched and widened varicose veins are produced. The skin which surrounds varicose veins darkens in time.

Some people have an abundance of blood flowing without any black bile being present; this blood pushes on the veins and dilates those that are naturally weaker. But even when there is not an abundance of blood, the same thing happens if blood mixed with black bile produces an enlargement of the veins. In these cases there is danger that those affected might be troubled by melancholia if the problem veins should be surgically removed. This often seems to happen, not only when the veins are dilated, but also when haemorrhoids are produced by black bile.

A patient who suffered from a chronic sore had the vein above it, which was rather varicose, removed. The sore was immediately cured, but by the same token what was left of the excised vein after surgery remained incurable. A year passed before one of my teachers from Pergamum, a man by the name of Stratonicus, a student of Sabinus from the Hippocratic school, cut a vein in the elbow of the same man.[6] He observed that thick black blood was being excreted. He drew a little blood again on the next day, then similarly a little on the third day and on the fourth day, and then after these three days he used a drug to purge him and so evacuated the black bile. By devising a diet for him which contained healthy humours, he was able to aim for the cure of the wound.

Therefore from this diversity of colour and consistency it is revealed that all the humours are contained within the veins and arteries. From what I have already said it is clear that, in addition to everything Hippocrates wrote in his work *On the Nature of Man* about which I have elaborated in greater detail in my work *On Elements*, one particular matter must be discussed now, starting with the following quote:[7]

> The human body has in itself blood, phlegm, yellow bile and black bile; these make up the nature of the body, and through these pain is felt or health enjoyed. The most perfect health is enjoyed when these humours are in correct proportion with each other – that is in compound, power or quantity – and when they are properly mixed. Pain is felt when one of these humours is lacking or excessive or is isolated in the body without being compounded with the other humours. When a humour is isolated and stands on its own, not only must the part of the body which it left become diseased, but the part of the body where it remains in a pool must, because of the excess, cause pain and discomfort. In fact when more of a humour flows from the body than is necessary to remove what is superfluous, the process of flowing causes pain. But if it is to an inner part of the body that this flow, movement and separation away from the other humours takes place, then from what has been said two areas of pain must necessarily be felt, the first in the part of the body that has been drained, the second in the part of the body that has been filled.[8]

Now anyone acquainted with the workings of medicine will acknowledge that Hippocrates is correct here, because the body is indeed healthy when these humours are in their correct proportion with each other, but is diseased either when there is an excess of humours throughout the body, that is in all the vessels, or when in a particular part of the body there is just one humour present.

For I showed, when I was discussing a little while back the diseases that begin in one part of the body because of black bile, that some people are filled with melancholy if their varicose veins or haemorrhoids are removed. It is reasonable to suppose that similar diseases occur in the parts that are hidden deep within the body as they do on the skin. Surely when yellow bile attacks in one particular place erysipelas will be produced, but when black bile attacks, carbuncles and cancer will be the result. But of course whatever lies deep inside the body has a state that cannot be changed, although still subject to the same diseases.

From these statements it is in fact possible to recognise for certain the effective cause, during which process both yellow and black bile clearly appear to gnaw at one intestine or the other, wherever in fact they are particularly lodged, and they render dysentery completely incurable. This is why Hippocrates wrote in his *Aphorisms*: 'Dysentery that starts with black bile presages death'.[9]

I said before that everything that is ulcerated because of black bile is incurable, unless you want to term as healing the excision of the whole of the affected part, that is the cutting round in a circle up to the parts that are unaffected. Therefore just as an intestine is incurably ulcerated by black bile, and ulcerated by yellow bile in a way that is difficult to cure, so it is clear that this is the case with each of the other parts that are hidden deep within the body and which are considerably more important than the intestines; in addition to which the treatment is easier in the case of the intestines, because the drugs, on being injected through the anus, immediately hit the affected parts, but in the case of the other parts this cannot be so readily effected.

Perhaps those who ignore black bile have left a considerable part of the art of medicine without scientific consideration; this is still more so for those who ignore yellow bile. It is impossible to enumerate those crucial theories of medical practice that are pushed to one side by people who ignore both these humours and phlegm. Erasistratus wrote absolutely nothing about black bile, and just a little about yellow bile, and even this is not wholly correct. For he says the following about it:

> Many of the diseases which trouble us are witness of the need to focus on bilious fluid: for example jaundice, inflammations around the liver and many other diseases in addition. But it is of no consequence to the medical art as to whether this process occurs internally during the digestion of food in the stomach, or whether it accrues externally through its inclusion in whatever is eaten.

That is what Erasistratus wrote in the first book of his *General Principles of Yellow Bile*. Those who contradict him state that, since he agreed himself that yellow bile in excess is harmful, it would make more sense either if black bile was not produced at all; or if, supposing this to be inconceivable, at least as little black bile as possible.

Yet it is neither possible in any way whatever to prevent it from being produced, nor could one try, even if it was in fact possible, but it is possible to ensure that only a very little is produced without understanding the reason for it being produced. The basis of this humour is therefore contained in food and drink. Certainly foods differ among each other: some contain more black bile, some less, while some perhaps have nothing of it at all. If it comes about in the body, doctors ought to know that it is formed particularly in some special parts of the body, since this is effected by some cause or other.

This discussion, however, is connected to a general discussion about the origins of the humours, concerning which Erasistratus wrote absolutely nothing. Which means that, whatever may be relevant, it is impossible to ascertain which foods are good and which are bad, or to learn about how to live, and more importantly, the nature of human beings. But it can be seen that some people, however they live, collect a lot of fluid that is either full of yellow bile, black bile or phlegm. That this is the reason for diseases that cannot be trivialised will be shown in another book. Erasistratus himself agreed that some diseases are brought about by such a fluid, but he continually hesitates to blame the cause on bad humours. He denied that thick and viscous humours were the reasons for paralysis by using the following argument: 'Therefore disease occurs when there is an influx of fluid into the vessels that are situated in the muscles of the lungs, by means of which the reflex movements are performed'. And a little further on he states: 'The influx is of food, by which the muscles are nourished; this influx is viscous, ductile and difficult to excrete'. But he does not even say that this influx, when collected, is the cause of apoplexy, lethargic fever, epilepsy and many other diseases.

I do not intend now to explain the power of the other humours, since my proposal was to discuss black bile. Hippocrates says that its production is necessary, but he advised on how it might not be produced in excess, beginning his advice with examples that were clearly visible. More black bile seems to be produced in people who are hotter and drier in temperament, and also at hotter and drier times of the year, and in hotter and drier places and constitutions, and in patterns of life that are wrapped in depression, stress and insomnia, and in the driest foods that consist of thick particles. The colour of the whole body is darker for those people who are prone to collect this bile and in instances of hot

disease, that is all those diseases that originate removed from any moisture; if, in these cases, there is a haemorrhage or slow loss of blood, the
bile flows dark.

So visible phenomena like this reveal the causes by which black bile is
produced. Purging whatever can be seen highlights the road to discovery.
If the spleen has been diseased for a long time, whether through inflammation, induration or enervation, the whole body loses its original
colouring and grows darker.[10] Black bile is also always darker than the
liver, especially in animals that have a hot and dry temperament, such are
those with sharp incisors; just as conversely the spleen is not completely
dark in animals that happen to be of a temperament which is colder and
moister either in combination or separately, for example pigs. In cows,
however, the spleen is by nature darker, and as they grow older the spleen
gradually becomes even darker. The taste too of this offal, even when it
is cooked, seems to hold some bitterness and never becomes like the liver.

Swayed therefore by these facts, the greatest doctors and philosophers
of the past said that the liver was cleansed by the spleen, which drew into
itself all that was slimy in the blood, this resembling, according to them,
lees in wine or the watery part of olive oil. But doctors recently have
preferred to follow the schools of philosophy, and just as they have been
mistaken in many of the things that they have said, so they also have
argued that there is no need in medicine for a doctor to be concerned
about the humours, adding before all of this that purgative drugs purge
without effecting anything, since they are equally purgative of all the
humours in the body, not just those which are thought to be harmful.

Hippocrates, however, by employing what is agreed to purge these
humours, proved that during the whole course of life the four humours
were contained in the human body. There was no time of life, no season
of the year, no natural disposition of the body during which all the
humours were not present. It was apparently evident to the ancients that
each of the purgative drugs attracts a particular humour, since the drugs
which draw yellow bile are of benefit to those suffering from jaundice,
whilst the drugs which are called hydragogues empty out watery
discharges in dropsy, whilst those drugs which remove black bile prevent
elephantiasis and cancer from growing.

If it were true that all the humours contained in the vessels are drawn
out after being affected according to the strength of a particular drug,
then a purge involving one of these drugs would be similar to cutting a
vein and bleeding. But why are hydragogues given in cases of dropsy
when it is possible to drain the blood by cutting a vein? How is it that
most of the watery matter is emptied out, but very little of anything that

contains yellow bile, or conversely, with patients who are jaundiced, how is it that a great deal of what contains yellow bile is emptied out, but little watery matter? Why are those suffering from dropsy helped by hydragogues, whenever they are gently purged, yet not one of those doctors who believe that purging with purgatives is of equal value to letting veins have dared to draw blood off them?

Some doctors also effect purges by using hydragogues, whilst the universal practice is to use diuretics. As far as those who maintain that urine is formed by the transformation of blood in the kidneys are concerned, you should bleed anyone suffering from dropsy by cutting a vein instead of treating with diuretic drugs. For it is better to drain the excess once rather than often, and for this to be done gradually over the space of several days.

In fact I have even written against this theory in a separate work entitled *Against the Strange Theory about Urinary Secretion*. I really think that the majority correctly commit themselves to wasting time without any logic rather than distorting the art of medicine through logic. At least some of what the former say is very true, since they understand what diet means for healthy and sick people far better than those who chatter like fools using sophistry, whilst the latter waste amongst other things my life, since first of all I have to read what the principals of their schools have written, then I have to listen to what their students say, and finally I am forced to refute their captious arguments.

I believe that Hippocrates was someone who was good and honest, chasing neither honour or glory, but loving only truth. If anyone claims that he wanted glory or honour for himself – and it would certainly have been easy for him to win both – yet it is however true that he did not wish to engage in academic rivalry with the established system of philosophy which was then held in high esteem. His successors clutched insatiably at a reputation that was undeserved, setting up their own ridiculous schools of thought and contriving arguments directed at their own predecessors. Even so, some of these people possessed abilities that cannot be ignored, among whose number Erasistratus springs to mind. But the war of rivalry that was being waged against Hippocrates forced Erasistratus to write what he thought himself. For surely it could not have been anything but rivalry which produced the statement that, while nature thoughtfully formed all the parts of the body, the whole of the inner section of the spleen was created for no reason? How can anyone fail to realise that some of those who hold the same ideas as Erasistratus are obviously in disagreement with what he said about the spleen? As a result of which, although they say that this organ prepares the juice from foods for the liver so as to make good blood, they then follow up this argument and allege that there is another membrane by which the intestines are attached to the omentum, without even considering that the veins leading from all the intestines, not just from the stomach, must convey to the liver the nutritious juices?

Erasistratus was contentious because he thought that speculation by doctors about the humours was futile. He did not discuss in detail where, why and how the blood is produced in the body. All this is clear proof that there is no mention by him of the diseases that are caused by black bile or in short by melancholy humour. In fact there is no recollection of any of the philosophers and doctors who came before him, nor of those who, in stating that some mental problem or other is melancholic, try to effect a cure by means of white hellebore. No one who has grown up in Greece is so ignorant as not to have heard or read that the daughters of Proetus, when afflicted with mental illness, were cured by Melampus after being purged in this way.[11] So this purge has been highly regarded, not just in the past two or three centuries, but also many more years back, and in the meantime everyone has used it as a drug.

Therefore it would have been better if Erasistratus, in the face of his contemporaries, had shown that he was arguing from a position of uncertainty, when he said that neither melancholia nor any other form of mental illness stemmed from black bile, just as in fact black bile was not the cause of cancer, elephantiasis, the wild ravings of phrenitis, varicoceles or haemorrhoids, without any caveat that many people are filled with melancholy when haemorrhoids are removed. But he could not bring himself to say anything of this sort, because he was frightened, I believe, of being judged unfavourably in the minds of those who carefully carried out the duties of medicine, seeing that doctors in the past made use of case studies rather than sophistic arguments.

I would like one of his students to tell me the reason for the spleen appearing so dark in animals of a hot and dry temperament that they cannot be eaten. Take pigs, for example: even if the spleen is not as good as the liver for eating, yet it is not inedible. On the other hand, anyone who eats lions, lionesses, panthers, leopards, bears and wolves for pleasure leaves aside the spleen as being inedible. Furthermore, if that person is to enjoy especially what is being eaten and drunk, the spleen must either be, if possible, a better food than the liver or, if that is impossible, it must not be in every way worse. So when Erasistratus said that in such an argument the different reasons have to concur wholly with each other, I cannot understand how some people agree to accept theories refuted by what is plainly evident, and which even the authors themselves were unable to defend in their entirety.

In fact Erasistratus was silent about the substance of the juice that nourishes the sinews, but he was compelled to describe it in his writings because of its value in aiding those who are paralysed. He said the sinews were nourished by something that is viscous, ductile, and hard to digest and pass as food. Moreover, the conclusion from this premise is that this nourishment is derived from nowhere else but from whatever appears around the lungs. These things have their dissolution in such a fluid after undergoing digestion and putrefying; normally they contain no blood whatever.

However, unless it is agreed that every part of the body is nourished by a special fluid with its own particular substance, the logic of this argument fails. If a special fluid did nourish each part of the body, it would be impossible for the spleen of animals with sharp incisors to obtain sweet food. So if in their case there is a particularly distinct appearance to the spleen, as there clearly is when it seems astringent and sharp in quality, it is evident that the fluid feeding this quality possesses an identical nature. The Creator of these animals did not forget to cleanse the blood of all its existing impurities and sediments, nor indeed its bilious and serous waste matter.

Hippocrates proved in his arguments that all the humours are contained in the body. In healthy people each humour can be expelled if drawn out by a drug linked with this humour. Thus the system which formed animals did not neglect to form an organ which attracted the waste which belongs to black bile. But you cannot invent another part of the body which is capable of attracting this humour and ignore the spleen. Presumably you cannot still be hunting for the vein by which the thickness of the blood is carried to the spleen? Surely you must realise that, during a long abstinence from food, the spleen and the stomach draw the special fluid through just one vein? If you remember what I proved in my book *On the Natural Faculties*, you will not have to search for any of this information, nor will you have to enquire how nutrition is conveyed through the same veins from the stomach to the whole body, and then once again carried back through the same veins to the stomach.[12] In purges using drugs – bearing in mind that anything which is to do with a crisis during an illness is cleared naturally, just as often happens too in those who are in good health – the most useful blood is conveyed to the stomach, nourishing it during lengthy abstinences from food. There is sometimes secreted through the veins a great deal of waste matter from the rest of the body.

I have demonstrated all this in my book *On the Natural Faculties*.

Anyone who contradicts me should not question the theories which I disproved in that book by referring to the conclusions of my arguments, but must instead show my whole arguments to be false. If that person cannot do either of these things, then it would be a good idea to show some respect and keep quiet, just as Erasistratus did.

Nowhere did Erasistratus mention the production and power of the humours. Where he did try to record a cure for paralysis, he was forced to mention the juice which nurtures the sinews. Similarly he was compelled, in the second book of his work *On Fevers*, to make reference to ancient writers, for he did not call the menstrual cycle an emptying, but rather a purging, thus employing the same terminology as is used with purgative drugs. In the same way doctors once termed even child-birth as purging, not simply emptying. When nature forms and develops the foetus during pregnancy, the very best blood is drawn off, so leaving in the veins the worst blood. The latter is discarded after giving birth, just as each month there is discarded blood that is in excess and useless, not just in quantity but also in quality. This sort of blood is far darker than the usual sort of blood.

This is what Erasistratus wrote in the second book of his work *On Fevers*, and I quote word for word:

> Anyone who wants to cure diseases ought definitely to be trained in the art of medicine. No symptom of any disease should be left without examination. Everything must be observed and treated systematically, according to whatever physical condition each disease causes. It sometimes happens that there is a secretion of dark urine when a woman is feverish and faint, but seems otherwise to be in no danger. However, the prognosis in this case is extremely pessimistic. The secretion should be checked to discover its origin in the particular physical condition and whether the menstrual cycle happens to be regular. If this secretion does not happen, then by its concentration it endangers the bladder. It can only be supposed that this secretion occurs more as an alleviation for a woman than a problem, which according to what is apparent seems to be the case.

Accordingly dark matter is often passed in the urine if menstruation does not occur. Women who are thus affected are relieved more by this than irritated. Since any evacuation through the womb can be designated as purging, Erasistratus showed, both in his diagnosis of the condition and in his prognosis of its development, that the statement which he made was useful and that his description was correct. He is witness to everything which has been said on this subject: that black bile is produced in the human body, in the same way as fluids full of yellow bile and phlegm.

I have shown that the humour which is called phlegm stems from phlegmatic foods during the initial stages of digestion in the stomach, just as whatever is full of yellow bile or black bile arises in the liver, as a result of which for the purging of blood there exists no special organ on the same lines as the kidneys and the spleen, the former for the purging of yellow bile and serous waste matter, the latter for the purging of black bile. Whatever is produced in the stomach, after it has been carried to the liver along with the humours distributed from food and drink, becomes blood at the same time as it is digested with these things; but whatever is left behind around the stomach, after it has been washed away by the fluid flowing down from the liver to these places, is secreted through the lower parts of the stomach.

Erasistratus is clearly shown as knowing these facts, because during his deliberations he was forced to recall them when he was applying his knowledge of medicine. He may have remained silent about many areas of medicine, but here he is detected as willingly trying to obscure and hide everything that the ancient doctors correctly stated about the humours. I can, by omitting the rest of what he said, highlight that idea, which in the extract which I have just quoted he circuitously mentioned in passing. There can be no reasonable excuse to explain this silence, because he himself wrote: 'It sometimes happens that there is a secretion of dark urine when a woman is feverish and faint, but seems otherwise to be in no danger. However, the prognosis in this case is extremely pessimistic'.

Earlier doctors had written that black bile is among the bad signs, so he said he realised that it exercised great force in those who were ill with acute fevers, since he had obviously read what had been written by these doctors concerning urine. Which is the reason why he had to treat his statement on urine rather more comprehensively in his work *On Fevers*, particularly in the second book where these descriptions of his can be found. For Hippocrates wrote in his *Prognostics*:

> Urine is best when the sediment is pale, smooth and even for the duration of the illness up until the crisis, since it indicates a brief illness and a definite recovery. If, however, the sediment should vary its appearance, the urine sometimes being clear and sometimes showing a pale, smooth and even deposit, then the illness will last longer and recovery is not so definite. If the urine is tinged with red and the sediment is smooth and also tinged with

red, recovery is certain, although the illness will last longer than in the case just mentioned. Sediments in urine that resemble coarse meal are bad, but worse than these by far are flaky sediments. Thin pale sediments are very bad, but even worse than these are those which look like bran. Clouds suspended in the urine are good when pale, but bad when dark. Provided the urine is thin and orange, it is a sign that the disease is unconcocted; if the disease is also prolonged while the urine is like this, then there a danger in case the patient cannot last until the disease is concocted.

The more deadly sorts of urine are smelly, watery, dark and thick: dark urine is worse for adults, watery urine is worse for children. If the urine remains thin and raw for a long time, and if there are signs of recovery, then pus will probably be found in the area below the diaphragm. An oily film resembling spider webs on the surface of the urine is a cause for alarm: the prognosis is consumption. Cloudy urine must be examined to see whether the clouds are at the bottom or the top, and to check on the colour of the clouds. If the clouds are at the bottom, and the colours are good, then this is a good sign; but if the clouds are at the top, and the colours are bad, then this is a bad sign. Do not worry if the urine displays bad signs because the bladder is diseased, for these signs will not be symptomatic of the general state of health, but only of the bladder.[13]

Since Hippocrates wrote this, and since Diocles and Praxagoras wrote much the same, whether they were telling the truth or lying, it might have been expected that Erasistratus should have said, by adding the reason for his own interpretation, that the same was true in cases of vomiting and diarrhoea, where there is present what is called dark matter, as well as genuine black bile. Consequently there was a need with melancholy humour to distinguish everything that was being confused by using lay terms, a need which I defined earlier. Erasistratus therefore omitted the whole of the medical aspect of the humours. But my intention was not to discuss all the humours, but only black bile. Everything that I have written connected with the other humours can be found in more detail elsewhere.

On the subject of black bile, I will now add what I know for certain through long experience, since this will be invaluable to all those who study not sophistic arguments but the practicalities of medicine. As far as all the diseases which stem from black bile are concerned, if you immediately purge with the drugs that evacuate this humour, you can prevent any developments that might lead to cancer.

Those people really are a source of amazement who either voluntarily or under pressure devise heated arguments to deny the existence of black bile. They claim that it is produced only in those who are suffering from some unnatural complaint, whereas nobody who is correctly producing healthy humours in the body contains black bile. If, as they say, you administer to an athlete who is in the peak of health some drug which is believed to empty out black bile, it will be seen that this bile is emptied, just as, if you employ a drug which is thought to purge yellow bile, it will be seen that this bile is purged. Following this they also state that evidently the power of the drug alters the blood and transforms it into the bile. Similarly, if you give an expellent of phlegm, you will see, so they claim, phlegm being emptied. Equally if you force someone who is generating very healthy humours to take those drugs which are believed to empty thin serous discharges, you will observe even in this case some thin serous discharge being emptied.

Before it is proved that each purgative drug works on one particular humour, where an element of attraction is intended by nature, their argument holds some plausibility; but once this has been proved, their mistake is made clear. For it has been shown that each drug attracts a particular humour, which results in some drugs administered to those suffering from dropsy causing on occasion such an evacuation as to fill a chamber pot completely; on the other hand the stomach is checked by other drugs in proportion to the evacuation, and patients are clearly relieved and can breathe more freely; yet other drugs empty out the bulk of the yellow bile in those who are suffering from jaundice and help those patients.

Conversely, if you give hydragogues to those who are ill with jaundice, and drugs that remove black bile to those suffering from dropsy, you will evacuate very little of the humour in question, and not only will you fail to help the patients, but you will cause a great deal of harm, just as you would if you were to cut a vein. And yet among those who believe that the humours in the body are transformed by purgative drugs, and that each of the drugs used for attracting these humours possesses an unique nature, the cutting of veins is of similar efficacy as purging. Just as we empty out excess fluid in those who have hydrous dropsy by administering hydragogues, and in doing so help the patients, so too anyone who subscribes to cutting veins can see to what end their help results.

I can only laugh at anyone who believes that there is no organ in the body which holds black bile, on the analogy of the bladder holding yellow bile, and claiming this proves that there is absolutely no black bile in perfectly healthy bodies. For they concede then that we do not have any phlegm at all, just as there is no yellow bile in pigeons; but the reason for pigeons not having any yellow bile is that they do not have their bladder next to their liver, as is the case with quite a few other creatures. By a process of homonymy they devise subtle arguments about melancholy humour for themselves, but certainly not for me. I say that melancholy humour is present in healthy people, because I listen to what is always being said about black bile, which I say is produced in those who have an abnormal condition. There is not the same black bile in those who are perfectly healthy as in some of those who have an abnormal condition, but nothing prevents me from calling both melancholy humour. These matters I have already discussed. But there is nothing wrong in revising all this in these short chapters for the benefit of all those who are caught up in sophistry with false arguments and all those who learn precisely what Hippocrates believed.

4

ON UNEVEN BAD
TEMPERAMENT

Uneven bad temperament happens from time to time throughout the whole body, for example in the case of dropsies that are specifically within the skin, in fevers that are named agues, and in almost all other sorts of fevers, apart from those that are termed consumptive; for it arises in every part of the body, when that part is swollen, inflamed, gangrenous, stricken with erysipelas or cancerous. In this category belong what is called elephantiasis, cancerous sores and shingles. However, all these conditions come about together with fluxes; but if the parts have been affected solely by the qualities, uneven bad temperaments happen without any suppurating material, when the parts have been cooled, burnt, exercised more than usual, left idle or subjected to some other similar state.

In addition, as a result of those problems which attack from without, more uneven bad temperaments spring up inside our bodies if they are warmed, cooled, dried or moistened. These are simple bad temperaments, as has been explained in my book *On Temperaments*.[1] From these simple bad temperaments derive four other bad temperaments, either when the body is heated at the same time as being dried, or cooled at the same time as being moistened, or cooled at the same time as being dried, or heated at the same time as being moistened. It is absolutely clear that such composite bad temperaments differ from those that are of a single constitution through not existing evenly in every part of the body that is in a state of bad temperament.

So I propose in this work to explain in detail what the manner of generation is for all uneven bad temperaments. In order to clarify my arguments, it is necessary to make mention of all the parts of the body, beginning with the largest parts, which are of course known even to the layman. For no one is ignorant of the hands, feet, stomach, chest and head.

Let me divide even further every part of the body that falls in this category into its relative sections: the leg, for instance, into the thigh, tibia and

37

foot; the hand conversely into the arm, forearm and end of the hand. To proceed further, the parts peculiar to the ends of the hands are the wrists and bones forming the palms of the hands, and the fingers. In addition, the fingers are composed of bones, cartilage, ligaments, sinews, arteries and veins, as well as membranes, flesh, tendons, nails, skin and fat. It is not yet agreed to divide these constituent parts into further sets, but they resemble each other and the whole body, except the arteries and veins; for these are composed of fibrous vessels and membranes, as has been stated in my work *On Anatomical Proceedures*. Moreover, there are many spaces between the parts that resemble each other and the whole body and those parts that are called primary, and these spaces are also more numerous and larger in the middle of the instrumental and composite parts, but sometimes too in respect of every part that resembles another and the whole, as in the case of bone and skin. All these matters have been discussed in my work *On Anatomical Proceedures*.[2] So the soft parts of the body, as they rest against each other, produce the spaces in between which are devoid of any sensation; but in the case of those parts that are hard and dry, the intervening spaces can be detected through their sensation, for example with the medullary cavities in the bones. These naturally have in them a thick white sap that makes up the nourishment for the bones. The way in which the passages in the skin are produced has been described in my work *On Temperaments*. For the sake of clarity what was then the intention of my discussion should be remembered.

But in the present discussion my intention is to focus on the nature of uneven bad temperament and the number of ways in which it can come about. That there is not one single temperament in every part of the body thus affected has been stated before. But the following observation is common in all cases of uneven bad temperament: that the different temperaments follow the nature of the affected bodies. For on the one hand flesh is of a single temperament, whilst on the other hand the whole muscle can move into a state of unequal temperament.

As soon as a hot flux rushes into a muscle, first the larger arteries and veins are filled and dilated, then after this the smaller arteries and veins, and so on as far as the smallest arteries and veins. At the point when the flux has reached saturation point and can no longer be contained, some of it is filtered through the mouths of the veins and arteries, and some of it through the membranes to the outside. While this is happening, the intervening spaces of the primary bodies are filled with flux, with the result that everything is both heated and awash with fluid. By everything I mean the sinews, membranes, ligaments and flesh. This condition affects first of all the arteries and veins, which suffer pain in a manner that is especially complex. The reason for this is that they are heated, stretched and racked by the flux from within; while from without they are both heated and at the same time compressed and burdened.

Of the other parts, some suffer through just heat or compression, others through a combination of these two problems. The resulting ailment is called inflammation, that is an uneven bad temperament of the muscle. For the blood that is in the muscle is already fermenting, and this causes first and foremost the membranes of the arteries and veins to grow hot, then everything which is positioned outside and which surrounds them.

One of the two situations will necessarily be encountered: if the flux is overwhelming, then the bodies that are overwhelmed will be corrupted; but if the flux is overcome, then for the muscle there is a return to its usual state. The flux should be overcome first, for it is better to begin from a stronger position, since in this case there will occur two types of healing, either when all the fluid which has been secreted is dispersed, or else when it has been concocted. But of these two types of healing, the most desirable is dispersal. There are inevitably two consequences of digestion, namely the production and the discarding of a discharge.

Sometimes the discharge withdraws into the the largest and least important of the adjacent cavities. This is in fact the best sort of withdrawal. At other times, however, it withdraws to a large and by no means unimportant cavity that lies adjacent, or to an unimportant cavity that is not the largest. Of those discharges that withdraw to the stomach, the best sort of dispersal is that which proceeds into the open space inside, into which the majority of things burst; the worst sort of dispersal is that which goes under the peritoneum. Of the discharges that withdraw to the brain, the best is that which proceeds to the front of the ventricles; the worst is that which goes under the membrane that covers the brain and to the rear of the ventricles.

A discharge in the sides breaks into the open spaces of the chest; a discharge of the muscles breaks under the skin, of the intestines either into the arteries and the veins in them, or beneath the surrounding membrane, which acts like a skin for inwards.

But if the parts of the body are overcome by flux, they will clearly arrive at such a state of bad temperament that any activity which they might have will be ruined and in time they will be destroyed. Only when the parts of the body resemble what has been changed does the pain abate. For it is not during the changing of the temperament, but when the temperament causes a change that the parts of the body suffer. This is what Hippocrates so admirably stated: 'Pains occur when the nature of anything is changed and corrupted'.[3] Everything has its nature changed and corrupted when it is heated, cooled, dried, moistened, or released from a set pattern. So in uneven bad temperaments the primary cause of change is heat and cold, since these qualities are extremely powerful; but there is also moistening and drying, in other words hunger and thirst, the former being a lack of what is dry, the latter a lack of what is moist. Release from a set pattern occurs with wounding, corroding, stretching, compressing and tearing.

So if the temperature of the blood in the inflamed parts is moderate, and the blood contained throughout the whole body is of average consistency, it is not at all easy for anything to be heated at the same time as the affected part. But if the blood flows very strongly, or if it should be bilious throughout the whole body, then immediately everything is heated, and even more so when there occurs simultaneously particularly hot blood in the inflammation, and bilious blood in the body as a whole. Any blood that is in the arteries is heated first, because it is by nature hotter and more aerated, and after that the blood in the veins. If the inflamed part is close to the inwards which are filled with blood, the blood throughout the whole body is heated more quickly.

If I may summarise, everything that is readily susceptible to heat, or is naturally hot, is heated first, just as everything that is readily susceptible to cold, or is naturally cold, is cooled first. Air is easily changed, because it is composed of the tiniest particles. Yellow bile is hottest by nature, phlegm coolest. Of the other humours, blood is the next hottest after yellow bile; black bile is the next coolest after phlegm. Hence yellow bile is easily changed by whatever it comes into contact with, whilst black bile is changed with difficulty. Thus everything that is composed of small particles is easily changed, but everything that is composed of large particles is changed with difficulty.

In the case of inflammations, there are inevitably many sorts of changes, because each body is differently disposed. Firstly the humour that causes the inflammation is either more or less hot, then its corruption occurs through its own nature, not least according to whether it is more or less trapped. Whatever is not dissipated through exhalation putrefies more quickly, just as in the case of everything that is outside, and particularly when these things are hot and moist in temperament. In addition the inflamed part is either close to or far from the inwards that are full of blood; and the blood is either more or less full of yellow bile, or black bile, or phlegm or air. Consequently these changes necessarily take on many forms, if one change is compared with another or even itself.

These are all uneven bad temperaments of the body, and this is particularly the case when the blood in the inflammation undergoes digestion, then in turn the blood in the inwards and in the heart. If, when the patient is still alive and not yet feverish, you wish to place your fingers over the left ventricle, you will feel a very intense heat. I have written about this in my *Practical Anatomy*. It is therefore not illogical that such heat should result in something so dire when the body is warmed in excess of what is natural. For the body contains blood that is made up of extremely fine particles and much air. This blood is continually on the move. But generally during fevers all the blood is heated as it absorbs all the unnatural warmth that arises from the putrefaction of the humours.

However, neither the membranes of the arteries nor the veins nor anything else in the surrounding parts of the body have their temperament completely changed; but they are still changed and altered when they are heated. If this happens over a lengthier period of time, the body is some-times overwhelmed and wholly changed, as it is no longer just being heated, but already has been heated contrary to what is natural. Alteration to each part of the body can be defined as the damage done to the usual function of this particular part. The range of alteration is circumscribed by the boundary of what is contrary to nature; in other words there is shared ground common to and in between the two limits, which can be defined respectively as whatever is in accordance with nature and whatever is absolutely contrary to nature.

During all this time the body that is heated suffers pain commensurate with the amount of change. Whenever all the solid parts of the body are completely heated, the resulting fever is termed consumptive, since no longer is it contained only in the humours and in the breath, but also in the bodies of those who have such a condition. This condition is painless, and those who suffer from such a fever regard themselves as not being wholly feverish, for they do not feel the heat, since all their bodily parts are heated equally. Moreover, in their arguments about perception, natural philoso-phers concur with the following statements: that there is no sensation without change, and no pain in what has already been completely changed. So all the consumptive fevers are painless and totally without feeling for those who are ill. It is not the case that one of their bodily parts is active, whilst another part is passive, since each resembles the other, and all have one corresponding temperament.

But if one part is hotter, and the other is colder, yet they may be hotter or colder in such a way that they do not affect whatever is next to them. Otherwise the parts that are thus contrary to nature would harm one another, so that they would differ from their own temperaments. Whatever is flesh is hot, whilst whatever is bone is cold. Yet in respect of flesh and bone and all the other parts of the body, the irregularity of a condition is painless if the excess is within moderate bounds. Thus the air surrounding us does not distress us until it takes on immoderate coldness or heat. Of the average differences, although they are very numerous and clearly possess an excess, we feel them without pain.

Therefore, in view of the facts above, it can be said that my argument is reasonable, and this is indeed what Hippocrates stated in passing, asserting that all diseases are ulcers.[4] For an ulcer is a break from the set pattern, but excessive heat and cold come close to releasing any continuity, the former by separating and severing the basis of solidity, the latter by compressing and squashing inside whatever is squeezed out or crushed. Anyone trying to set limits beyond which heat and cold are immoderate will not appear to be reckoning without logic.

But whether one or another limit is set on what is out of proportion, it is quite clear that all disproportion must set in relation to something. The body as a whole is not disposed in the same way to what is hot or cold. Hence some creatures emit secretions that are mutually suitable for each other, whilst others are not only unsuitable, but are deadly, such as those of humans and vipers. The saliva of each is in fact fatal to the other. Thus you can kill a scorpion by spitting on it if you are fasting, but one man cannot kill another man by biting, nor can one viper kill another viper, nor can one asp kill another asp. That which is similar is suitable and benign, whilst that which is opposite is hostile and troublesome. Everything grows and is nourished by whatever is similar, but is killed and destroyed by whatever is opposite. In this way the preservation of health is through whatever is similar, whilst the cure for diseases is through whatever is opposite. But I have discussed this in another book. A consumptive fever that takes hold of the body is not perceptible to the sick person. Of the other fevers, none is perceptible, but some are more and some are less troublesome to sick people. Some of these fevers cause shivering. This is a symptom, just like many other symptoms, of unequal bad temperament. However, it is not the time or place to explain the generation of unequal bad temperament in the present book, since I have discussed this in my work *On the Natural Faculties*. As to how many bad temperaments there are, how they are categorised, and what each is disposed by nature to do, I have explained all in my book *On the Causes of Symptoms*.[5]

Let me return once again to the differences among unequal bad temperaments. I have already stated how all fevers arise from inflammation; and how all inflammations and fevers (apart from those that are termed consumptive) spring from diseases that are unevenly composed. When there is no inflammation, fevers come about from a putrefaction of the humours. For whatever is not contained, and whatever is not dissipated by exhalation, putrefies most definitely the quickest of everything, but much else besides that is ripe for putrefaction also putrefies. Concerning what is the most suitable of all these states has been discussed elsewhere.

But to return to the subject in question: in some ways it could be said that unequal bad temperament exists throughout the whole body, sometimes when particled exhalations are blocked in, sometimes when excessive exercise or unusually hard work augments the body's temperature, sometimes when the blood flows at an increased rate through anger, and sometimes when the outside of the body is warmed by heatstroke. I think it is clear that in all these fevers, just as in the case of the inflammations mentioned above, as a result both of the relative strength of activity and of the condition of each body, some people become more fevered, others less so, and some not at all. Moreover, since on occasion bad temperament affects the humours, it is no less clear that in the case of all such chronic fevers those which are termed consumptive follow.

And now my argument has almost come to the point of showing that sometimes this unequal bad temperament occurs when the composition of any part of the body runs hot or cold, just as has been stated in the case of inflammations; but often it does not happen like this, the temperament of the body being altered according to the state of the qualities, that is hot, cold, moist and dry. Of the causes of change, some arise from the body itself, whilst others come about from without. They arise from the body whenever a fever is exacerbated solely through putrefaction, or through some form of inflammation; they come about from without whenever the body is disturbed because of heat stroke and exercise. This has been discussed at greater length in my work *On the Causes of Diseases*.[6] In the same way that a fever arises from heatstroke, when the temperature of the body has been altered, so death can even be the result, when some people violently cool their whole body in icy cold water. How everyone feels pain when subjected to this process is clear.

For everyone quickly feels pain when, after rapidly cooling themselves in icy cold water, they eagerly try to warm themselves up. Many people sense a violent pain around the base of their nails when they bring their hands up suddenly to a fire. So how can anyone, who understands clearly the cause of pain as stemming from uneven bad temperament, still be in doubt about pains inside the body? Or be amazed at how the colon, or the teeth, or any of the other parts of the body often experience pain without the presence of inflammation? For none of these conditions is amazing, nor is it amazing how some of those who are ill shiver and are fevered at the same time. If the cold phlegmatic humour, which Praxagoras called vitreous, and the hot bitter bile are present in excess at the same time and pass through the sensitive parts of the body, then it is not strange that a sick person senses both of them alike. If you keep a man in the heat of the sun, and you pour cold water over him, it is not impossible that he will feel at the same time both the hot sun and the cold water. But then both of these sensations are from without and affect the major parts of the body.

Agues work from within and affect the minor parts of the body, which is why the whole body seems to feel both of these sensations, since hot and cold are drawn forcibly through the narrowest of passages, making it impossible to find a sensitive part in which neither of the two sensations can be felt. And yet, during the incursion of paroxysms, some of those who are fevered both shiver and suffer thirst and simultaneously feel excessive cold and heat, although not in the same way as in the previous example, for they can distinguish clearly the hot from the cold parts of the body. This is because they feel the heat from within the body and in their inwards, whilst they sense the cold in all the exterior parts of the body.

Some chronic fevers are still called intermittent malignant fevers, that is a type of bilious remittent fever that is destructive. Whatever happens during these fevers to the large parts of the body also happens during agues to the small parts. The bad temperament of these fevers is unequal, as is the bad temperament of all the other fevers, except for those that are categorised as consumptive. Bad temperament is unequal too among those who shiver, but not in those who are termed consumptive, since that particular symptom is rare, and occurs generally in women and but rarely in men. For it to come about, one must lead a life of idleness, or eat large quantities of food over a long period, the result of which is the slow, cold, raw and phlegmatic humour which Praxagoras considered to be vitreous. Long ago, so it seems, no one suffered like this, because to live with such ease and abundance was unheard of, and as a result doctors once wrote that fever followed upon shivering.

But both I and the majority of contemporary doctors do not generally consider fever as a necessary step from shivering. Ague is compounded from such bad temperament and also from the bad temperament of those who are fevered. Thus I designate a fever in which both symptoms occur simultaneously; but a fever in which an initial shivering is followed by fever, as in tertian and quartan fevers, I do not call ague. So that ague is a combination of uneven bad temperaments, as are nearly all the other fevers, except for those which are called consumptive.

Similarly all those diseases of any part of the body whose symptoms are swelling, and nearly all those diseases whose symptoms are inflammation, are the result of uneven bad temperament, namely cancer, erysipelas, carbuncles, shingles, tumours, inflammations, sores and gangrene. An origin from an influx of the humours is the common element in all these conditions. What is different is that some arise from phlegmatic humour, others from bilious humour, others from melancholic humour, others from blood that is either hot, thin and bubbling, or cold, thick and contrastingly composed. It will be shown elsewhere what the differences are between them according to type.

For the present discussion all that need be said is that whatever the flux, it produces according to the same pattern each of the diseases already mentioned, in the course of which inflammation has been shown to come about through whatever is hot and full of blood; and that each of the parts of the body that are both simple and also akin to one another and to the whole body, after being affected by the flux, move to a state of bad temperament, although when each is heated, cooled, dried or wetted externally, depending on the sort of flux, they are not in any way affected to the same degree internally. But if everything is completely altered and changed, then at once such a condition becomes painless, although it is very difficult to achieve a state like this. This is as much as needs to be known before anyone tries to follow first my treatise *On Simple Medicines* and then my work *On Therapeutic Method.*[7]

5

ON THE CAUSES OF DISEASE

I have explained in another work the total number of diseases in existence, when divided according to sort and kind, both simple and composite. But there remains for me to discuss the causes of each of these diseases, beginning with the simple and similar which are named according to the constituent parts of the body, and then passing on to the composite and instrumental. Now by those who believe that in birth and in death the substance of the body undergoes a process of uniting and changing respectively, every illness and bad temperament too has been shown to arise from a body that in terms of sensation is both simple and composed of similar parts, and divisible according to the continuity of its parts; but for those who hold that the parts of the body are not united, and that spaces are an integral part of the fabric of the body, there are innumerable ways of dissolving and dispersing any perceptible union.

Hence I am now going to consider the causes of each of the diseases by basing my argument on the first hypothesis, which I certainly believe holds the truth. There are, I posit, four simple and four composite diseases, sometimes arising only from an immoderate increase of the hot and the cold, or from some clash between one or other of these things, such as between the dry and the moist; and sometimes from a combination of those things that have increased to such a degree of excess as to cause a disease, that is hot at the same time as dry, or cold and dry, or hot and moist, or cold and moist.

So I shall look at the reasons for the origins of each of the diseases, beginning with disease that is the consequence of a bad temperament brought about through a disproportionate amount of heat. In all bodies a level of heat in excess of what is normal appears either when there is an increase in heat through motion, or putrefaction, or interaction with another hotter body, or a blocking of the pores, or the necessary intake of food.

In the case of motion, especially among those who exercise in the gym, it is just as when stones are rubbed against each other, or pieces or wood, or when a flame is fanned; in the case of putrefaction, and particularly of semen and faeces, I know for a fact that sometimes pigeon dung on putrefying spontaneously combusts. Furthermore, it is clear to everyone, who bears in mind public baths, the summer sun and fires of every sort, that through proximity with what is of a higher temperature the adjacent parts of the body are warmed. So if you light a fire during winter in a large house, after closing all the doors and windows, you will trap the heat inside; but if you allow all the doors and windows to be opened, the house will be no hotter than before. By this example it is evident that the act of closing was the reason for the greater heat. The study of materials too adds weight to this argument: dry reeds easily send up flames to the greatest height, whilst green wood, and particularly if you pile more of the same on top, weighs down the flame for much longer and almost smothers it, only increasing its power after a considerable lapse of time.

How, then, in the living body do each of these actions take place? After exercising comes exhaustion. This is because there is immoderate heat in the limbs and muscles in excess of what is natural, these parts being the first which moved. If the heat should remain there and disperse before spreading through the rest of the body, weariness would be the only thing of consequence; but if the heat should spread through the entire body, the resulting illness is a fever, that is an immoderate heat of the whole body. So anger, which is heat seething around the heart, can sometimes by immoderate motion spread through the whole body and fuel a fever.

Of all the things that putrefy in the body, some cause excessive heat only in those areas in which they putrefy, such as is the case with erysipelas, shingles, carbuncles, inflammations and swellings of the glands; whilst others spark fevers and make the whole body as hot as they are.

The third reason for excessive heat is now revealed: from the way it is started in people and from that condition which is called heatstroke. In the case of swollen glands, inflammations, erysipelas and all diseases that are hot in this way, the part that is touching and always contiguous is the first to be affected by this heat, and then to pass a portion of this heat to whatever is near, which in turn passes the heat to whatever is next to it. Thus when this bad temperament reaches the usual source of heat, the whole body quickly absorbs an element of the incipient illness. Spending a long time in the sun without any clothes on, except for a hat, occasionally overheats the skin. This is dubbed 'heatstroke'. But if this heat should permeate through the whole body, then fever will ensue.

The fourth reason for an exacerbation of the natural level of heat can

be seen to arise from whatever is cooling or astringent. If you are particularly chilled after swimming in water that contains either astringent
substances or something similar, you block and contract the skin, thereby
trapping inside whatever should be exhaled. If this happens, the smoky
vapour collects and causes fevers.

The fifth cause of excessive heat lies in foods that have hot and harsh
powers, such as garlic, leeks, onions and so on. Immoderate use of these
foods sometimes sparks a fever. People have in fact fallen to a fever as a
result of hot drinks, for example when drinking too much old rough
wine on a weak constitution, and when taking harsh medicines, remedies
and drugs.

Why then, some people ask, do these things not always start a fever?
It is because the level of active element is unequal, because the resulting
condition has parameters of excess or deficiency that are individual to
each body, and because everyone has a body that is unique in the way
that it changes with ease or otherwise from what its nature usually is. So
you should not be puzzled if not all movement causes exhaustion, for it
must be clear by now that unless this movement happens to be greater
and stronger than the capabilities of the limbs and muscles, it will not
cause exhaustion. Similarly it should be noted that the same condition of
exhaustion, unless it is particularly strong and chronic, cannot by itself
harm the body as a whole. Can it be that a modicum of movement does
not cause exhaustion, but that a modicum of exhaustion in general sparks
a fever? Or can it be that movement has the means to achieve all this, but
exhaustion does not? The reason is that athletes can undergo lengthy and
violent movement without exhausting their bodies, but everyone knows,
even the most ignorant, that us ordinary mortals at once feel physical
pain if we exert ourselves a little more than usual. So it is not surprising
if one does not in general develop a fever if one is exhausted. For either
the exercise is modest, or of short duration, or it is of lesser strength than
the body. If exercise of the body is of a brief duration, without violence
and weaker than the constitution of the person exercising, then no
exhaustion is caused. Exhaustion causes fever, even if it is short, even it
is brief, even if it is weaker than the strength of the affected body.

This can be seen when the most efficient fire is considered, and how it
does not heat those who are cold without time and strength. For sometimes, when we come indoors from the icy cold, we pass our hands
through a large flame. In fact fire does not readily kindle all material: dry
reeds might at once catch fire on their first contact with the flame, but
wet green timber has to have a long period of time and a strong flame to
be kindled.

You are not amazed at any of these facts to do with fire. So how is it that you are puzzled by exhaustion, even if it needs excess, time and a body provided with what is needed to be kindled? It would be better if you did not stay puzzled, but looked at what sort of body grows hot with ease and what sort of body becomes cold with difficulty. You will hear about this later. Meanwhile, do not be surprised by any of this, if what has to be achieved demands a great deal of time, besides being on the brink of whatever can be endured. No fire can burn without these things, no sword can cut, nor can anything be done effectively to whatever is stronger without a considerable lapse of time.

You would not pour oil all over the flame in a lamp, and certainly not water; you would not try to cut stones with a sword, even less diamonds. But do you not always consider exhaustion, warming, cooling and other such things as the cause of fevers, even if on the body as a whole they have a heating effect that is of minimal intensity, of short duration and of little consequence. For whatever is hot readily heats excessively, just as whatever is cold readily cools excessively. So whatever is opposite is not suitable.

Any difficulty over research into this must therefore be ascribed to stupidity and ignorance. One ought to pity the mental obtuseness and hate the contentiousness of those who readily and recklessly declare that no fever arises from any of the causes listed above. In fact their insidious arguments have been refuted in a separate work of mine about the primary causes of disease. However, now is not the right time to refute those who are in error, but rather it is my intention to explain the truth.

So once again I shall return to my original proposal which was, I think, to talk about the antecedent causes of each of the simple diseases as far as their initial stages of development. For one cannot do worse than to be guided by those who, for the sake of clarity, define precisely those words in common use. These people designate on the one hand the antecedent causes of disease as those which actually occur inside someone, whether bodily conditions or movements contrary to nature, whilst on the other hand they designate the initial causes of diseases as those which happen outside of someone, thereby inducing change and alteration in the body.

I have discussed in general terms the causes of hot diseases, but now I shall turn to those that are cold. The latter have many causes, such as, for example: proximity to what is cold, the quantity and quality of what is being drunk, constipation and diarrhoea, and finally a sedentary lifestyle or immoderate exercise.

These external causes extinguish even a fire. If you place a lot of snow on a little bit of charcoal, or some ice, or if you pour some cold water over it, you will extinguish it immediately. If the air should be extremely cold, as it is especially around the Danube in winter, not only would you observe how a lamp, set in the open air, is extinguished at once, but also every other small fire.

Thus what puts out a fire is: juxtaposition with whatever is very cold, smothering by an excess of whatever usually feeds it, starvation from a lack of the same, or through some harmful quality that is unconnected with these things. For if you pile a heap of logs on top you will smother a small flame through an excessive quantity; conversely if you do not provide anything at all, or at least very little, you will see the flame die away because of a lack, or just a paucity, of fuel.

So we can see a flame in a lamp decreasing and running the risk of being extinguished from an excess of suitable fuel. Whether you do not pour enough oil into a lamp, or whether you add too much oil, you will affect the flame quite markedly; and if you feed it fuel ungrudgingly, but do not allow it to burn completely on its own or without interference, you will at once make the flame smaller, just as if you had poured oil mixed with water into the lamp.

In addition, if you block off the air from the flame and cause it to be overly depleted, you will soon see the flame growing smaller and on the verge of being extinguished. You can do this by placing around the flame a surgical cup, or a lid from a stove, or some other such instrument. The same happens if you block the opening to a oven.

Yet if you place the flame in the hot summer sun outside of any shade, or if you place another larger flame beside it, you will notice the smaller flame being strongly diminished and dissipated by the adjacent and more powerful heat. Equally clear is that, by fanning a fire, you will cause it to blaze up, provided you do this gently; but that, by fanning it violently, you will weaken and enfeeble it. So in fact the size of a fire is commensurate even with the wind, if it causes a blaze to spread; but contrastingly strong winds do not encourage a fire, but rather extinguish and do not fan it.

From this example it can be seen that flames require some external movement for their increase, although this movement should not be too violent, for a flame that is not gently fanned is feeble, but it is enfeebled and dissipated when it is subjected to any external movement.

Working on the first premise, any cold disease is caused by a chill penetrating the body from the outside, either just through contact or through its force. So you can be harmed by bathing in cold water, both by being badly washed and because of entering something that is freezing. I have been witness to some people actually dying before they got home from such a bath.

Working on the second premise, by excessive drinking you can suffer from an abnormality in movement or sensation either through paralysis or epilepsy; or you can be chilled in some other way. Certainly wine in moderation bolsters the natural temperature of the body, as does a proper diet; but an excessive consumption of food, however nutritious and excellent, is the cause of cold diseases. Among the cooling drugs are poppy, mandrake, henbane and hemlock, the last of which is lethal because of its violent chilling action. We designate the blockage as the third and worst cause of cooling diseases, since it engenders torpor, lethargy and apoplexy.

Let me refer here to Hippocrates, who stated that what was troubling the body of someone who suddenly lost their power of speech was a blockage in the veins. Like the other doctors of antiquity, he referred to the two sorts of vessels that are full of blood as veins, unlike modern doctors who only designate as veins the sort of vessels that do not pulsate. Whenever the arteries in a body have seized up, that is they have become engorged with blood, the innate heat is smothered so that no empty space might still remain into which, by being dilated, they might suck in air from outside, and those who are affected like this quickly grow sluggish and numb throughout their whole being.

I have shown in my work *On the Use of Pulsations* that the arteries pulse for the sake of preserving in all parts of the body a moderate heat in harmony with what is natural.[1] In my work *On the Use of Respiration* I showed that one should maintain a moderate heat in the whole of the body.[2] Just as you can immediately extinguish external flames by depriving them of any contact with the air, either by setting over them the cover of a stove, or a cupping instrument, or some other similar thing, so you will quickly extinguish the heat in the body by confining it in such a way that it has no association with the air around. The heat in the heart is linked to the outside through the passage of the windpipe, and if you block this you will at once smother the heat and shut down any life.

Throughout the whole body the arteries vent themselves into the atmosphere both through the heart itself, since this is connected with the windpipe, and through the skin, first being fanned during the expansion of the lungs, then shedding any smoky waste during the contraction of the lungs, thereby preserving through both these actions the natural symmetry. So when the arteries become blocked either, as I have already said, by an excess of blood, or by some obstruction to their mouths, and they can no longer breathe, the vital heat is extinguished and the body is as a consequence reduced to a state resembling death.

However, when the blockage is light, a condition of this kind does not necessarily involve the innate heat; for example, there should be present anything sooty or smoky, then because of the existence of excretive matter in the body the innate heat will be affected in one way, whereas if only good and pleasant vapour should be exhaled, then the innate heat will be affected in another way.

For each of these two conditions there are two categories, and their differences may be set out as follows. When the blood in the body is definitely good and is not muddied by any bad sediments, but instead a good vapour is produced from it as it grows warm, and nothing fiery or harsh is transmitted with it, then a moderate blockage of the body quickly becomes either plethoric or hotter than it would otherwise be: plethoric in those who live without exhausting themselves, since they should drain themselves by means of exercise, or else any waste will stay inside the body; hotter in those who exercise, since the innate heat is increased by movement, which cannot disperse because of the blocking of the body.

When the body is blocked and smoky excretions are produced, either a fever is kindled, since the smoky exhalation is trapped inside, or the innate heat is choked and extinguished. Each of these actions will be consequent to the quantity of excretion and the degree of blockage. For if there is present a great deal of smoky waste and severe blockaging that has need of evacuation, there is a danger that the innate heat will be smothered and extinguished; but if there is not so much excretion and the blockaging is minor, a fever will be started. So it is clear that it is vital to have some acquaintance with both the normal and the abnormal state of the body, in which either sooty, smoky or vaporous matter is dissipated through exhalation. This has been described in my treatise *On the Therapeutic Method*.

Now let me return to the topic at hand. Just as blockaging is often the cause of cooling through the process that I have delineated, so also unblocking, when it dissipates and disperses the innate heat in an immoderate manner, causes the body to grow colder. Such things happen not only to the body as a whole, but also to each part of the body individually, either through blocking or through unblocking. For if the body as a whole suffers the same condition through the blocking and filling of the arteries as an individual part, even if the arteries alone have been affected, it is of course a foregone conclusion that the body as a whole will also have the same illness as the individual part.

Moreover the remedies which present themselves, both cold medicinal waters and the surrounding air itself, can produce in the individual part either a blocking or an unblocking. In addition the restrictions that sometimes spring up around this particular part, or in the parts above, mortify and chill the part, depriving it of any connection with the force of life in the body, through which both the innate heat maintains its flow and the power of movement furnishes the arteries.

I have said enough about hot and cold diseases. Let me now turn to dry diseases. If anyone exercises and pants more than usual; if at the same time this person eats less and makes use of foods that have drier properties; and if this person is drier in temperament; then a dry disease will easily occur, particularly if there is any stress or an unusual level of insomnia at night. In fact the dry nature of the surrounding atmosphere clearly dehydrates the body, as does swimming in water saturated with sodium carbonate, sulphur, astringent substances, asphalt or the like. In fact all medicines that are dry in power, whether they are employed internally or externally, dehydrate the body. There is a fuller discussion of this in my work *On Medicines*.

These are the causes of dry illnesses. All such causes are opposite to moist illnesses, which are a surfeit of foods that are moist in power, too many drinks, an excessively luxurious mode of life, sex and frequent baths in soft water, particularly after a meal. Hence a life spent wholly in idleness and without exercise, showers of rain, getting wet and medicines have the capacity to effect the same.

Obviously the causes of composite illnesses are invariably composite. So if, for instance, one cause that is hot and and one that is dry run concurrently, the illness will necessarily be hot and dry; and if the causes are hot and moist, the illness will be hot and moist. The same is true for the other two combinations, namely moist and cold, and dry and cold. Now is the moment to explain what this treatise contributes and distinguishes.

The body is often changed by causes that are of a similar nature to one another, sometimes overwhelming those causes that are more numerous or of a longer standing, whilst at other times the body derives an equal share of harm from both these things. Even if it seems impossible for one and the same body to be made hotter or colder than normal, and more moist and more dry, yet this is the case. Appropriately this break with normality is called bad temperament. What is germane to this condition has been described elsewhere by me in another book, so there is no need to discuss it any further here.[3]

It is time, however, to turn to the remaining categories of illness, the causes of which I intend now to examine. Yet it would be relevant to think back to what was stated in my work *On the Differences between Diseases*: that sometimes the body is parted from its usual state through the four qualities alone, without anything else besides these qualities entering from outside, whilst sometimes the body is filled with a flux that appears at first sight to be completely moist, but has anything but a moist action.[4] The question of the power of these sort of moist things was discussed by the doctors and philosophers of antiquity, as well as by me in various treatises including my work *On Simple Medicines*. Nevertheless everything that is of relevance to the present debate can be stated now: yellow bile is hot and dry in power, whilst black bile is dry and cold; blood is moist and hot, whilst phlegm is cold and moist; sometimes the humours each flow unmixed, at other times they are mixed with each other; the appearance of swollen, indurated and inflamed parts of the body are thus varied to a wide degree. Hence carbuncles, cancers, shingles, erysipelas, gangrene, swollen glands, cankers and satyriasis are generated like this. In fact other diseases of the humours that are related include white leprosy, tumours full of matter that resembles soup, scurf, cysts, encysted tumours on the tendon and sebaceous tumours.

Both these and all the other illnesses mentioned previously differ from one another in that some are a result of just phlegm, others just of blood, others just of yellow bile, others just of black bile, others just of a humour that is not wholly abnormal. Whatever this humour might be, it will definitely belong to one of the types already described: for it is not possible for it to be anything but hot and dry, hot and moist, cold and dry, or cold and moist. Yet since it could not be thicker or colder, it no longer appears at first sight to be normal phlegm, but rather another sort of humour that is through its whole nature abnormal. This is not, of course, the truth. Whatever is moist and cold in power is categorised as phlegm. By the same criteria whatever is dry and hot has the general characteristics of yellow bile. All this has been discussed in greater detail elsewhere, so it is not necessary now to debate these problems at length, for there is an examination in depth of such matters in my work *On Therapeutic Method*. Let me return at once to what is relevant to this book.

All these diseases occur every time that nature dumps what is superfluous on to the less important parts of the body. Lots of other people have said exactly this, but the process of dumping has not yet been delineated. I attribute to nature some sense of logic and design, even if I say that it simply dumps anything that is not useful from the important to the unimportant parts of the body. In an illness the good crises are clearly generated through a process like this, but how these crises happen has not been expounded accurately by any of my predecessors, because they were incapable of showing properly the number, type, existence and function of each of the natural faculties, on something about which I have deliberated in another book.[5] However, there is no problem about detailing all of this now and making use of the ideas contained in the other books.

There are four powers, which every creature and plant shares: absorption, retention, transformation and rejection of whatever is superfluous. Superfluity can be divided into two types: either superfluous in quantity or quality. Not all the parts of the body are equal in strength: those that have the greatest importance are, from the start, made stronger by nature. Therefore in a body that has not been cleaned or is full of waste products something surely flows to the less important parts. Since what is superfluous is expelled from the stronger parts of the body, and cannot remain anywhere, it arrives at whatever is the weakest point. There follows a chain reaction: the part is either harmed when the body is initially formed, or is harmed afterwards, or it must be like this naturally, such a part being skin.

The skin is created not for any specific activity, but for its use alone, so it should be expected that it is weaker than those parts that do something. It can be likened to some natural covering or clothing on the body, but affording neither digestion, nor assimilation of food, nor conversion into blood, nor pulsation, nor respiration, nor self-generated movement, nor in short any activity in the body. At the same time, since it is situated outside everything else, it receives the waste products of the whole body.

Right from the outset nature created lots of organs to evacuate waste matter, and these organs suffice to preserve health, since no harm comes to the body from the air that surrounds it, nor does the body as a whole produce the excessive amount of waste matter seen if the diet is faulty. When a mistake in the diet does occur, then the normal functions of the organs are not sufficient to evacuate the bulk of the waste products, and the fluxes flood the skin after being driven from the stronger to the weaker parts of the body. These constitute the initial stages of the illnesses I have just described. Whatever is bad then increases in the limbs, when waste matter is trapped and putrefies, and when what is bad gets worse, the humour that flows afterwards is corrupted, even if this humour was initially good.

I have now discussed the diseases that are particular to the body as a whole. There remains to investigate the diseases of the organs, beginning with what is the first among these diseases in its style of formation. This illness arises sometimes from an alteration of what is normal in appearance and sometimes from the smoothing or roughing of a channel that has been damaged. The reasons for the alteration of a normal appearance can be detailed as follows: first, the formation of anything that is conceived in the womb is bad, since it is full of a substance that sets up a hindrance to, or is of an unsuitable quality for, the usual movement of the sperm; second, the birth itself and any mistake in the wrapping of the baby in swaddling-clothes.

Since the bodies of babies that have just been born are still soft and somewhat fluid, they can be easily distorted, such as when the midwives do not pick them up properly as soon as they are born and do not wrap them correctly in swaddling-clothes.[6] In all these cases the regular appearance of the limbs is readily tampered and damaged, unless they are handled in the correct manner.

In addition there are many cases of limbs being twisted after the initial birth during nursing, some through overfeeding, others through inappropriate movement either in being permitted to stand or walk prematurely or in being moved too violently. This is because overfeeding hinders natural activity, whilst premature and excessive movement disturbs and makes the limbs move round in an unnatural way. With the weight of the body pressing down from above, the legs are twisted either out or in according to the particular curve of the tibia. Among those who have legs that are by nature straighter than average, the tibia is more crooked; but among those with more curved legs, it is bent. What I mean by crooked is a curving out, by bent a curving in the opposite direction.

The structure of the chest is often distorted by wet-nurses binding it badly during the first feed. Where I live you can observe this being done all the time to little girls. Their wet-nurses want to stretch the area around the hips and thighs to make it larger than the chest; so they wrap everything round with some bandages, binding the shoulder-blades and chest firmly, but the tension is often not even, and either the breast seems pushed out to the front, or the area round the spine to the other side of the breast seems convex.

So, in addition, the back is, on occasion, broken and directed sideways, so that one shoulder-blade appears discrete, small and tucked in closely, whilst the other shoulder-blade projects, slopes and is altogether larger. All these problems associated with the structure of the chest are caused by the fault and stupidity of the wet-nurses who do not have a clue about what is properly symmetrical.

Even doctors often cause distortions when they fail to bandage and set limbs properly that have been broken. Conversely when there is no mistake in the medical treatment, the patient can be the creator of the distortion if he tries to use the limb before the callus that unites fractured bones has properly hardened.

A regular appearance can be ruined when the nose is bruised, or indeed when the rims of the joint sockets are crushed and the splinters of bones are surgically removed and the folds of skin do not afterwards heal evenly. An outward appearance can be harmed through excess or shortage, for instance among those who are too fat or too thin, either in one particular part of the body or throughout the whole body. The diseases called elephantiasis and atrophy visibly alter a profile: with elephantiasis the nose turns up, the lips and ears become thick and extended, and the general appearance of sufferers resembles satyrs; with atrophy the nose looks pointed, the temples are contracted, the eyes are hollow, and the shoulder-blades and shoulders project like wings. In all these cases appearances are ruined.

They are destroyed too by paralysis, intermittent convulsions, inflammations, indurations, the severing of sinews and tendons, and by hardened scars. Without fail, the particular part of the body is distorted for one reason or another. With those who are paralysed on one side or the other, the particular part of the body is dragged down by the action of the muscles, and this is the case as well with convulsions which incline to one side or the other through the spasms of the muscles. Inflammations, indurations, hardened scars and all similar problems affect whatever is adjacent to them and so a particular part of the body is distorted. This is what happens when sinews and tendons have been severed, just as with paralysis whatever acts for and whatever acts against nature draws the particular part of the body to itself, which is why all these factors can be summarised as an inclination to one side or the other distorting the particular part.

I have said enough now about the differences between appearances that are contrary to nature. The cavities inside the particular parts or their passages are either completely destroyed or harmed through continuity of substance, narrowness of space, obstruction, pressure, collapse and opening. Sometimes when what is visible of the interior surface is ulcerated in its own cavity, all that is ulcerated blends into a single mass, with nature delineating the differences in formation. At other times when either the skin forms a protuberance; or there is some other unnatural growth; or an induration, inflammation or abscess is produced in the heart of the organs; and when this unnatural tumour fills their interior cavity; then there is created a restriction on space.

In addition, this obstruction brings the cavities to the same condition through thick and viscous humour, and through lumps and callosities. So if you squeezed hard on whatever can be seen on the outside, the tumour occupying the cavity would necessarily be forced into the inmost section of the cavity. If these parts should withdraw into themselves, just as they do when they are drawn together by astringency, contracted by cold and dehydrated by dryness, they will of course close the passages, and in particular the bowels. The mouths of these passages are not only closed, but also they often become completely blocked up under such conditions. Nevertheless even the excessive force of what is termed the retentative power is, by drawing together and absolutely restraining the mouths of the passages, the cause of blockaging too, just as the cause of loosening is often the excessive force of the secretory power, whilst at other times it is often the weakness of the retentative power, or some medicine, or water that has a laxative effect, or our predominant temperament changing to moistness and excessive heat. These are the reasons for conditions in the bowels and in the passages.

Some people think that the body is made up of masses and passages. From what I have already said, it is clear how these people would like to assign reasons for disease in the parts that resemble each other and the whole body. It would be a waste of my time to discuss these ideas one by one, considering that the whole of their premise is false. Let me return to my original proposition, that is to explain the causes of the remaining diseases, beginning once again from the type of their composition.

There is left diseases of a double nature, for instance when the organs are roughened or smoothed abnormally. The organs that were once smooth are roughened, and those that were once rough are smoothed, the former when purged by harsh humours or medicines, the latter when lubricated by an oily moisture or a viscous humour. These phenomena appear distinctly in the bones, sometimes when they are not treated properly by doctors, and sometimes when they arise from the nature of the humours in the body.

Asperities of the eyes and windpipe come about not just because of these factors, but also because of harsh vapours, or because of dust and smoke, just as, in my opinion, asperities in the oesophagus, stomach and bowels from the excretions produced in the body itself and from the quality of whatever is eaten or drunk, in which there lurk noxious substances. It is evident that an excess of the roughening agents is the cause of a certain degree of ulceration or erosion of the flesh, but of caries in the bones. These, then, are the causes of the first category of diseases.

By way of contrast the second category of disease is concerned with number. If any part of the body which accords with nature dies, it is as a result of cutting, burning, putrefaction or violent chilling. The causes of chilling have already been discussed. Some parts putrefy because of drugs that have a putrefying tendency, or because of secretions that occur in the body; whilst some parts putrefy because they are not able to vent their waste matter through exhalation. What precedes this inability to vent waste matter has already been described.

If any disease occurs contrary to nature, it is also contrary to the number of the parts of the body. However, if the disease has an element that accords with nature, then it forms the basis of something useful to nature; but if it has an element that does not accord with nature, then it forms the basis of something that disagrees with nature. The power inherent in both these instances has the ability to be enhanced, otherwise it would neither create anything good, nor would it eliminate anything bad.

This power is creative at conception, since it can produce a sixth finger, or some other such phenomenon; and it is creative among adults, since it can cause healthy skin to grow over diseased parts of the body, such as with cataracts over the eyes. Any excess this power possesses results in encysted tumours on the tendons, cysts, sebaceous tumours that are full of pus, and other such problems.

Thus the size of the bodily parts increases with a quantity of good material and strengthening power, but diminishes when the opposite is the case, whether that is cutting, burning, putrefaction or mortification. Excessive cooling can destroy part of any organ, so that what remains is mutilated.

Some diseases that fall into this category have movements that precede with suddenness and violence, whilst others come about as a result of a disproportionate moistness in the joints which both lubricates and loosens the ligaments, and makes the whole articulation slide with slipperiness. Sometimes joints that have splintered around the hollow of the bone-socket readily overlap at the far ends of the limbs; sometimes right from the start the sockets have their concave side uppermost and incline forwards. These are all causes of dislocation.

In cases of intestinal hernia and what people call hernia of the omentum it generally happens that the passage leading down from the peritoneum to the testicles is dilated, although on occasion it can be broken, and then the same thing occurs to the passage leading to it, since it either slips down to the testicles, or to the omentum, or to one of the intestines. The intestines are parted from their correct position whenever they project beyond the divided peritoneum.

The lobe of the lung is often dislocated as a result of wounds to the chest. When the external coat of the eye has been abraded, the torn membrane is slackened to its greatest extent. If a lobe of the inwards becomes a little wrinkled because of a violent collapse or pressure, a disease will ensue as a result of the causes already stated that is an alteration both in positioning and in appearance. The coexistence of the adjacent parts is disrupted when some of these parts unite with each other in an unsuitable way, either through the relaxation, straining or severance of some ligament or ligature. It is quite clear that each individual complaint arises from these external causes.

However, I must still explain the reasons for the origin of the one type of disease that is common to all parts of the body, whether these parts resemble one another and are absolutely basic, or whether they are by nature composite. I usually call this type of disease either a loss of unison, destruction of unity, breakdown in continuity or some other such title, depending on how I want to make my point clear to my audience. What I do not admit is any name formulated by my predecessors, since in some cases they designated as fracture and caries the breaking of continuity in the bone, but in other cases ulcer or wound the breaking of continuity in the flesh. As for the bones of the skull, there are even more names, for just as in the study of the other bones, so there are also in the skull fractures, breakages and breaks; but there are incisions, gashes and slashes, when these bones are attacked and split with a sharp instrument. The technical name for caries is *teredon*. This seems to have had a letter *e* added, for it is thought to be derived from the word *trema* which means a perforation, that is a type of caries. It is the result of harsh humours that corrode, yet at its onset it falls under the category of another type of disease, when it is then called a roughness rather than caries of the bone. When the perforation has grown larger, and looks complete, it is called caries.

In fact bruises can be classified under this heading, since they arise for the most part in the fleshy areas, but sometimes also in the bones of the head, especially among children, for the areas must be soft and not wholly hard. So bruises are found when fleshy areas and soft bones are struck hard from without. Therefore whenever the external appearance of the affected area is still kept continuous, many small divisions are apparent deep down, and this injury is called bruising; but when a hollowness appears which has been produced in the part that has been bruised, then this injury is called a pressure point.

Consequently it must be the case that everything is hollow which either has been forcibly compressed into itself through being struck or which has been bruised, otherwise it is not pressure which has caused the indentation. Yet the hollowness does not have to remain after whatever has caused the hollowness has been removed. In general everything that is soft returns to its former state when what has struck has been taken away.

However, if the blow not only penetrates the bone in the head, but also a fracture is added to whatever has happened externally, then such an injury is called composite, and I do not know of any ancient name by which to refer to this. So I have to explain it by using a phrase or even in the last resort, as is the practice among many more contemporary doctors, to use foreign nomenclature. A relaxation of continuity is both lesion and rupture, the former condition existing in fleshy parts, the latter in sinewy parts. What causes this to happen is sudden, irregular and violent motion, especially when an unexercised body or a body that is uneven, unheated and intractable is moved, for many of the parts in a body of this kind are wrenched apart under such conditions.

To sum up: all causes of these sorts of diseases either force their way in from the outside, or else they stem from the body itself; from without come all injuries that can bruise or wound, from within come excessive and irregular movements of the body, and any bad elements in the humours that have the power to corrode. Such are the reasons for the disease which is common to all the parts, both simple and primary, which are designated as resembling one another, and of those parts that are made up of them, which are called organs and or which serve as organs. There is no problem over ascertaining the causes of the composite diseases since they are composed of what has been described. Hence everyone can supply the answer to whatever is being investigated whenever it is required. However, it is now time for me to bring this treatise to a close and to move next from this subject to *On the Differences of Symptoms*.

6

ON BARLEY SOUP

Not long ago I found some physicians using the juice of pearl barley on one of their patients, although they neither specified in what cases it helps or hinders those who are convalescent, nor did they determine the manner and amount of the dose, or the correct time for administering the soup.[1] Instead, so it seemed to me, they considered the use of barley soup to be suitable whenever they wished, which made me think that it would be useful to set out more clearly for the layperson everything Hippocrates wrote concerning its use: that is an explanation of the method of boiling; its power and effect; the correct time, amount and manner of the dose; the range of benefits it confers on those who are ill when properly administered, and conversely the troubles it causes when administered incorrectly; and in addition to all this the sort of people to whom it is, or is not, right to give.[2] Since the topic is pearl barley and its juice – made from barley that has been properly winnowed, husked and boiled in water – I have decided to summarise first its constituent parts. For if these facts are not determined from the outset, then major problems will arise, even if all the other ideas are correct.

I do not think that anyone is in doubt that the purest water should be chosen for the preparation of barley soup. The best water can be judged by its consistency, taste, smell and colour. As regards taste and smell, there should be no strange quality present, in other words nothing sweet, salty, sharp, bitter, odorous, rotten or, in short, any other extraneous quality. It should be completely neutral, without anything extraneous and without any taste or smell.

What is also essential is for it to be translucent, clean and without any mud, as if it has been carefully filtered and rid of any suspended particles. Water like this is good to use, but its properties are not so clear since it is not composed of perceptible elements.

If the water is as I have described, then of course it consists of fine particles, is readily digested and assimilated, and quickly passes through the body. Not only is it easily transformed when in proximity to the heat of the body, but also it is warmed in a short space of time when placed next to a fire.

Hippocrates is witness to this fact: for he believed that water which heats quickly and which again quickly cools to be extremely unsubstantial, not light when judged by its weight, but composed of fine particles and readily absorbing alien qualities into itself. Such water is cold and moist; this is genuine water.[3]

Waters that are polluted by some substance or quality – for example bituminous, sulphurous and aluminous waters – are polluted to the same degree as they are removed from the true nature of water. If you are looking for proof that water cools and moistens, then this is not the purpose of this book, which is designed rather to elaborate on barley soup. Just remember that water is cold and moist: this is what all the ancient authorities say, and experience bears witness to this. I take this supposition as unanimously agreed, so I shall move on to my discussion of barley.

As is universally acknowledged, barley is cooling and drying, but has a purgative and flatulent element. Its exterior husk, since it is like bran, is drier and more purgative. Its interior, resembling a sort of nutritious flesh, is purgative too, but less so than bran, although it has in itself a flatulent quality.

The other husk, situated inside the bran, is thin and enfolds the barley; compared to the other parts it is midway in power, so it is less purgative than the bran but more purgative than the barley. In addition you must recognise which barleys are best; which barleys contain no rotten matter or excrementitious moisture; and which barleys are neither too new or excessively old.

For new barley is full of excrementitious moisture, absorbed from the soil which is filled with dampness and wind. Old barley in time becomes feeble and weak, after losing its peculiar power. A sign of this process is wrinkling, diminution in size, and emission of what looks like dust when pounded.

A most suitable choice in the making of soup is plump barley which is neither too young nor too old and removed from any alien quality. However, this test alone is not sufficient, for only experience can prove which barley is genuinely plump. If, in addition to what I have just said, the barley during boiling increases through swelling to a greater weight, then the barley must be used for cooking, provided that it really is the intention to make it as good as possible.

So I shall state briefly what the best water is and how it may be judged; and what the best barley is, and by what evidence we may judge it.

The third topic to discuss is the cooking. People prepare the barley first by pounding it in a mortar into small pieces, then after it is quickly boiled some add reduced wine, others add starch, and some also cumin and honey.

This recipe is bad. The best recipe that entails the correct preparation is as follows. First soak the barley beforehand in water while it is still raw, then rub it between your hands to remove the skin. Using the same method, again rub the barley between your hands until all the chaff is removed, unless you want it to be more laxative, in which case it is better to boil it with its skin. You should boil it like this: first over a high flame, then afterwards on a gentle flame until it has liquefied.

If it is boiled like this, everything flatulent is removed and – as Hippocrates testifies – all that is gained is good.[4] For he says that its thick mucilage is smooth, clinging, soothing, slippery, moderately watery, quenching of the thirst, laxative and easy to excrete (if there is any need for that) and without astringency. It neither disturbs other foods nor does it swell up in the bowels, because it has swelled during boiling as much as it can be swollen.

Clearly pearl barley contains nothing glutinous and adhesive, although it is completely sticky, because it not only rids the body of waste, but also clears phlegm from the stomach when administered in a particular way. Vigorous boiling and a careful mixing of the ingredients produce this apparent stickiness.

Within its gluten there is no roughness, but rather absolute smoothness, uniformity, permanence and density. Since it has no share of astringency or harshness, which causes roughness, it of course is smooth, not only to the touch, but also in power.

Other viscous foods, such as olive oil, honey and so on, appear to anyone touching them as smooth, consistent and with nothing uneven in them, since a part of them is smooth, another part thick, even when separated or divided. It is through this that they derive their smoothness to the touch, whilst in their activity and power they are in no way like anything else.

The reason for this is that they do not saturate every part of the body to which they draw near in an even or continuous manner, but, with the exception of pearl barley, the constituent parts of everything that is sticky are different from one another in this respect, because pearl barley is smooth, consistent and whole both to the touch and also in terms of its power. The other ingredients provide no pleasure to the taste, whilst pearl barley, in addition to its other qualities, provides both pleasure and smoothness to the taste, particular for those who are ill.

Although it is better than everything else in goodness, yet bread has a considerable degree of unpleasantness, even if it is soaked in water, as it requires chewing. Here too barley has the advantage in that it does not cause any unpleasantness through chewing. It does have slipperiness, especially the juice, although as it passes through the body it leaves nothing behind, and this is what all viscous foods do, with the exception of pearl barley.

Passing through to the chest because of its purgative element, it is suitable for evacuation and assimilation, particularly among those people whose convex livers do not easily allow for the movement of food.

It is moderately watery, by which I mean moist and hydrating. Its moisture is derived from the water, although this power is diminished through the moderately drying nature of the barley, because whatever is made up of opposite qualities escapes extremes by acquiring some other additional property. Its hydration is derived from the moistness, since this is more thirst-quenching than water, although its power is diminished because it is assimilated more quickly and because its moistness lingers through stickiness, besides which it is also cooling.

Hence it is most beneficial for burning fevers, holding the opposite qualities as it is cooling, moistening, purgative of putrefying juices, furnishing considerable nourishment to the body, whilst at the same time digesting semi-putrid juices and converting them into good juices.

All these powers it possesses, since it has no astringency or tendency to upset the stomach. Astringency may be suitable for strengthening the stomach, but it also thickens the juices; conversely moistness, since it cannot thicken, is easy to assimilate.

Pearl barley escapes all this through having no excessive badness. It does not cause upset or rumbling in the bowels, because any harshness or flatulence is lost in cooking.

These, then, are the beneficial properties of pearl barley which are acquired during effective cooking and which my discussion has delineated at length. Let me sum this up again. Barley soup is smooth, uniform, consistent, and homogenous to such a degree as not to allow one part to appear thin and another thick or uneven. This is not only to the touch, but also indeed to its power and activity.

It is also soothing to the taste, because it has no unpleasantness, and it is moist and hydrating, because of the stickiness in it. Whatever is smooth, moist and soothing has been rid of astringency and any other strong quality. In addition, it possesses no flatulence because it has been cooked properly.

Hence it is suitable for acute fevers, not only because it is the opposite to them in every way, but also because it is extremely easy to digest, cleansing the putrefied juices through its detersiveness and digestive of those that are still only semi-putrid.

You must not simply administer barley soup when a disease appears, for you need to determine several other factors. It is neither correct to dose people with it who are in a critical state, nor is it correct to give it to those who require the letting of blood, purging or a clyster; nor to those whose stomachs are filled with waste matter; nor to those suffering great pain; and certainly not to those needing a medical vapour-bath, the letter of blood or purging; nor yet to those affected by very dry diseases.

You must also consider the correct time, the dosage, the particular characteristics of the patient; then you ought to consider the juice on its own, or the pearl barley, or both of these together, or neither of them.

The correct time for the administering of the soup – whenever you intend to use it after weighing up the situation – is when the body is evenly disposed, that is when no part of it is hotter and no part of it is colder. Such a disposition can be found at the abatement of a disease, for then the heat of the body is spread evenly through every part.

But it is essential that the soup is neither too much nor too thick. Filling a stomach, according to Hippocrates, is dangerous when done all at once, but it is safe when done gradually. You should therefore mix and measure the soup according to the usual habit of the patient. So if a patient usually eats just once a day, then the soup should be provided only once a day; but if the patient eats twice a day, then you can double the dose of the soup.

There is no need to increase the quantity of the soup or add anything to it in the case of drier diseases. What is required in such instances is for drinks to be taken before meals that are stronger than barley soup, for only then will the diseases be moistened more.

Dry diseases are pleurisy, inflammations of the lungs, and generally those illnesses of the lungs which do not involve expectoration; and complaints of the liver, stomach and bowels, when nothing is excreted that is hard or circumstantial or negligible. Any dryness in the arteries and veins can be diagnosed by looking at the tongue and skin, as can problems with the head, when nothing is expelled through the mouth or nose.

This is the way that inflammations and dry sores occur, from which nothing is removed by serous discharges. In these cases it is not right for barley soup to be made, for it does not have the power to moisten them, since whatever is not particularly moistening requires a considerable degree of strong moistening power, and it is moreover harmful to the body by causing repletion.

If, however, the body is rather moist, and if the patient spits anything up from the lungs, then you ought to use sufficient quantities of barley soup.

By moistening and at the same time cutting through whatever is moist in the body, as well as furnishing strength to the parts of the body through nourishment, barley soup in no time at all helps clear any state of the humours that might be troublesome and unwholesome.

When both these properties occur together, the harmful waste matter is easily removed. Besides, nothing else that is offered either as a medicine or as food possesses both these properties, since they either attenuate too little and so are extremely moistening and nourishing – for example, bread, groats, eggs and fish – or they have cutting powers and so cannot moisten and nourish – for example, honey and vinegar sauce and other such things.

Yet everything that is good is assembled in barley soup. Nevertheless, it affords no benefit if administered without careful forethought, and on occasion what is administered has instead been the cause of death.

When a patient requires a clyster for the purging of waste matter or a phlebotomy for the removal of excess blood, since the pain can scarcely be withstood because of its intensity, the administering of barley soup is the cause of death, for it quickly doubles the level of pain.

So barley soup must not be given to a person suffering from a fever, whether the fever is with or without pain, or when after a little food the patient tends to become fevered and has not yet defaecated. These considerations apply not only to barley soup, but also to pearl barley itself.

As for patients for whom barley soup is usually beneficial, you should not give it to them at once, but rather just the liquid at first, or at least more liquid and less pearl barley, then both these in equal proportions, then pearl barley on its own. For pearl barley contributes a great deal to the strength and nurture of the body, whilst the liquid is easy to digest, concoct and assimilate.

This is my summary about pearl barley. You now have enough information to understand how to regulate its dosage properly and to apply the necessary considerations for its use.

7

ON THE POWERS OF FOODS
Book 1

Introduction

A considerable number of the most outstanding physicians have written about the powers of foods. Yet they have set down their ideas in a great deal of haste, even though this is probably the most important of all medical subjects. For other remedies are not always used at every possible opportunity, but without food it is impossible to live either in health or in sickness. It is therefore reasonable that the majority of the best physicians should determine to ascertain the powers in nutrition, some of them making statements based on practical knowledge alone, others wanting to make use of scientific theory too, whilst a few put all the emphasis on just theory.

If in these writings it was the case that there was a general agreement about food, just as there is about geometry and arithmetic, there would be no point in me now writing statements about these things to supplement so many worthy gentlemen. But since in their quarrels they have viewed each other with suspicion (for it is impossible for them all to be telling the truth), it is essential for impartial judges to be appointed to test what they wrote, because it would be wrong to believe only one person without any proof.

There are two initial stages of proof (since every means of proof and persuasion arises either from perception or from rational thought), and I must use either one or both of these for the answer to the question that presents itself. Seeing as decisions through reasoning are not easy for everyone in the same way, because a knowledge of their nature is essential, it is better and preferable to begin with experiment, because through this means alone not a few of the doctors have declared that they have discovered the powers of foods.

The practical efforts and studies of the Empiricists are perhaps to be ridiculed since they work to make capital out of contradicting whatever has been discovered through argument; although Diocles belongs to the Dogmatists, he nevertheless wrote in the first book of his work *On Health to Pleistarchus*:[1]

> Those who presume that everything that is similar in juice, smell, heat and so on all possess identical powers are mistaken: for anyone can detect the dissimilar in what is similar. Of course regarding laxatives, diuretics and anything else with some other power, it must be supposed that each exists on its own, since not all sweet, bitter, salty and the rest have the same powers; but the whole of nature must be considered as the reason why this generally happens to each of them. Taken this way the truth can hardly be missed.
>
> Those who believe that in every case they must explain the reason why each food is nourishing, laxative, diuretic or the like appear to be unaware first that this is not necessary every time for their use, and secondly that many things that exist are in their origins naturally alike, so that they do not admit to an argument based on reason. Moreover, quite often they grasp things that they do not understand, which are not agreed upon, and which are unlikely, and make mistakes when they feel that they have explained the reason satisfactorily. It can be concluded that there is no need to listen to those who propound reasons in this way and think it is necessary to give a reason for everything; instead trust should be placed in the discoveries achieved over the course of time. Where possible the reason must be sought, since it is the intention that whatever is said on this subject should be intelligible and reliable.

This is what Diocles said when he became convinced that he could understand the powers in foods through just one experiment and not from an indication either of the temperament or the humours. He makes no mention of any other substance in the parts of plants. By this I mean indication about the parts of plants, which Mnesitheus shows that, in addition to their other properties, some powers reside in the roots of plants, others in the stalks, just as other powers are in the leaves, in the fruits and in the seeds.

Everyone knows, even if they only have a little intelligence, that experience serves as a teacher, just as of many other things, so too of which foods are easy or difficult to digest, which are helpful or harmful to the stomach, and which are purgative, laxative or costive of the bowels. Those who believe that they can conduct an experiment without guidelines make no small error in this particular area, as has been shown in my work *On Simple Medicines* and in the third book *On the Temperaments*, the mistakes being equal on each side. So in this book I will state my definitions carefully, just as I did in those books, in which anyone interested can find without problem their particular powers, although not according to my original plan, which was to write about each subject just once, whilst not running through the same things about them in lots of treatises.

This is my usual method, and I do not intend abandoning it now, since I will use only the main outlines of the definitions, by means of which it should be possible to mix conciseness with clarity. Since it has not been accurately described by Erasistratus, I will start from that fact which everyone has on their lips: that a blend of honey and milk does not relax the stomach for everyone, nor do lentils check it, but that there are some people who, besides experiencing neither of these two effects, yet fall into what is opposite, so their stomachs are checked by a blend of honey and milk, but relaxed by lentils. Some people are even found who can digest beef or rock fish with ease.

I myself have always asked these people – for I will begin with the final category – what the nature is of the symptom which reveals the indigestibility of rock fish, since there seems to lie in the bowels a weight like lead, stone or clay (at least this is how some people report the feeling in such cases of indigestion); or else there is evident a definite biting sensation in the bowels, or flatulence or a sensation of unpleasant belching. After that some people have said the belching has become greasier, others the biting, others both. By carefully examining the physical state of these people, I have found that a lot of yellow bile has collected in their bowels through some bad temperament or peculiarity of their constitution.

I say 'peculiarity of constitution' when the bile in some people flows down to the bowels from the liver and returns to the bowels; but I say 'bad temperament' when there occurs by nature a bitter and biting heat that is, one could say, like a fever. Understandably these people digest foods that are not easily spoilt more than foods that are easily spoilt, since things that are easy to digest are easily changed and spoilt, but things that are not easy to digest are difficult to change and are not easily spoilt. In fact these things, whenever they are in contact with a lot of heat, are digested better than when they are close to a stomach that has a moderate amount of heat. So according to this system some people digest beef more easily than rock fish.

Yet with some people lentils upset more than check the stomach: this has been explained by me in my books *On Simple Medicines*, for just as some of the medicines I prepare are composed of contrasting substances and powers, so in the same way not a few of what appear to be simple medicines are compounded by nature. Such is the case with many foods too, for it is not just lentils, but also cabbage and the seafood called shell-fish which have a nature composed of contrary powers.

Thus the solid part of each of these is hard to pass and constipates the stomach, whilst their moistness encourages it to evacuate. A clear proof comes from cooking, since the water, in which each of these things has been cooked, empties the bowels, although their bodies check. On this subject you can hear some people saying that, if before other foods you eat a cabbage that has not been cooked for too long, and you transfer it as a whole from the pan to a pot containing olive oil and fish-sauce, it will move the bowels; but you will hear of others preparing a dish for checking the bowels which carries the name of twice-cooked cabbage.

The recipe for this sort of cabbage is as follows: boil the cabbage in water, carefully drain off all this water from the pan, add more hot water, boil the cabbage a second time in this to ensure that if any of its own moistness is retained after the first boiling, it will be removed. Everything boiled in water experiences a shift of its own power and also a transfer of the power belonging to itself and the water. It is essential for you to realise that this occurs every day with things that are cooked in sauces, whether some pulses are being boiled, or part of an animal or a vegetable. Whatever has been boiled reveals through its taste and smell the quality and power of the sauce, whilst the sauce discloses the quality and power of what has been boiled in it.

You can test the truth of the whole argument that has now been set out in front of you like this: if you boil lentils or cabbage or one of the sea foods which I have just mentioned, then season the dish with olive oil, fish-sauce and pepper, and then serve it to whoever wants it as you would with cabbage that has been boiled twice, you will observe the liquid passing through the bowels, but the solids closing them.

It is not surprising that, on occasion, colic and flatulences are caused by such foods, whenever the whole of their solid part is eaten at the same time as their juices. For this results in a struggle between each other, the solid part of the food clinging and moving slowly, the moistness promoting evacuation. So if the biting sensation is removed, the symptoms stop; but while it remains, the bowels are bound to be subject to colic and flatulence. The limit to all of this is the evacuation of whatever is causing the disagreement.

Since for some people the stomach is ready for evacuation, but for others it is dry and constipated, each stomach derives its symptoms from these foods according to its individual nature, seeing as it is sometimes assisted by the power of the juice, at other times by the power of whatever is solid. These two effects are set up in opposition to one another, with one bound to follow up its victory, the other yielding. This occurs in accordance with certain conditions of the stomach which are not innate, but happen at a particular moment. Sometimes phlegmatic juice collects in the stomach, at other times bilious juice. The phlegmatic can be sharp, salty, sweet, without any perceptible quality, moist, thick, viscous and easily dispersed.

The bilious can be yellow, pale, and holding overall more or less each of these, so that I will leave aside the other biles in the bodies of those who are already ill. Each of the juices I have mentioned is either readily disposed towards the evacuation of the stomach or to its checking, and whenever the whole of the solid parts of the foods just described arrive in the bowels together with their particular juices, they either help towards whatever has the same power, or act against whatever has the opposite power.

The two reasons according to type for the different appearance of foods when digested in the stomach have been explained before. But now a third reason has been found to add both to the natural state and to the moist and solid parts of whatever is eaten. It does not matter whether whatever is eaten is called either provender or food. In fact people use these terms no less than foodstuffs and edibles. Thinking of which, Hippocrates wrote in his *Epidemics*: 'You should test foodstuffs and drinks, to see whether they remain for an equal length of time'.[2] And again in another passage: 'Physical work, food, drink, sleep, sex: all these in moderation.' Nomenclature should not cause any problems, as I keep saying, because all of these names can be used, since the Greeks are conversant with every one, but pursuing an understanding of practical problems does matter.

Foods seems to have a swift or slow passage through the body depending on the constitution of the stomach at the outset, or a condition that is acquired. I am talking of what is eaten and drunk, since some of these things are moist, others dry, some slippery, others friable and easily broken down, some containing an element of pungency, others sharpness, bitterness, sweetness, saltiness, harshness, astringency or, beyond these properties, some medicinal power with the general character of a purgative drug.[3]

Through their viscosity and moistness orach, beet, mallow and gourd pass through the bowels more quickly than anything without these properties, particularly in those who take a gentle walk after eating them, for they slide down more easily when shaken than if one reclines without moving.

In this category lie mulberries, sweet cherries and those wines which are sweet and thick. Watermelons and what people call melons are suitable for evacuating the bowels because of their moistness and slipperiness. In fact watermelons contain a moderately purgative property, melons even more so, which can be understood by rubbing a dirty part of the body; for they remove the dirt from it immediately, and they are also diuretic.

Among the foods that are moist and watery in constitution are apricots, peaches and in short all the foods that seem to have nothing by way of smell or taste to mark them out. These foods are easily passed, if the stomach is ready for evacuation, but if not, they remain undigested and do not help evacuation in any way. For whatever makes up these foods lies midway between the costive and the laxative, although there is a tendency to swing a little to one action or the other, depending on whether the stomach is in no way ready for evacuation or is vigorously engaged in assimilation, for sometimes these activities check the stomach.

A blend of honey and milk does not encourage an evacuation of the stomach in those cases where it races to be assimilated, but it does assist with the digestion of foods mixed with it. But if this blend is in no hurry to be assimilated quickly, it encourages evacuation, seeing that yellow bile is included with it because of its bitterness and biting effect. These sorts of food and drink, since they are only biting, encourage the parts in the bowels to evacuation.

It is evident that the substance of the intestines is subsumed under the term bowel.[4] So the general public in fact give this term to pot-bellies and paunches. Some substances relax the stomach as they have medicinal powers mixed in them, so for example scammony, large gourds, hellebore and all other such things; for their nature is a mix between food and medicine, exactly as if a small amount of scammony juice should be put into barley water.[5] Although their sensation fails to be noticed, their action does not remain hidden, but clearly relaxes the stomach.

This appears to be what Hippocrates meant when he said: 'In food medicine'.[6] Thus it is good not only to lend an ear to these ideas, but also the argument can be explained from those foods that possess no nutritive or purgative quality. For they say that these things not only serve frequently as foods, but also as medicines by heating, moistening, cooling and clearly drying us; just as consequently, when none of these things is active in the human body, but is only feeding it, this would not be included under the topic of medicine.

73

There are very few foods of this sort; but all that are like this only hold the category of food properly by not changing the body in quality when ingested. For whatever has been heated, cooled, dried or moistened is altered in quality, whilst whatever derives from foodstuffs in terms of weight as their substance is assimilated, is used only by foods themselves.

So everything of average temperament has no pronounced quality: it is only a food, not a medicine, since it does not relax the bowels, or check, strengthen and evacuate the stomach, just as it does not encourage, or even discourage, sweating and urination, nor does it set up in the body any other condition of coldness, hotness, dryness and wetness, but in every way maintains the body nourished in the same state that it was encountered. At this point some sort of distinction in between a food and a medicine is vital, although not the one delineated by Diocles, nor indeed any of the others that I have so far discussed.

For if the human body should really be average in temperament, it should be kept in its present state by nourishment that is of average temperament. If, on the other hand, it should be cooler, hotter, drier or wetter, it would be wrong to serve food and drink that was average in temperament, because it is necessary for each of these bodies to be shifted in the opposite direction by as much as they depart from the genuinely median state. This will be by means of whatever is the opposite to the existing bad temperament.

The opposites occupy a position as equally removed from the median as their counterparts are on the other side, so that, if the body happens to be shifted by three degrees from the harmonious and median state towards something hotter, it is important to leave off by the same amount food that is median for food that inclines towards what is cooler, but if it moves by four degrees towards what is moist, then food that is drier than the average is required in equal proportions.

With this it is of course again possible to find many completely contrasting expositions on the same foods. In fact just recently two people were having an argument with each other, the one declaring that honey was healthy, the other that it was harmful, each offering as proof whatever the honey had done on an individual basis, but ignoring the fact that not everyone has the same temperament at the outset. For even if they do have just one temperament, they cannot preserve it unchanged throughout the stages of life, just as similarly they cannot preserve it through changes of season and place.[7] So I will leave aside for the time being how these people alter the natural states of their bodies by their way of life and their diet.

To return at once to the argument about honey, the older of the two was by nature rather phlegmatic, lazy in his way of life and towards all other activities, not least the exercises in the public baths, which was why honey was beneficial; by nature the other was choleric, aged thirty, and worked out a great deal with exercises every day. Understandably in this instance the honey quickly turned to bile, and thus was very harmful.

I personally know of someone who complained about the area that is around the mouth of the stomach, and I reckoned from his description that phlegm had collected at this point, and so I advised him to eat his food with mustard, leeks and beets, since phlegm is cut by these foods. He excreted a great deal of phlegm from his stomach and was completely cured of his complaints. But then conversely he suffered from indigestion after eating biting foods and felt biting pains in his stomach. He had eaten mustard with beet, and not only was he taken unawares by the biting, but also was made considerably worse. He was of course amazed that he should be hurt so much by what had before been so beneficial, and he came to me to find out the reason.

It is natural for anyone not versed in the art of medicine to be baffled by these facts; but it is unpardonable for doctors to leave many of the most useful theories undefined. For it is not right for them simply to say first that rock fish are easily digested by the majority of people, then that they have found some people who can digest beef with ease, but rather to distinguish both groups; just as indeed it is not right for them simply to talk about honey, but to add in the middle of this for which stage of life, nature, season, place and way of life it is beneficial or harmful. For example, that it is completely opposed to hot and dry things, but is most beneficial to wet and cold things, and whether this sort of person has the temperament because of age, nature, place, season or a particular lifestyle.

It appears absolutely essential for the present discussion to examine the temperaments both in humans and in foodstuffs. A full list of human temperaments and how they must be distinguished has been written in my work *On Temperaments*, and similarly as regards medicines in *On Simple Medicines*.

For the moment it is the ideal opportunity to mention the temperaments of foods, as has been set out in the book on diet that some people ascribe to Hippocrates, others to Philistion, or Ariston, or Euryphon, or Philetus, all ancient authors.[8] According to some editions it begins as follows: 'It is vital to discern like this the power of each type of food and drink, both that which comes from nature and that which is acquired through art'. And in other editions like this: 'It is vital to discern like this the setting and nature of each place'.

When this book is circulated by itself, it is entitled *On Diet*, although there is a second section, seeing as the work as a whole is divided into three. When the complete work is found in one undivided volume made up of three sections, it is entitled *On the Nature of Man and Diet*. The second section, in which foods are treated, might perhaps with good reason be thought worthy of Hippocrates; but the first section very often strays from Hippocratic doctrine. But let this be said as a kind of side-track. Yet whoever it is of the writers mentioned, it seems that diet with respect to foods refers back to one system in general.

For whoever knows that barley is by nature cold and moist even when boiled, also understands how to recognise the temperaments of the body, both those that occur naturally, and those that come about through some acquired condition; and how to use barley effectively for consumption, not just with healthy people, but with those who are ill too; and how to employ poultices made with barley flour properly. That is what the person who understands temperament can do.

Not only the principal and primary temperament of each food must be known, as has been shown in my work *On Drugs*, but also the temperaments that stem from them. Essentially many of the useful temperaments, if not all, happen to reside in the juices, but some are also in the smell. For from the blending of so much heat, cold, dryness and wetness come their sweetness, bitterness, saltiness, astringency, harshness or sharpness.

Salt signifies nothing else besides saltiness, but one fact is explained by two words, just as astringency and sharpness are included under the generic term astringent. Every flavour is discussed at length in the fourth book of my work *On Simple Medicines*, and it is absolutely essential for anyone who is about to follow what is written here to read that book, so that I can avoid having to say the same about these things in this work.

Some foods, as I said a little before, exhibit no distinct quality regarding smell or taste; they are in fact called inert and watery. But other foods have a very obvious astringency, innate sweetness or bitterness, just as indeed some appear rather salty and others have a clear element of bitterness. It is obvious that such foods have in them the same power as medicines, which they resemble in flavour. The reason why some astringent substances do not have the same effect as other astringent substances is discussed in my work *On Medicines*, for example bitter aloes, burnt copper, copper sulphate, copper slag, flaked copper and rock-alum.[9]

For by mixing these things on their own with something that has an astringent substance their effectiveness is changed. This is the case if scammony is mixed with quince, which I do of course on occasion, the core around the seeds being removed and the hollow which is thus created being filled up with scammony. After the fruit has been wrapped in dough, it is baked and given to eat. When prepared like this it loosens the bowels without upsetting the stomach, since what predominates is the cathartic effect which the fruit takes from the scammony, whilst the particular characteristics of the fruit remain, because when prepared properly it appears neither harsh nor sweet to the stomach.

Therefore a few of the things that are eaten have some power inherent in them which is either laxative or the cause of another effect. In this respect there is no need to disbelieve the powers of their juices, since they succeed in whatever they naturally have to do. However much astringent quality exists it contracts, squeezes and cools the neighbouring bodies by the same amount. But the same body can, on occasion, have constituent parts that are heating, and some that are cooling, just as I showed in my book *On Simple Medicines*, since these qualities are mixed together by nature like this, and also a few doctors sometimes mix pellitory or pepper with one of the heating things. These facts, as I stated in my work *On Simple Medicines* in the fullest detail, are extremely useful for what is being taught now.

The recipes for each food in turn can be found from those who already know about these things. So I sometimes serve a dish of beet and lentils, and before me Heracleides of Tarentum often used to serve it without any trouble both to healthy people, and also to those who were rather ill.[10] First I put in plenty of beet, next after seasoning it either add a little more salt or sweet fish-sauce, because then it is more laxative. If after removing their husks you boil lentils twice – since you must discard the first lot of water – and then add some salt or fish-sauce, you can also mix in a little of those things that check a stomach but do not ruin the overall taste. In this way you will make a pleasant, but extremely useful medicine, which serves as a food for quite a few people who suffer from chronic diarrhoea.

For in general nothing can be tested properly through experience without first discovering the precise reason for the condition, with which whatever is being tested is connected, whether it is food, drink or medicine. For the substance of remedies provides the knowledge for conditions of this kind, but not the actual remedies. Since it is impossible, without a precise knowledge of their powers, to help people who need those substances which we use, it is necessary at this juncture to discuss the powers in foods, just as elsewhere we discuss the powers in drugs.

What can only be recognised with difficulty after some considerable time spent in motivated experience is the nature of vapours and humours: whether they exhibit what is being examined, in addition to their consistency, which is realised in their viscosity, looseness, sponginess, compression, lightness and heaviness. All these things contribute to their own discovery, so that if, on arrival in a foreign country, some food is seen that has not before been observed, many clues will be available for the recognition of its powers.

What Mnesitheus wrote about roots, shoots, leaves, fruits and seeds certainly does not have a firm basis in thought, if it is judged according to defined experiment, as will be revealed by what follows.[11] For I am conscious of discussing each food individually. Yet if my work is rather too long or has the potential of becoming so, I can of course summarise it in a second much shorter book, which will be of use to those who are learning medicine, because only practice and training through detailed exposition will produce skilled practitioners.

For this reason I believe that most people are right in saying that the best teaching comes about through direct communication, because it is not possible to see a captain of a ship or a practitioner of another skill emerge from a book. For books are memorials to erstwhile scholars, not perfect training manuals for the ignorant. But of course if anyone lacks a teacher and wants to read carefully what has been written clearly and in the sort of detail that I employ, then great benefit will be derived, especially if there is no hesitation over frequently revising these things.

Wheats

It seems quite understandable to me that the majority of doctors should begin what they propose to explain with wheat, seeing as this grain is by far the most useful and most used among all the Greeks and most foreigners. The most nourishing wheats are those that are hulled and whose whole substance is dense and compressed, so that they can only be broken by the teeth with difficulty. These wheats furnish the body with a lot of nourishment from just a little volume. The opposite of these wheats can be broken up easily by the teeth, appears loose in texture and spongy after chewing, and furnishes little nourishment from a large volume. If you want to compare an equal volume of each wheat, you will find the compact wheat far heavier.

In colour, these are more yellow than the spongier wheats. Their nature should be tested, not simply by examining their outward appearance, but by cutting them open and breaking them in pieces, as has been stated; for many wheats on the surface appear light brown and dense, but inside are observed to be thin, spongy and pale. Such wheats contain a lot of bran and if, after milling, the finest flour is sieved off and from what remains a bread is made (which is called bran-loaf), it will be proved that they contain little nourishment and generate a great deal of waste in the body, and for this reason they are easily passed. At the same time, on account of the purgative nature of the bran, their passage through the body is understandably swift, because they stir the bowels to excretion.

Contrasting with these are the genuinely white breads that manage a great weight in a constrained volume. They are the slowest of all breads to pass. You will notice that their dough is particularly sticky, so that it weighs most when unseparated, which is something that is peculiar to a sticky body. These breads of course require more yeast, must be kneaded most of all, and should not be baked immediately after rising and kneading. On the other hand, bran-loaves only need a small amount of yeast, light kneading and a short time in the oven. Thus white breads must have a longer time in the oven, bran-loaves a shorter time. There is a considerable difference one way or the other between the whitest and the darkest breads, since some are called and really are white, whilst others are dark.

There is also a type of bread that is precisely halfway between these breads. It carries the name of wholemeal bread, although doctors in the past called it unrefined. It is made from unsifted flour, or in other words from the plain flour from which the bran has yet to be separated. From this derives the name, since every bit of the wheat without any separation is used to make wholemeal loaves, whilst unrefined bread is so called because unrefined flour is gathered together for its manufacture. But even with these breads, which seem to be positioned between breads made with bran and perfectly white breads, there is a considerable difference regarding the nature of the wheat, because superior breads come from compact and heavy wheats, but inferior breads are made from wheats that are porous and light.

Among the Romans, as among nearly all the people whom they rule, the whitest bread is called *silignites*, whilst that which is not quite so white is called *semidalites*. However, *semidalis* is an ancient Greek name, but *silignis* is not Greek, although I cannot think of another term. The most nutritious bread is *silignites*, then comes *semidalites*, in third place comes bread from partially unbolted flour, whilst the fourth place is occupied by bread made from unsifted flour, of which bran bread is the most extreme, and this lacks anything nutritious as well as being more purgative of the bowels than other breads.

The breads that are best for the digestion are those which contain plenty of yeast, have been kneaded very well, and have been baked in an earthenware hearth tile with a moderate fire. For a stronger fire as soon as there is contact immediately bakes the outside to a burnt shell, and the bread becomes bad in two respects, because the crumb is raw and uncooked, whilst the crust is overbaked, dry and resembles a shell. A fire that is less than moderate does not finish the bread off well, but leaves it rather undercooked, particularly the whole of the crumb. All breads that are fully and evenly baked with a moderate fire for a longer time are digested extremely well in the stomach and are also most valuable through the subsequent energy. The worst types of breads are obviously all those that share none of the aforementioned properties.

The defining limits of what is good and what is bad in these breads is not difficult for anyone to grasp (even without me), some breads being close to the best sort or the worst, others being further removed, and some others, as has been said, straddling the midway point between the two. As I stated before in the case of honey, one must not simply set out what is good or bad for the health, but what is valuable for a phlegmatic nature. In other words, what is valuable for a nature that is wetter and colder than the ideal mixture, even if it is only colder without any more moisture, or wetter without any more coldness. But it is not suitable for hot temperaments, still less for temperaments that are hot and dry. So any bread that is not properly baked is suitable for an athlete, since it does not contain much yeast, whilst anything that is well-baked in an oven is suitable for an ordinary old man, since it contains a lot of yeast, whilst whatever is completely without yeast is of use to no one.

If you add some cheese, as is the habit of the farmers who live round me when celebrating a festival, and these breads are what are called unleavened, then everyone is harmed, even if they are the most healthy of reapers and diggers, and yet these people seem even better than sporting heavyweights at digesting unleavened bread, just as beef and goat too. Why must lamb and goat be mentioned in addition to these foods? In Alexandria donkeys are also eaten, whilst some people eat camels. It is partly habit that contributes to their digestion, partly and not negligibly the small quantities that are eaten, and the hollowness of the whole body that is an inevitable consequence for those working the whole day in their own areas of activity. For the empty flesh seizes from the stomach not just partially digested juice, but also on occasion completely undigested juice, whenever it is struggling for food, and as a result these people later catch the most intractable diseases and die before they are old.

The ordinary people in their ignorance thank the strength of their body, since they see themselves eating and digesting what none of us would be able to take and digest. As most of those who are engaged in manual labour sleep very heavily, something that contributes greatly to the digestion, they are consequently harmed less by bad food; but if they are forced to stay awake for several nights in a row, they immediately fall ill. These people therefore possess this one advantage in the digestion of bad foods.

On the other hand, athletes eat foods containing good juices, although the heavyweights among them take thick and viscous foods. Wrestlers in particular are called heavyweights, but also boxers and all-in boxers and wrestlers. Since the preparation for the contests is everything for them, during which they are sometimes compelled to wrestle and box for the whole day, they require food that is not easily spoilt and hard to disperse. Such food is composed of thick and viscous juices, especially for example food from pork and (as has been said) specially prepared bread which only athletes customarily eat. If indeed an ordinary individual who does not exercise should partake in such food, the swift consequence will be a plethoric illness, just as if someone who exercises should live off vegetables and barley juice, the whole body will quickly be in a sorry state and waste away.

If one of us eats any of those breads which athletes use, there is an excess of a thick and cold juice which I tend specifically to call 'raw'. There is phlegmatic humour that is raw and cold, but not thick, since it contains a lot of moisture and flatulent wind; in contrast what is specifically called raw juice appears suspended in urine and sometimes looks like pus. However, pus smells bad and is viscous, while raw juice resembles pus only in thickness and colour, since it is neither malodorous nor viscous. A considerable quantity of raw juice is suspended not just in the urine of those who have a fever, as I said, but also in the urine of those healthy people who, after hard manual labour, eat food that is tough and hard to digest.

I shall speak in turn about the other foods, but breads are my current topic for discussion to add to what has already been said by me, since it was my original intention to survey breads first. The best breads are those that are baked under a dome.[12] Their method of baking and the preparations for their baking have been discussed. After these come breads baked in an oven, which obviously use the same recipe, but fall short because their crumb is not cooked like breads baked under a dome. Breads baked over a grill, hot ashes or a hearth tile used like a dome are altogether bad, their composition being uneven: for their crust is overcooked, whilst their crumb is undercooked.

The ash adds a bad element to hidden bread, so called because of being baked hidden in the ashes, which makes it run the risk of being the worst of all breads in relation to the type of baking, compared to all the others begun in this way. It is essential to pay attention each time to what has been set out like this, since there is only a difference in these things when they are compared one to another. So if in fact a comparison is made between things that are in many respects different, all these ideas that are described individually will in turn form a complete collection of facts. Enough has therefore been said about the differences in breads.

Pastries

Now is the opportune moment to elaborate on the other sorts of pastries that are made with wheat flour. What are called griddle cakes by the Athenians, but girdle cakes by Greeks like me from Asia, are cooked in olive oil. The olive oil is poured into a frying pan which is placed over a smokeless flame. When the oil is hot, wheat flour kneaded with lots of water is spread on top. Fried quickly in the oil, this mixture becomes as firm and thick as the soft cheese that sets in wicker-work baskets. Then the cooks turn it, making what was the top the bottom, so that it comes into contact with the frying pan. When it has been sufficiently fried, they turn it so that the underside is now upperside, and when this has set they turn it two or three times more, until it is certain that the whole cake has been evenly cooked.

This food is, of course, full of thick juices, blocks the bowels and produces undigested fluids. So some people mix in honey with the dough, others sea salt. This is one sort or type (whatever term you want to use) of flat cake which, along with lots of other flat cakes, those living both in the country and the city make in a rough and ready way. All thin cakes that contain no yeast and which are baked in an oven, should be taken out and dipped at once in hot honey so as to saturate them. These are one sort of flat cake, as are all the honey cakes made with wafer biscuits.

Wafer biscuits

There are two sorts of wafer biscuits: the superior is called *ryemata*, the inferior *lagana*. Everything made with wafer biscuits and finest wheat flour has thick juices, is slow to pass and liable to obstruct the passages for food in the liver, exacerbates a weak spleen, produces stones in the kidneys, and yet is reasonably nourishing, if it is digested and converted into blood properly. All those things made with honey have a mixed power, since the honey itself has a fine juice and comminutes everything with which it comes into contact.

Understandably everything that absorbs a lot of honey in its manufacture, and which is subjected to longer baking, is less slow to pass, produces a juice that is a combination of thick and thin, and is better for the liver, kidneys and spleen – provided that these organs are in good health – than whatever is prepared without honey. But if these organs are at the initial stage of a blockage, either through inflammation or induration, then the cakes made with honey are no less harmful than those without honey. There are even occasions when they are more harmful, especially with those cakes whose flour is rather sticky. The juice derived from these cakes is not only prevented from moving on because of its thickness, but also furs up the narrow limits of the vessels and causes blockages that are difficult to shift. When the spleen is affected in this way, a feeling of weight is created, which requires the help of attenuating foods and drink. This has been discussed elsewhere in my book *On Attenuating Diet*.

It certainly does not harm the chest or lungs when prepared like this. But I have in turn written about the foods which produce thick and viscous juice. My present argument asks you to commit to memory the other matters which I have gone through up to this point, and especially about the powers of breads, since we use bread all the time. In fact there is nothing wrong in reviewing the main points of what was said about breads.

The best bread in terms of health for someone who is neither young nor does physical exercise is that which contains a lot of yeast, a lot of salt, and has been kneaded for as long as possible by the baker, before being shaped and baked. It is cooked in a moderately hot oven, as has been stated before. Its flavour should be your test as to whether it has too much yeast and salt, because the distress caused by too liberal a mixing of these ingredients means bad bread. So as long as ones taste does not register any unpleasantness from the mixing, it is better to increase the quantities of the ingredients.

Refined bread

Those who have devoted thought to the preparation of refined bread have discovered a food with little nourishment, but it does avoid, as far as is possible, the harm that comes from blockages.[13] This bread is the least thick and viscous, since it is more airy than earthy. Its lightness is observed from its weight and from it not sinking in water, but rather bobbing on the surface like a cork.

Although the people who live in the countryside around me cook large quantities of wheat flour with milk, it should be understood that this food causes blockages. All such foods that contain good juices and are nourishing, harm those who use them constantly, by creating blockages in the liver and generating stones in the kidneys. For when the raw juice acquires viscosity – whenever the passages through the kidneys are in some people by nature rather narrow – whatever is very thick and viscous is ready to generate the sort of scale that forms on pots in which water is heated, and is deposited around stones in many of the waters that are naturally hot. The temperament of the kidneys is a contributory factor, especially when its heat is fiery and sharp.

In this category lies the scale that forms in diseased joints. For everything superfluous always flows into the weakest areas and causes whatever condition is appropriate to the nature of the individual. There will shortly be a discussion on its complete use in the section about milk, just as there will be one on fattening foods, since there are some other foods that contain the same power.

Groats

Groats are made from a type of wheat. They are fairly nourishing and contain a viscous juice, whether, after being boiled in just water, they are eaten with honey mixed with wine, or with sweet wine or with astringent wine (for each is used at a given time); or whether, they are eaten after being stirred about with olive oil and salt. Sometimes vinegar is also added. Doctors call this recipe groats, adding that the seasoning belongs to barley soup; some suggest that soup from groats nourishes anyone who is ill. But a few of the doctors in the past, like Diocles and Philotimus, gave the name of wheat soup to groats prepared in this way. This is why the term is rarely found in these ancient authors, as for the same reason 'spring wheat', because they referred to it by the common term of wheat.

It is stated in the work *On Diet* by Hippocrates that breads made from groats are extremely nutritious, but pass through the body less well; but it is also stated that fine wheat flour and boiled groats are strong and nourishing. So it is right to guard against their excessive use, especially with those whose liver is prone to blockages or who have kidneys that are inclined to generate stones.

It is particularly important to keep an eye on those thin soups made with what are called refined groats. For the juice of groats, when mixed with water, requires considerable boiling. Those preparing it can be deceived: although they think they have boiled it enough, it does in fact cause no little harm to the patients for whom it has been made, because it quickly congeals and thickens through being glutinous. So it must be mixed with plenty of water, boiled over charcoal and stirred frequently, until it has been properly cooked, at which point some salt should be added. Olive oil does no harm, if it is added at the beginning. But this subsidiary discussion is appropriate for therapy, not for the task now at hand.

Whenever at any time those in good health need a drink for severe stomach ache or the passing of much bile, boil groats for a long time until it becomes soft, then stir it and blend it, so that it resembles strained barley juice, and finally give it to drink. The seasoning is the same as for washed groats.

Wheats boiled in water

If I had not at one time eaten wheat boiled in water, I would never have considered there to be any purpose in eating it. For no one, even during a food shortage, would arrive at such a practice, since bread can be made if there is a good supply of wheat. And although chickpeas are eaten at dinner as a side-dish either boiled or fried, as are other seeds prepared in the same way, nobody serves boiled wheat. I would never have expected anyone to have eaten boiled wheat for the following reason.

Once, when I was walking in the countryside far from any city with two young men the same age acting as guides, I came across some peasants who were at that moment making their supper. Their wives were about to make some loaves because they had run out of bread.[14] One of them straightaway poured some wheat into a pot and boiled it. Then, after it was seasoned with a little salt, we were invited to eat. Since we had travelled far and were hungry, it was quite reasonable that we should decide to do this.

So we ate a lot of it, and felt a heaviness in the bowels, as if clay was lying there. Even by the following day it was not digested, so we passed that whole day without food, unable to eat anything because of flatulent bloating, headache and blurred vision. For nothing was passing downwards, which is the sole remedy for indigestion. So I asked the peasants if they ever ate boiled wheat and how they coped with it. They replied that they often ate it through necessity, as we too had been forced on that occasion, and that wheats prepared like this were a heavy and indigestible food.

The logic of this was clear even without any testing. Since, as I stated earlier, wheat flour when eaten is not easy to digest (unless it has been mixed with salt and yeast, worked and kneaded, and put in the oven), how could anyone not realise that it is the most powerful of indigestible foods? In fact wheats, when eaten like this, possess great power, provided they are digested, and they strongly nourish the body, thereby affording remarkable strength to those who eat them.

Starch

This is made from wheat. Its power is en... ... of whatever is harsh. This action is shared by all substances that are dry in consistency, and have no astringency, harshness or any other pronounced power. Understandably such substances are dubbed neutral to the senses. Even in moist substances there is water like this.

Starch is similar in power to refined breads, although it affords less nourishment to the body than unrefined breads. This power does not heat, just as these breads do not heat, although other breads do heat. There is no need to compare it with wheats boiled in water, since they are obviously strong on heat and nutrition, if digested, because they are difficult to digest, as has been said.

Barley

The use of this grain is widespead, although it does not contain the same power as the wheats. For the latter are conspicuously heating, whilst barley not only fails to heat (just like some foods that lie between what is heating and what is cooling ... ... and refined bread), but also seem to have something cooling about it in every application of its use, whether breads are made with it, or it is boiled for soup, or whether groats are made from it.

Barley falls short of the nature of wheat and in the appearance of its juice, which both of these grains produce, because wheats yield for us a thick and viscous juice, but barley a thin and cleansing juice. However it is prepared, barley never heats the body, although different recipes do either moisten or dry.

For groats made from parched barley obviously appear drying, whilst pearl barley moistens when it is properly prepared, that is to say when the grains have swollen to their greatest extent during boiling, and then after this are made into a soup by long simmering over a gentle flame. As soon as it has fully swelled some vinegar is mixed in. When it has been carefully cooked, you should add some finely ground salt, but not too much. If, at the beginning, you also add oil you will not affect the cooking. Nothing else needs adding, apart from some leek and dill when you start cooking.

I make the observation that barley soup is universally made in the worst possible way by cooks, for they pound it in a mortar when still raw and do not break it up by boiling it over the fire. Some even add some starch to make it appear as if it has been made into a decoction through sufficient boiling. Not surprisingly this recipe is very flatulent and rather difficult to digest.

I ought to add what I omitted regarding the correct recipe. You should soak raw barley in water for a little while, then put it in a mortar and pound it by hand with something rough, such as what is called 'Spanish broom' from which people plait shoes for pack animals.[15] The objective when pounding is to strip away the surrounding husk because, when barley is winnowed, the thin casing that surrounds it is not completely removed. This is why it is soaked and pounded in the mortar. If, on the other hand, not all the chaff is discarded, the barley when boiled will be more purgative, but it will not cause any other difficulty.

The worst recipe for barley soup is when the cooks pound it when raw with water in a mortar, then boil it for a short time and add what they term reduced must or wine. Some even add honey and cumin with these ingredients and so make a stew rather than barley soup. Yet the correct recipe confers on both healthy and sick people the benefits that were delineated by Hippocrates, since its gluten is, as he says, light, homogenous, soothing, moderately moistening, thirst quenching and easily passed – if this is required – neither does it contain any astringency or unpleasant disturbance, nor does it bloat the bowels, because during cooking it swells up naturally to its fullest extent.

Enough has been said on the power of barley in the present work, although not enough for the purpose of therapeutics, but then I am only explaining the powers of foods. Yet even a cursory glance at the argument elucidates some of its uses.

Barley breads

It is the right time to move over to a discussion of breads made with barley, which some people prepare in almost the same way as breads made with wheat. The more crumbly breads are made not only with ordinary wheat, but also with emmer wheat and still more with einkorn wheat, since the last variety contains nothing glutinous as do the others. Barley breads obviously furnish little nourishment to the body, especially when they are made from the sort of inferior grains that Hippocrates requested should not be used for barley soup, since they do not release much juice when they are boiled.

The best barley grains appear white after winnowing and have the maximum density and weight that is given to barley. Full grains with an exterior surface that is smooth are clearly better than grains that are shrivelled and wrinkled.

This should be the common mark of all seeds, unless perhaps they have far more weight than is usual, as well as being softer and spongier. You should realise that these grains contain an excessive amount of moisture and are worse than those that I mentioned before, which is why it is not a good idea to use them after the harvest, but instead to store them in dry places to allow, over the course of time, some evaporation of excessive moisture and a certain amount of digestion until they become dried and moderately shrunk.

For there flows out of all plants, seeds and fruits, when they are laid up after being harvested, first all the thin watery excretions that are contained in them, then any moisture that occurs naturally. Whenever grains are drier in substance than usual, they are worse than those grains which approach the pinnacle of excellence, although even in this state they are not completely bad, but are quite useful in certain conditions of the body which need to be dried. Those grains that have been stored for the longest period of time are less in power, their limit being reached when they are dry, on being broken in half, what looks like dust. You should bear all those things in mind now they have been stated once, because I am not happy about continually repeating the same ideas, unless on occasion it seems essential to recall just the bare outline.

Returning to the discussion, let me say something by way of summary about barley breads: the differences between them are similar to those which I mentioned a little way back about breads made from wheat, for all barley breads are far less nutritious than breads made from wheat, although breads made from the best barley are not so inferior, whilst bread made from barley that is spongy and light is similar to bran bread. Bread made from this sort of barley, no less than the other types of barley, is particularly laxative when compared with breads made from wheat. All the other recipes for barley bread fall between these two types, following the same pattern as the wheat breads that have been described.

Barley groats

From fresh barley that has been gently parched come the best groats. When barley is in short supply, I sometimes prepare groats from other grains too. Since every sort of groats smells sweet when it has been properly prepared, groats made from premium fresh barley are especially sweet smelling if the ears are not completely dry. It is customary for a lot of people who enjoy good health, to combine the groats with a mixture of reduced wine, sweet wine and honeyed wine and also in summer to drink them with just water two or three hours before a bath. This drink feels thirst-quenching they say. Taken with astringent wine it heats the stomach.

Some countries use groats in place of bread, as I have observed among the peasants on Cyprus, even though they do in fact produce an abundant harvest. In ancient times groats were prepared for soldiers, but nowadays the Roman army does not use them because they are recognised as being weak since they furnish little nourishment to the body. But they suffice for ordinary individuals who do no exercise, although they are not enough for those who do some form of exercise.

Barley cakes are made from groats that have been soaked and kneaded. I will come to these cakes in a moment, especially since Philotimus in the first book of his work *On Foods* discussed these cakes at length, but left vague what was most useful about them.

Flour

You can judge the power of each food by its nature even before a determining experiment. Anyone with any intelligence should not need convincing that flour which is genuinely fine, white and free from all branny material is converted more efficiently and quickly in the stomach and because of this is digested better, as well as being distributed more easily, furnishing nourishment more readily, so that it is completely assimilated and absorbed by the bodies that are being fed; whereas whatever contains bran and is hard, since at first sight it appears not to dissolve in water, cannot by the same argument be dissolved in the stomach even when soaked, but will stay completely undivided and undigested, that is in the same state as when it was eaten.

It therefore cannot be properly digested or distributed because it wholly lacks any correspondence with the mouths of the veins that run to the stomach and the intestines through which, of necessity, it must run, whilst the excessive faecal matter which results from it quickly passes down because of the weight of its mass and because in addition all bran has a purgative quality.

It is obvious to anyone who understands these things that barley wafers as a food for the body fall short of barley breads to the same degree as barley breads fall short of wheat breads. Since barley naturally already contains a considerable amount of bran, when dried it contains what is drier and more difficult to break up, but that dryness is its strongest feature, from which the body derives it nourishment, and accordingly barley wafers are less digestible than bread made from wheat and fill the stomach more with wind, and if they linger any more in the stomach they cause upset. They pass through the body more quickly if they have been kneaded and worked for longer. But if honey is added, they encourage an evacuation of the bowels ever more quickly.

Philotimus therefore thought that from all barley wafers came a thick, glutinous and cold juice, which he and his teacher Praxagoras called 'glassy'.[16] But this is not the case, because barley groats do not contain the sort of viscosity that is present in wheat groats, nor are they nourishing. He was even more mistaken over barley wafers soaked for a long time in sweet and reduced wine which, like the Athenians, he called 'crushed'. Compared with wheat dough these are malleable and glutinous both from being kneaded over a long time and from combining with the thick and heavy moisture the groats.

Just as a lot of kneading coupled with thick liquid makes the flour that has been kneaded sticky in appearance, even if it is millet flour, so by the same token the juice of barley soup appears viscous, although it contains nothing that is glutinous or resembles glue, but is purgative and cutting, with the result that it even seems to clean dirt from our skin. If you give it to someone to drink, you will later cause that person to be sick and bring up the phlegm which lies in the stomach, and everything will be expelled with the vomiting.

Einkorn, emmer and rice-wheat

Mnesitheus ranked einkorn in third place after ordinary wheat and barley, but Diocles went through these grains quite carelessly, preferring brevity in his writing rather than the accuracy of a detailed account, so in fact he wrote an abridged account of wheat, barley and many other foods. Praxagoras and Mnesitheus wrote a little more about these grains than Diocles, although they too are inadequate.

Philotimus recalled some grains at great length, others summarily and some (such as rice-wheat) not at all. It is obvious that Praxagoras was not his teacher, since Philotimus omitted nothing which Praxagoras mentioned, but gave detailed explanations and added much.

What is surprising is that the author – whoever that man was in antiquity – of the treatise on diet which is ascribed to Hippocrates makes no record of rice-wheat. For if he thought that rice-wheat was called one-seeded wheat by some people, then he ought to have explained this. But perhaps it would be better to define these terms.

Diocles wrote in the first book of his work *On Health to Pleistarchus*, at the point where he goes over the powers of foods: 'After barley and wheat in order of excellence come especially emmer, one-seeded wheat, rice-wheat, panic and millet'. In some manuscripts rice-wheat is not always included, although in other manuscripts it is not their excellence that is described as follows but their usefulness: 'After barley and wheat, in order of usefulness come especially emmer, one-seeded wheat, panic and millet', as if emmer were one sort of cereal and one-seeded wheat another. But Mnesitheus actually states that two terms were conferred on one cereal by writing: 'Wheat and barley are the most appropriate cereals for nutrition. It is said that after these come two cereals, although they are in fact the same cereal, some people calling it one-seeded wheat, others emmer.' Following on this he writes: 'after these come rice-wheat, millet and panic'.

Consequently all those grains to which I have just referred only apply in Diocles for describing rice-wheat and one-seeded wheat, although Mnesitheus in turn treated these cereals using the same method, discussing first emmer wheat and barley and then rice-wheat in these words:

One-seeded wheat is the best of the other cereals because it provides sufficient nutrition and is digested without too much effort, but no one who eats lots of bread made from rice-wheat can enjoy good health, whilst those who who are unused to such food will be ill, even if they eat just a tiny amount, because it is heavy and difficult to digest. Those living in northern climates are forced to live on it and sow it, because it resists the cold very well, and they usually eat it in small quantities, because its food does not smell pleasant and good harvests are rare in those areas. But then, through their familiarity with it as a food, it makes for an easy working up in their bodies. In short it must be said that rice-wheat is heavy, difficult to digest, strong and fibrous.

Through these words Mnesitheus showed very clearly which cereal he wanted to be called rice-wheat since it is farmed in cold countries. I have not seen every northern country, nor have I heard from anyone else who has seen these places of a cereal grain which is called by the locals one-seeded wheat (*zeia/zea*), for the word is found written both ways, in some texts with the first syllable ending in e and i, in other texts with just an e.[17]

One can observe, however, that the Greeks use the above name for this grain, whilst foreigners affix to it their own term. Noticing many fields in Thrace and Macedonia that contained a plant that both in its ear and its entirety resembles the einkorn growing around me in Asia Minor, I asked by which name those people called it, and they all replied that the whole plant (including its seed) is called rye (*briza*), the first syllable being written with a b, an r and an i, the following syllable with a z and an a when in the nominative case, but obviously with an n when in the accusative case. The bread made from this grain is black and does not smell nice because, as Mnesitheus wrote, the grain contains a very fibrous substance. If he had added a postscript to the effect that bread made from rye is black, I would have more readily believed that he was calling this grain *zeia*.

In the coldest areas of Bithynia there is a cereal called one-seeded wheat (*zeopyron*) without an i in the first syllable, just as it appears in Homer: 'emmer and einkorn and pale broad-eared barley'.[18] With this is made a much better bread than the one in Macedonia and Thrace. Just as the term one-seeded wheat (*zeopyron*) embraces both the other terms (that is einkorn and emmer), so its substance lies almost midway between these two cereals, being as it were a blend of them. It is, of course, as inferior to emmer wheat as it is superior to Thracian rye.

The names of the cities where this cereal grows are Nicaea, Prusa, Crassopolis, Claudiopolis, Heliopolis and also Dorulae, which is situated in Asia Minor on the borders of Phrygia. Phrygia too, just like a few other cities that border on it, has this cereal growing in the countryside. It is to be observed that the bread made from this cereal is as superior to the rye bread in Thrace and Macedonia as it is inferior to the bread made from emmer.

Theophrastus also mentions one-seeded wheat in the seventh book of his work *On Plants*. He says as follows:

Of all the plants that resemble barley and wheat – such as rice-wheat, einkorn, emmer, oats and haver-grass – the strongest and most exhausting of the soil is rice-wheat. It has many deep roots and lots of thick stalks. Its seed is extremely light and agreeable to all animals.[19]

Then he adds: 'Einkorn is the lightest of all the cereals, for it has a single stalk that is slender, which is why it requires thin soil, unlike rice-wheat which needs good rich land'. He adds after this: 'These two cereals – rice-wheat and einkorn – are very similar to emmer'. That is what Theophrastus wrote about one-seeded wheat.

Herodotus wrote in his second book as follows: 'Most people live on wheat and barley. Yet when Egyptians live off these cereals it is a very big disgrace, but instead they derive their food from emmer which a few people call rice-wheat'.[20]

Dioscorides writes in the second book of his work *On Medicinal Substances*:

> There are two sorts of rice-wheat: one is called simple, the other is called two-grained because the seed is joined together in twin glumes. It is more nourishing than barley and is wholesome, but when made into bread it furnishes less nourishment than wheat. Coarse meal made from rice-wheat and ordinary wheat is in its manufacture thicker than the meal from which porridge is made. It is fairly nourishing and easy to digest, although it checks the bowels when made from rice-wheat, especially if this has been parched beforehand.
>
> Emmer belongs to the same species as rice-wheat, although it is to a certain degree less nourishing than the latter. It is, however, made into bread, and similarly a coarse meal comes from it.
>
> Gruel is prepared with rice-wheat milled finely. It is taken as a liquid like a runny porridge, so it is suitable for children, and it is useful too for poultices. Spelt has a grain that resembles groats, but it is far less nourishing than rice wheat and contains lots of bran.

That is enough on the subject of rice-wheat. Anyone would be amazed at Mnesitheus not knowing the difference between einkorn and rice-wheat. Both varieties grow abundantly in Asia, especially in the country which lies above Pergamum, so that the peasants always use it to make their bread even after taking their share of wheat to the cities. Breads made from emmer are the best after those made from naked wheat, provided the emmer is the finest available, whilst second to these are breads made from einkorn. None of these breads is inferior when the emmer is bad, but when the einkorn is best, breads that are hot and which are made from this wheat are much better than breads made from emmer. But when these breads have grown stale, they are worse than these, since their sticky dough becomes much more dense, especially when they have been made carelessly, so that after a day or two, and even more so after this, anyone eating this bread supposes that a lump of clay is lying in his bowels.

But while they are still hot they are eagerly eaten by those who live in the cities with a cheese which is called locally *oxygalaktinos*. This cheese should be fresh and the bread should be still warm from the oven. Bread baked in this way is popular not only in the country, but also in the cities. But after three or four days this bread is unpleasant to eat even for the peasants, and it is quite difficult to digest and passes through the stomach very slowly, an attribute it does not possess when hot. Compared even with barley bread it is not too far behind in its laxative effect, although it is not to be blamed as much as bread made with millet; yet it still nourishes the body since it is quite hot, so it is not far behind bread made with unbolted wheat flour.

The grain of one-seeded wheat has a husk on the outside, just like emmer and barley, but after this has been removed the cereal serves very usefully for the making of bread. It is also eaten after being boiled in water. This recipe is called *apothermon* by the peasants when there is added what I refer to as reduced must (*hepsema*), but which some people call boiled new wine (*siraion*).[22] Sometimes it is served with salt too, in the same way as I said I ate emmer.

Whenever people winnow the best sort of emmer using the correct method, they make what is called *tragos*, which many people use after boiling it first in water, then discarding the water and adding reduced wine or sweet wine or honeyed wine. They also stir in some pine nuts soaked in water until they have swollen to their maximum size. Some people say that this grain belongs to the same species, others that it does not.

But there are many other grains that have a similar appearance, although accurately speaking they do not belong to the same species as the grains I have just described, some being between barley and rice-wheat, others between emmer and rice-wheat, or between ordinary wheat and emmer. Some are closer by nature to emmer, others to barley, rice-wheat or ordinary wheat, just as some are closer to panic or to millet. Some of the names they have are simple, like what they make groats from in Italy, others are composite, like what in Cappadocia is called naked-barley, but in Bithynia is called one-seeded wheat.

But it is better to bring this research into names and grains to a conclusion, and to discuss a single idea that is common to all of them. All grains that hold a great deal of thick and viscous matter in a confined space are wholesome and extremely nourishing, although they are not easily excreted; conversely all grains that contain soft and spongy matter with a proportion of bran, pass through the body more readily, but are less nutritious.

Obviously those grains that smell unpleasant and have something disagreeable about their taste are all unwholesome and difficult to digest. Your proof that grains have a great deal of matter packed into a small volume should come from their weight when weighed in a balance, and from the quantity of flour they produce, since a lot of flour is made from grains that contain this compressed matter.

Before consumption and absorption into the body their difference in warmth and coldness can be reckoned by their colour, taste and use when applied externally; after consumption and absorption into the body a precise determination and awareness is provided for those who have eaten them because, once taken, they either heat the stomach or cool it or clearly do neither of these things.

The colour in barley and emmer is naturally white, whilst in ordinary wheat it is pale yellow. Rice-wheat is more yellow than ordinary wheat. Its body is compressed until dense, and this perhaps contributes a little towards the smallness of the grain, for it falls far short of the size of ordinary wheat. But some people place this grain under the heading of wheat. The statement in Homer about horses, when Hector says to them that: 'he hastened to set delicious wheat before you' is said by some people to refer to the grain of rice-wheat since horses eat that without trouble, whilst ordinary wheat really does cause problems.[23] It is not surprising that rice-wheat is called 'little wheat' since it resembles its power both in colour, density and heat.

Oats

This grain is common in Asia, particularly in the part of Mysia that lies north of Pergamum, where there is also an abundance of einkorn and emmer wheat. It is a food for animals, not humans, unless the exigencies of famine at any time necessitate it being made into bread. When there is no shortage of food, it is boiled in water and eaten with sweet wine, reduced wine, or honey mixed with wine, just as with einkorn.

Like the latter it has a sufficient share of heat, although conversely it is hard, which is why it affords very little nourishment to the body. The bread made from it is otherwise unpleasant, but it does not constipate or relax the stomach since in this it is classed as average.

Millet and panic, which some people call Italian millet

A bread is made from these seeds whenever famine makes the cereals scarce that I have just described. It provides little nourishment and is

95

cold. Obviously it is friable and crumbling, since it contains nothing oily or glutinous. It is therefore logical that it should dry a moist stomach. Those living in the country boil the flour, and then eat it served with soft lard or olive oil.

Millet is in every way better than panic: it is more pleasant as a food, it is easy to digest, it does not check the stomach so much and is far more nutritious.[24] Sometimes peasants cook the flour with milk and eat it just as they do with wheat flour. This food when eaten on its own is clearly better since milk exceeds the nature of both these cereals in goodness and everything else.

By everything else I mean digestion, evacuation of the stomach, assimilation, and sweetness and pleasure in eating. For there is nothing sweet in these seeds, particularly in the panic that grows in my area of Asia, although in other places such as Italy they are much better.

Pulse

The term 'pulse' is used of cereals from which bread cannot be made, such as broad beans, peas, chickpeas, lentils, lupins, rice, bitter vetch, marrowfat peas, wild chickling, birds' peas, calavances, fenugreek, tares and similar such things. I will therefore discuss the power of all these in turn, so that they can be understood and used with the minimum of harm.

Rice

This grain is universally administered to check the stomach. It is cooked using a method similar to that employed with groats, although it is harder to digest than groats, contains less nutrition, and generally falls short of groats in culinary terms. [25]

Lentils

Nobody makes bread with lentils. This is because lentils are devoid of anything fatty in their construction and are friable, having an astringent husk and a flesh that is full of thick juices, earthy and with a small amount of the harsh quality of which the husk has so much.

Their juice, as I have said before, is the opposite to astringent. So if they are boiled in water, and this water is taken seasoned with salt or fish-sauce, together with olive oil, the resulting drink is laxative. When lentils are boiled twice (as has been said), the dish made with them also has the opposite power to the juice, since it dries fluxes in the stomach, and imparts energy on the stomach, intestines and the whole belly. For this reason, therefore, they are a specific food for bowel troubles and dysentery.

When the husk has been removed, the lentil loses the force of its astringency, and obviously whatever accompanies this force, but it does on the other hand become more nourishing than the unwinnowed lentil, since it is then slow to pass and contains thick juices that are bad. However, it does not dry the fluxes in the stomach, as the unwinnowed lentil does. So understandably anyone who eats excessive amounts of this food contracts what people call elephantiasis and cancer; for thick and dry food necessarily engenders black bile.[26]

Lentils are only useful as a food in the case of those affected by a watery indisposition of the body, just as it is extremely harmful for those who are dry and desiccated. For the same reason it also harms the sight since it parches anyone who is in a fit state, but it is beneficial for those contrarily disposed. It is not suitable for monthly periods, since it makes the blood thick and slow to flow, but it is excellent for what in women are called discharges.

In this respect pearl barley has the opposite effect to lentils, so an excellent dish can be made by combining these two ingredients. Those who live round me call the dish lentil and barley soup, although the lentils and barley are not added in equal proportions, less barley being used since with cooking it expands a great deal in volume, whereas lentils only swell a little when boiled.

The seasoning for this dish is the same as for barley soup, except that savory and pennyroyal are added for taste and to aid the digestion, although barley soup has no need of these ingredients, but suffices with just dill and leeks on their own. The worst recipe for lentils is that made by cooks for the wealthy with reduced wine, because it does not require the addition of thick ingredients, rather moist ingredients that cut through its thickness. Lentils mixed with reduced wine generally cause obstructions in the liver and exacerbate inflammations in both this organ and the spleen, unless some honey is added to improve it. It is clear that they also irritate indurated conditions of both these organs. But if you want to cook it with pork, you will find fresh meat goes well with barley, but cured meat with lentils, just as what is midway between these meats, which people call freshly salted, is of use for lentils and barley mixed together in terms of pleasure and digestion.

However, eating lentils with cured meats results in an increased production of thick juices, for such food produces even thicker blood with larger amounts of black bile. So it is important not to eat too much of these foods, especially when the body in question is inclined towards either black bile, or an excess of thick juices or bad juices in general. With each foodstuff you must be aware of locality, season and climate, in autumn being abstemious with foods that are drying or productive of black bile, but using them in winter, just as of course in summer using foods that are moist and cooling. But in spring, which is average in its temperament, foods that are average in their powers should be served.

Yet there is no single category of average foods. For some of these foods generally have something in common with the extremes, whilst some acquire a central position through two things of equal power being blended, just as I said a little earlier in the case of barley being mixed with lentils.

Thus Heracleides of Tarentum gave lentils and beet not only to healthy people, but also to the sick. For this food lies midway between the opposites, since beet passes through the body less easily, whilst lentils pass through more easily. It is obvious that the juice which is distributed to the body is blended from the two different powers of lentils and beet.

Beans

Beans have a multiple use: from them are made soups, both the watery sort in a saucepan and the thick sort in a casserole.[27] They are also an ingredient of a third recipe with pearl barley. The gladiators with me use a lot of this sort of food each day when building up the condition of their bodies not with dense and compressed flesh, as does pork, but instead rather more spongy.

But however it is made it is a flatulent food, even if it is cooked for a long time, although barley looses all its flatulence during the time that it is boiled. For anyone who pays attention and attends closely to the state of the body that follows from each food, a sensation arises throughout the whole body of stretching due to flatulent wind, especially when that person is unused to this sort of food or eats it without proper cooking.

The substance of beans is not solid and heavy, but spongy and light. They also possess a cleansing action like barley, for it can be clearly seen that their meal wipes dirt off the skin, something which slave-dealers and women have realised since they use bean meal for washing every day, just as other people use sodium carbonate, which is suitable for washing thoroughly too. They smear their face with it just like barley because it removes superficial blemishes which go by the name of burrs. By the same power, therefore, it slows nothing down in its passage through the body, which is a problem with viscous foods with thick juices that contain no purgative element, the examples we have mentioned being groats, spelt, finest wheat flour and starch.

The soup made from beans may be flatulent, but it becomes even more flatulent when the beans are used boiled whole. If they are roasted – for some people eat them like this in place of sweetmeats – they loose their flatulence, but become difficult to digest and slow to pass through the bowels, whilst for nourishment they distribute a thick juice to the body. Eaten when green, before they have been ripened and dried, they share the same attribute as all other fruits which we serve before their peak has been reached: namely that of supplying nourishment to the body that is moister and consequently more productive of waste, not only in the bowels, but throughout the whole body. So understandably such food is less nourishing and passes through the body faster.

A lot of people not only eat green beans when still raw, but also cook them with pork just like vegetables, although in the country they cook them with goat and lamb. Other people, realising that they are flatulent, mix them with onions when they are making a thick soup in a casserole. Some people even serve raw onions with this soup without cooking them together, because with all foods any tendency towards flatulence is mitigated through heating and diluting.

Egyptian beans

Since it differs very much in size from our type of bean, the Egyptian bean thus has a moister and more excrementitious composition. So if you recall what was said about related beans, but remember that these are by temperament moister and hence more excrementitious than what has already been mentioned both as regards digestion, passing through the body, distribution and nutrition, there will be no need to hear about this particular bean, since you can transfer the information you heard about these to the Egyptian bean.

Peas

Peas are very much the same in composition as beans, but although they are eaten in the same way, they nonetheless differ in two respects: firstly, they are not as flatulent as beans; and secondly, they do not have a purgative power. They are therefore slower to pass through the stomach than beans.

Chickpeas

Chickpea soup is not generally made in the same way , just as they also cook their wheat flour with milk. For the same fine grinding is not attempted with both broad beans and peas when what is known as meal is made with them. Chickpeas boiled in water are customarily eaten among many peoples, some serving them plain, others seasoning them with a little salt. Those around me make a sort of flour out of dried cheese and sprinkle the chickpeas with this.

Chickpeas are no less flatulent than broad beans, but they nourish far more effectively, and incite the need for sex, being reputed at the same time to generate sperm, so that they are given to stud horses for this very purpose. There is also more purgative power in them than in broad beans, which even means that some chickpeas clearly break up stones that have formed in the kidneys. This type of chickpea is dark, small, grows mainly in Bithynia, and carries the name of 'ram'. It is better to drink just their juice after boiling them in water.

Chickpeas are also used before they have ripened when still green, just like broad beans. The common property of all immature fruit has been discussed under the chapter heading of broad beans. So take what was said about grilled broad beans as applying to grilled chickpeas. For everything that is grilled loses its flatulent property, but becomes harder to digest and more costive, whilst affording thicker nourishment to the body.

Lupins

I of course know that this seed too is useful, whatever the interpretation of the word useful. It derives its name both from being appropriate to many conditions of the body, and being useful to everyone (or at least to the majority), even if all these people only require it for a one type of use. So according to this second interpretation, the lupin is a most useful pulse. For when boiled, then soaked in sweet water until it loses all its innate unpleasantness, it is eaten seasoned with fish-sauce, fish-sauce mixed with vinegar or, instead of these, a moderate amount of salt, but not like barley and other foods that are prepared in complicated ways.

It is hard and earthy in substance, so that it is necessarily difficult to digest, and it produces a thick juice from which, if it has not been properly processed in the veins, the humour specifically called raw is collected. Everything that sheds its bitterness when cooked becomes like those foods which have no effect on the senses. It is logical, therefore, that such foods are not serviceable when it comes to evacuation or to the checking of stomach flux, as are astringent foods, but are understandably slow to move, difficult to shift and hard to pass. Doctors classify all those foods which do not contain an excessive quality of power either to excite the bowels to evacuation or prevent them from evacuating like this.

Such qualities belong to them not when they act as foods, but as medicines. Everything that has no such pronounced quality is with good reason called inert by doctors, according to the difference between them in moisture and viscosity, so that it is categorised either with foods that are swift or slow to pass, or with foods that lie midway between those that are moist and slippery and move quickly, or conversely between those that are hard and dry, such as lupins. Everything that is midway between the differences I have just described does not promote either a special swiftness or slowness in the passage through the body. It is important to understand the following factors that are shared by all these foods in the same way.

Everything which is moister in consistency furnishes the body with little nourishment, since it is quickly turned into vapour and dissipated, whilst whatever is hard and earthy lasts for a long time and hardly dissipates. This all happens very much more obviously if they also contain a glutinous element. It is evident that it is not easy for these foods to be digested as they are not converted into blood or assimilated into the hard parts of the being. If this is the case, then they do not nourish quickly, but once they have been digested, they provide the body with plenty of nutrition.

Fenugreek

This seed is not only called fenugreek, but also bird's foot and Greek hayseed. It is clear that it belongs to the category of foods that heat and provides the same culinary use as lupins. It is eaten with fish-sauce to purge the stomach, and for this purpose it is much more useful than lupins, since it contains nothing that is awkward to pass.

It is served with vinegar and fish-sauce, just like lupins. Popular too is fenugreek and lupins with wine, fish-sauce and olive oil; and also with bread. In fact it makes an adequate accompaniment for bread, since it is not so purgative of the stomach, nor does it affect the head as much as fenugreek with fish-sauce does for some people, and it does not upset the stomach, as it can in the case of some people.

Some eat fenugreek even before the plant had run to seed, dipping it in vinegar and fish-sauce, whilst others pour olive oil over it and use it as an accompaniment to bread. Some even eat it with vinegar and fish-sauce. It affects the head when eaten to excess, and still more if it is not accompanied by bread. With some people it can upset the stomach.

The juice of boiled fenugreek taken with honey is good for cleansing bad fluids from the intestines, since it is gentle in its viscosity and soothing in its heat. Through its share of laxative power it encourages the bowels to evacuate. A little honey should be stirred in with the juice in case it might be too sharp.

For chronic chest pains without fever, fenugreek should be boiled down with oily dates. When the juice has been expressed, plenty of honey should be stirred in, and after this has been reduced over a flame until moderately thick, it can be used as a substitute for a much greater quantity of food.

Calavances and birds' peas

As with fenugreek, these seeds are soaked beforehand in water, and the whole length of the root is eaten dipped in fish-sauce as a starter to loosen the bowels. They contain a nutritious juice which, when distributed through the body, is digested better than fenugreek.

I knew a young man – a student at the school of medicine in Alexandria – who for four years used as his accompaniment with bread only the following pulses: fenugreek, calavances, birds' peas and lupins. He sometimes also touched olives from Memphis, vegetables and a few fruits which can be eaten without cooking, because he had resolved never to light a fire. He stayed healthy during all these years and his body was in no worse a condition than at the beginning. Of course he ate these foods with fish-sauce, on one occasion adding just olive oil to the fish-sauce, on another occasion also wine, on another occasion vinegar too, but otherwise only salt as with lupins.

What this book repeats about a healthy diet in these brief chapters has been treated in more detail in my treatise *On the Preservation of Health*. But for the moment let me add the following to what I was saying about birds' peas and calavances. As food, they lie midway between whatever contains good and whatever contains bad juices, the digestible and the indigestible, the costive and the laxative, the flatulent and without flatulence, the less nutritious and the more nutritious. They therefore hold no active quality, unlike some foods which harbour sharp, astringent, salty, bitter or sweet juices.

Marrowfat peas

Marrowfat peas are nearly the same in substance as birds' peas, and in my part of Asia they are used a great deal by the peasants, particularly in Mysia and Phrygia, not only like birds' peas and calavances as they do in

Alexandria and several other cities, but also cooking them as if they were making barley and lentil soup. They contain a juice that is closer in power to birds' peas and calavances, but thicker in consistency, which suggests that they are perhaps more nutritious than them.

Wild chickling

I have found the last syllable of the word *arakos* written with a k in the *Merchant Ships* by Aristophanes where it reads: 'wild chickling, wheat, pearl barley, groats, one-seeded wheat, darnel and fine flour'. The seed is similar to that of chickling, and some people do not think they are separate species, for the general use and power of wild chickling is similar to that of chickling, except that wild chickling is harder and more difficult to boil and so is harder to digest than chickling.

Where I live there is a wild variety that is round and hard, smaller than vetch, and found in cereal crops. It is called *arachos*, pronounced not with a k in the last syllable but a ch. Harvesters throw it away, just as they do with axeweed.

Calavances

The word calavance appears in Diocles along with the names of other edible seeds, but it also features in the work *On Diet* by Hippocrates, a work I have made mention of before.[28] I think that this was the name they gave to the the cultivated plant which today is generally called by two names in the plural. Some people call them *loboi*, or pods, whilst other people call them *phaseoloi*, giving the word four syllables and so making the term *phaselos* with three syllables refer to something else. Some claim that *phaselos* is another label for chickling, whilst others state that it is just a variety of chickling.

Proof that the cultivated plants are called calavances can be found in what Theophrastus wrote in the eighth book of his treatise *Enquiries into Plants*. The relevant passage states:

> Some again have erect stems, such as wheat, barley and in general the cereals and summer crops; some have by contrast a crooked stem, such as chickpeas, vetch and lentils; some have a creeping stem such as ochros, peas and lathyros; while calavances, if long poles are set up next to them, climb and produce a crop, but otherwise are unhealthy and have a tendency to attract fungus.

From the instructions about the erecting of long poles next to the plants, and the assertion that fungus will result if this is not done, it can be concluded that his discussion is about what people now call *phaseloi* and 'pods'. He also uses the word 'pod' for what surrounds the seeds of these pulses, as is the case with lentils, vetch, peas, beans and lupins. Just as ears surround the seeds on cereals, so it is the same for what are now termed pods, and pods surround *dolichoi* too. I therefore think that people today use the word pod for all the pulses and the word ears for every cereal crop. It is common knowledge that many individual foods that are in frequent use have attached to them the name of the whole crop species, for example – to use things that I have written about – reeds and apples.

In his work *On Diet* Hippocrates wrote: 'Peas are less flatulent, but more laxative; whilst birds' peas and calavances are more laxative than nutritious, but are less flatulent'. By comparing in this passage peas with beans, which he earlier describes as a flatulent food, he shows in the course of describing birds' peas and calavances that the calavance has seeds similar to the other pulses, particularly birds' peas. But the fact that he does not mention *lathyroi* and *phaseloi* is grounds for suspicion, since it is agreed that one of these seeds can be called *dolichos*. If *phaseloi* are included among chickling, it would then of course be impossible to deny that chickling are called calavances in the passage I have just quoted.

In his list of pulses, Diocles mentions first beans, then peas, and then writes: 'Calavances are no less nutritious than peas, and then are equally without flatulence, but they are not so pleasurable or laxative'. But he also mentions in turn birds' peas, lentils, chickpeas and vetch. By omitting *lathyroi* he leaves the question open. There is no problem over designating these pulses as a single species – that is chickling, birds' peas and calavances – although the nomenclature is wide. A parallel can be seen with the synonyms 'column' and 'pillar'.

There may be some apparent differences, but the idea of calavances being as nutritious as peas, and almost as free from flatulence, ought to be indicative that Diocles was talking about what we now call calavances. Chickling is no less free from flatulence than peas, and similarly birds' peas and *phaselos*, whether they belong to one species, as I have just said, or whether they are varieties of one species.

Philotimus and Praxagoras make no mention of these foods, apart from just beans and peas, so that there is nothing in these authors to connect with the name of calavance, on which this discussion is centred. Call those pulses which the majority of people know as calavances and pods whatever you will, but learn about their power from what Diocles wrote concerning calavances.

Hippocrates comes to almost the same conclusion in his work *On Diet* when he says that birds' peas and calavances are more laxative than peas, but less flatulent, and adding that they are nutritious. And this is the truth. Calavances are generally eaten whole with the pods when still green in olive oil and fish-sauce; sometimes wine is added. But unlike peas they are not used for preserving, since they are rather moist and so tend to have their nature ruined. Anyone who wants to store them safely should follow what my father used to do, and that is carefully dry them; in this way they keep without rotting or going off for the whole winter, and they can be used prepared in this way just like peas.

One of my friends, who was at the time living in Rome, used to say that in Caria, around his home at Ceramus, there were sown in the fields like the other pulses a calavance which had a more elongated appearance than chickling.

Vetch

Where I live cows eat vetch, whilst elsewhere people eat vetch that have been sweetened beforehand. But you should really leave off this seed, for it is unpleasant and contains bad juices. However in a famine, as Hippocrates remarked, they come into their own out of necessity.

If you prepare them first, you can use them like lupins with honey as a medicine for purging the thick humours in the chest and lungs. Among the vetches, the white variety is less medicinal than those which have a hint of yellow or cream. When boiled twice and sweetened in water their unpleasantness is removed, but in this unpleasantness is held their purgative and cutting power, so that of their general substance only the earthy part is left behind, and this is a drying food without any distinct bitterness.

Sesame and hedge-mustard

Sesame seed is greasy, so when stored it fast becomes oily. This is why it soon satisfies those who eat it, but it upsets the stomach, is digested slowly, and furnishes the body with a greasy sort of nourishment. As with anything else that is greasy, it is clearly unable to provide the parts of the stomach with tone or strength. It is full of thick juices, so it does not pass through the body quickly. It is eaten not just on its own, but with raw honey, mixed into what are commonly called sesame cakes. It is also sprinkled over breads.

Italian millet, which I said is called panic, is similar to millet, but generally worse; in the same way hedge-mustard is similar in substance to the general character of sesame, but is more unpleasant to eat, furnishes less nourishment for the body and is altogether worse. Both seeds are hot in constitution and because of this generate thirst.

Poppy seed

The seed of the cultivated poppy is useful as a seasoning spread on bread, just like sesame seed. The whiter seed is better than the darker seed. It possesses a cooling power, hence it is soporific and, if taken to excess, causes lethargy. It is difficult to digest and stops the expectoration of matter from the lungs and chest, but it helps those who are subject to thin catarrh from the head. For the body it provides nothing of note by way of nutrition.

Flax seed, which is usually called linseed

After drying it some people use linseed either like medicated salts or as an accompaniment to bread mixed with fish-sauce or honey. It is sometimes sprinkled on bread, although it is bad for the stomach, is difficult to digest and provides little nourishment for the body. It cannot be faulted for loosening the stomach. It possesses some diuretic power, something that is highlighted when it is eaten after being dried, although to a certain extent it then checks the stomach. Farmers often use it after drying it, finely grinding it, and mixing it with honey.

Red-topped sage

It is used after being dried, then ground until it is reduced to flour, and finally mixed with honey. Red-topped sage furnishes little nutrition, being by nature between hedge-mustard and cumin.

Hemp seed

Although the hemp plant in some ways resembles the chaste tree, the seeds do not have the same same power, but are completely different, for they are hard to digest, disagree with the stomach, cause headaches and contain bad juices. All the same, some people eat the seeds after they have been toasted with the side dishes.

What I mean by side dishes are those foods eaten for pleasure after dinner during the drinking. They are particularly heating and so affect the head, when just a few too many have been eaten, by sending up to the head a hot and medicinal vapour.[29]

Chaste tree seed

The seed of the chaste tree is eaten both as it is and toasted since it is believed to damp the libido, but it furnishes the body with little nutrition, and even this is drying and cooling, although it is sufficiently without flatulence.[30] In all it is suitable for anyone who wants to abstain from sex, which is the reason for the name of this plant. Unlike hemp it does not affect the head.

Tare and vetch

The shape of these seeds is not round, like broad beans, but instead flat like lentils in some way. Farmers store the whole of these plants together with their pods to use as fodder for their cattle. I know that, during famine and particularly in spring, farmers eat them when they are still green, in the same way as they usually eat both chickpeas and broad beans. They are not only unpleasant, but also hard to digest and costive of the bowels.

Since they possess this tendency, it is clear that the food which is assimilated from them is thick and certainly far from being composed of good juices, but instead is ideally suited to the production of melancholy blood, just as I said in the case of lentils. But in the latter there are present many commendable qualities, whilst in these there is nothing of the goodness of lentils. Where I live the name vetch (*bikos*) is well established, but this is not something that is universal, for among the Athenians it is called both *arakos* and *lathyrus*.

Different types of seed which appear in separate and mixed crops

A good deal of darnel is often found in wheat. This plant also grows in barley, but sparsely, for instead there is a lot of haver-grass in this crop, whenever problems arise with the initial stages of growth or germination.

In the latter part of his life, my father became interested in farming, and he once sowed wheat and barley, mixing both types of seed together after carefully selecting them, hoping in this way to find out for certain whether darnel and haver-grass appeared through mutation, or whether these seeds possessed a peculiar nature. Since a lot of darnel happened to appear in the wheat grown from specially selected seeds, but in the barley only a little darnel and plenty of haver-grass, he tried the same method in the testing of other seeds. So he found that inedible seeds such as the hard round wild chickling and axeweed appeared in lentils as a result of mutation, whilst there were clivers that are not only inedible, but also smother the lentil shoots as they are growing, by choking and strangling and dragging them down, just as dodder does to bitter vetch.

These are therefore altogether worthless seeds. Dark wheat is so called from a change that occurs in wheat, but this is far from the badness of darnel. He discovered similar such changes in other seeds, so he instructed those who were using them to pick out everything that was bad, whenever the seeds were being used to maintain health, and not to ignore them, as the bakers do who serve the general public.

For sometimes when the course of the year turns out badly, there springs up in the wheat massive amounts of darnel, and since the farmers do not remove it in sieves designed for this purpose – because total wheat crop would be small – and bakers act similarly for the same reason, the immediate effect is for headaches to trouble a lot of people, and when the summer comes for sores to appear on the skin of not a few of those who eat it, or some other symptom which is indicative of bad juices.

It is therefore important for us to sift the seeds that are going to be used for food, understanding that, even if we do not sense the harm caused each day because of its low level, yet after a long time the harm accumulated from it finally becomes noticeable.

8

ON THE POWERS OF FOODS
Book 2

Introduction

We feed off plants and animals. This is why everyone before me in their books about food has begun with cereals, because in these is that most useful nourishment of bread. So throughout my discussion in the first book of the present work I examined both wheats and barleys – that is einkorn and emmer – and added what are referred to as pulses and legumes. In this book I felt it important to move on to all the other foods which we enjoy from plants, and then to all the foods derived from animals that are particularly valuable to humans. The logic of this seems sound.

Some people do not go through every food that shares a similar nature, nor, on following on from cereals, do they give instructions about all the foods derived from plants, but instead they always base their discussion primarily around those foods which are most useful to humans. It is certainly the case that pork, kid, goat, veal, beef and lamb afford no less use to people than everything that hunters chase up in the mountains, as is in fact the case with the majority of fowl and sea food.

Then, reflecting that it would be impossible to include each type of food in a single book, I concluded that it would not make a great deal of difference if, of the designated foods that remained, I discussed in the second book those from plants, whilst in the third book I discussed those from animals. When selecting the particular book that delineates the power of the foods which are most wanted, the reader has the option, if so wished, of referring on one occasion to the first book, on another occasion to the second or the third book. As the plan is to conclude the discussion about plants in the first two books, I will start with the remainder of what I set out to say, thereby establishing this as the start of my reflections.

In the first book all the foods were seeds; now I will begin with fruits, after making a prior distinction between them and seeds, especially because

109

many people think it makes no difference whether you say fruit or seed. The seeds that have already been discussed are little different from fruits, but there is no small divide between what is now under discussion. For the fruit of the fig tree is the fig, but the seed of the fig tree is the pip, just as the fruit of the vine as a whole is the grape, yet the pip alone is the seed of the vine. In the same way the fruit of the pear tree and the apple tree are the pear and the apple, but the seeds are the three or four pips in their cores.

Why do I need to say anything more about large gourds and cucumbers – how many watermelons there are, or are not, and how many melons there are, or are not – and about all the other fruits that resemble them? For the whole fruit is radically different from the seed. Of the bean, lupin, calavance, lentil and all the other things that have a pod guarding the seed, the fruit consists of both pod and seed. The greatest part of the whole fruit is contained in the seeds. Only the seed is eaten of almost all the other foods which I discussed in the first book, with just the whole fruit of the calavance being eaten, provided that the fruit is still green; for when they are dried the pods that surround the seeds are useless to humans. The pod of the green bean is not edible, nor is the pod of the chickpea, nor the pods of any of the other things that Theophrastus generally called podded.

Understandably I have mentioned what most people designate as pods, but which some people call calavances, since only in their case is the pod edible. But I have described their power before, as I in fact believe some of the ancients applied the name of bean to them. Fruits come both from trees and from vegetables in the garden, among which some doctors list watermelons, melons and large gourds. It is with these that I shall make a start with the instructions in this book.

Fruits that are called autumn

The Greeks designate as autumn that part of the year during the middle of which the Dog Star happens to rise.[1] This period lasts forty days. It is then that all the fruits appear that are called autumn, although some are already past their best, some are not yet ready, and some are just right, either after the peak of the season or before it. They are called autumn fruits, not only because of the time at which they reach their prime, but also, I think, because they must be distinguished from foods that are suitable for storing, since wheat, barley and the other cereals which have been discussed in the previous book grow every year in the summer, but do not rot quickly, as do gourds, mulberries, melons, round melons, peaches and all other such things. For if they are dried, put into storage and kept for the winter, their original state is completely changed to something different.

Of course some people remove the seed from gourds, then dry the flesh, store it over the winter, and generally use it far more than some of the other foodstuffs. Yet the state of wheat and barley, as indeed all the other cereals, does not change to anything different in storage; because every cereal holds to those basic properties which were formed right at the beginning of the summer.

Evidently anything that possesses a body with a dry constitution, since it is stable in its condition, is therefore solid, earthy and hence nourishing; whilst anything that is moist in consistency both rots, affords a negligible nutrition and passes easily out of the body. It is for this last reason that such foods go through the stomach more than solid foods, particularly when they contain anything alkaline and laxative, some of the autumn fruits, as I have shown, being quite powerful in this respect; even though I said they were full of bad juices, yet they have no perceptible quality of taste, just as the finest water has no perceptible quality.

So all these things, particularly everything that we eat before it has fully ripened, are flatulent, but pass through the body quickly, seeing as everything that has a thin juice is also quickly distributed. These things are all replete with bad juices, and the only sort of person who would derive any benefit from them is someone exhausted after a very long journey and from excessive heat; in this instance they are of benefit, firstly by rehydrating a dried out body, and secondly by cooling to a moderate degree, if they are eaten when cold.

So they always hold the ability to rehydrate, but their cooling property is not kept if, as I have said, they are served hot to patients; for in their own particular constitutions they are not so cold as to cool the stomach even if they are served warm. An additional cooling agent is required, which can counteract the heat that belongs to the parts in the stomach and the liver, with which the initial contact is made. Since these ideas about all such foods have now been introduced and discussed in general, I shall now move on to the powers peculiar to each individual food.

Large gourds

When raw these are unpleasant and bad for the stomach, since they are extremely indigestible. So that if you are forced, through want of some other food, to eat a large gourd, as by now you will have summed up the necessary courage, a cold weight will be felt lying in the bowels, the stomach will be upset, and vomiting will be induced, the only way in fact that the ensuing symptoms can be alleviated. So everyone tends to serve the large gourd and many of the other autumn fruits either immediately after boiling, or further fried in a pan or baked. You should bear this statement in mind, for it applies to everything that requires some alteration through heat.

The large gourd, which is the topic of this section, has no recognisable quality in its flavour after it has been boiled, unless you mean by flavour a lack of sharpness, saltiness, sourness, bitterness and anything else of this sort that is clearly defined. Water can be classified like this. It is the universal practice for everyone to designate such things as inert, and I would like to follow this concept in order to keep my discussion clear.

Since the large gourd is like this, it is understandable that it does not lend itself to many methods of preparation, because it is set midway between all extremes, and hence it has the potential of being brought equally and easily to these extremes. None of those foods that naturally have something extreme in them is brought easily to that state through contradictory preparation.

The large gourd furnishes the body with nourishment that is moist and cool, and therefore also scanty, as was said a little before about everything that has thin and watery juices. It passes down easily through the stomach through the slipperiness of its substance and following the principle that is common to all moist foods that are clearly devoid of any astringency.

It is not digested badly, provided it does not rot first. This rotting occurs through faulty preparation, whenever a bad juice collects in the stomach, sometimes as a result of the food lingering there, an occurrence typical of all the other autumn fruits that are moist in composition; for they rot in the stomach if their passage is not anticipated quickly.

The large gourd contains a juice that is without quality as far as the senses are concerned. It distributes all the juice it has as nourishment to the whole body. So, by the same token, whenever it is served with anything that has a strong power, this is readily absorbed: for example, if it is eaten with mustard, it is made bitter, but the juice that is distributed from both mustard and the large gourd has at the same time a pronounced heat; whilst in the same way, if it is eaten with anything salty, just as it is prepared by some people with pickled fish in a casserole, it produces a salty juice in the body. Served like this it is an excellent food, provided the pickled fish belongs to the kind from the Black Sea which people nickname 'apple'.

If large gourds are boiled together with quinces and are suitably seasoned, they have a bitter juice which is effective for the digestion. When baked or fried they lose a great deal of their their special moistness, and what remains does not acquire any strong power, something which does not happen when they are prepared in a simple sauce. Naturally, oregano accompanies large gourds well because of the watery quality that is innate in them; for everything of this sort demands to be mixed with bitter, sharp, astringent or salty flavours, if the intention is for them to be eaten without unpleasantness and without causing nausea.

Watermelons

The nature of watermelons is generally rather chilling and contains a great deal of moisture. Yet they possess a certain purgative quality, which means that they are also diuretic and pass down through the bowels more easily than large gourds and melons. Their cleansing action you can discover for yourself: just rub them on dirty skin. Watermelons will remove the following: freckles, facial moles, or epidermic leprosy, if anyone should have these conditions.

Watermelon seeds are more purgative than what is known as the flesh, so they are excellent for kidneys troubled by stones, but they produce bad juices in the body, especially when they are not properly digested, which is why they usually trigger cholera. This is because even before they have been digested, they are prone to induce vomiting, and if too much of them is eaten, they certainly do cause vomiting, unless they are accompanied by something that contains good juices.

Obviously the popular name for this fruit has come about from the same sort of association as the adjective black has with ink, for the word for watermelon (*pepon*) has connections with the adjective ripened (*pepanon*), that is to say what has been ripened, which to other people signifies everything that has ripened. A bunch of grapes can be described as ripe, when it it fully ripened, so anything that has not yet reached this state cannot be called ripe, since it is in fact unripe and not in season. By the same token all the autumn fruits, such as pears and large gourds, can be called properly ripe, and just like melons embrace the concept of what is described as ripe.

Hence some doctors do not think it right simply to call them watermelons, but urge that the term 'watermelon-cucumber' should be used. Such discussions are not, I believe, the subject of this present work, because they contribute nothing to the art of medicine. A clear explanation is far more valuable than clouding learning with futile arguments of this kind; clarity can best be reached by choosing terms most familiar to the majority of people and keeping to their basic meanings.

Melons

Melons are less moist than watermelons, do not contain so many bad juices, are less diuretic, and not so good at passing down through the bowels. They do not have the power to induce vomiting like watermelons, just as they do not rot nearly as quickly in the stomach as do watermelons, since in watermelons either the accumulation of a wretched juice or some other cause sets off the rot.

Although they fall far short of summer fruits that are good for the stomach, they do not possess the characteristic of being bad for the stomach which watermelons possess, nor do they induce vomiting like watermelons. People do not eat the flesh of watermelons inside which the seeds are contained, but they do eat the flesh of melons with the seeds, and this contributes to their passing through the body. Anyone eating only their flesh passes melons through the body less effectively than watermelons.

Cucumbers

These have a certain diuretic quality, too, just like large gourds, but less pronounced, and their substance is not so moist either. This is why they do not rot nearly so easily in the stomach as do large gourds. Some people digest them (as they do many of the other foods that people for the most part do not cook) through an affinity of their nature with them, a phenomenon described in my work *On the Temperaments* and with even more stress in my book *On Simple Medicines*, which show foods are peculiar to each species of animal due to their wholly unique composition: thus for mules and horses bran, straw, oats and so on; but for lions the raw flesh of animals; and for humans all such flesh cooked, and bread made, as I have said, from cereals.[2]

Furthermore, quails eat hellebore, just as starlings eat hemlock, but come to no harm, in the same way as cows that eat vetch. What therefore remains crucial to distinguish is that foods are each digestible and indigestible, either through the uniqueness of their composition or through some attribute that surfaces during testing. The sort of thing I mean by an attribute has been explained in my first book, for foods either contain bilious juice, or completely wretched waste matter that often collects in the stomach as in some people who have a constitution that is hot without being moist, and a rather bad temperament that is dry and fiery. For these people rot whatever in others is easily transformed and digestible, and a belching occurs which is completely greasy.

Always remember that, even if someone digests whatever most people

114

find indigestible, the juice distributed from this to the body possesses the same nature. Thus it is impossible for a thick and earthy juice to appear from large gourds, even if they are digested extremely well, just as from lentils and beef it is impossible for there to appear that watery and moist juice, which of course is even described as thin in consistency.³ In this especially lies the means for the maintenance of good health and protection against diseases, as has been shown elsewhere and will now, since the discussion is under way, be repeated in a brief summary.

So in the case of those who digest cucumbers well, whenever they ignore any qualms about eating a lot of them, a collection of cold and relatively thick juice occurs in the veins over a long period of time, which in addition cannot, without problems, be converted into good blood through venous digestion. It is for this reason that I would recommend that all foods that contain bad juices be avoided, even if they are easily digested by some people. As a result of eating cucumbers, a wretched juice that is the cause of malignant fevers collects unnoticed in the veins over time, whenever there is a minor reason for putrefaction.

Fruits that grow on trees

Clearly pears, apples, peaches, pomegranates and all such similar things that are fruits from trees are useful as food, although there are other fruits which are not eaten and which I do not intend to discuss in this present work. In general, as regards edible fruits, it is important to have knowledge of their basic background: that is moist fruits distribute their moist and thin nourishment to the body; and that in addition foods of this sort pass rapidly through the whole body and are excreted either through the urine or through the skin.

This is why doctors are quite right in saying that these foods afford little nourishment. By way of contrast is the consistency of hard fruits, from which much more nourishment is incorporated into the body, for their passage through the body is slower, especially when there is contained in these fruits some thick, viscous or astringent juice.

Figs

Figs not only have what is a trait common to all summer fruits, but also to all fruits that are called seasonable, and that is they cannot avoid having an element of unwholesomeness, although this trait is less noticeable in them compared with all the other seasonable fruits. But they also contain something good which readily passes through the stomach and easily goes through the whole body. They possess a considerable facility to purge, as a result of which their consumption promotes the expulsion of sandy sediments in people with kidney problems.

Since all summer fruits afford little nourishment to the body, ripe figs have next to no nutrition; in fact they do not make strong firm flesh, as does bread and pork, but rather spongy flesh, as do broad beans. They fill the stomach with flatulence, and so cause pain, unless on being eaten their passage through the body is swift, and if this is coupled with a prompt evacuation, they cause flatulence of short duration, and so they are usually less harmful than autumn fruit.

Compared to figs that are not ripe, the excellence of ripe figs is considerable, and this excellence is manifest in all other fruits without exception. Figs that are perfectly ripe come close to causing no harm at all, just like dried figs which have many uses, but they are bad for those who eat too many of them. For the blood which they produce is not altogether good, and so the result is a large number of fleas.

They have an attenuating and cutting power, which is why they encourage the stomach to evacuation and cleanse the kidneys; but they are harmful to inflammations of the liver and spleen, just like fresh figs, although this is due to a property inherent in all sweet foods and drinks, and not because of some special power.

For those affected by blockages or indurations they afford no help or harm; but mixed with cutting, attenuating and purgative medicines they are particularly beneficial, and because of this some doctors administer them with thyme, pepper, ginger, pennyroyal, savory, calamint, oregano or hyssop before any other food is eaten so as to help such problems in the liver and spleen. By the same token, if dried figs are used when one of the other ingredients has a power that is harsh, generally attenuating and cutting, then what is eaten is useful not just for those who have this complaint, but also for healthy people. It is safest for the alimentary passages through the liver to be open just as much in the case of the sick as of the healthy.

Thus many people give figs with medicated salts that attenuate in both vinegar and in fish-sauce, having through experience found them useful. It is reasonable to suppose that some of these people will share this knowledge with lots of others after some doctor has encouraged them to do so. Anyone who eats fresh or dried figs with one of the fattening foods does not suffer any harm.

Grapes

Figs and grapes are what one might call the chief of the autumn fruits. They nourish more than all the other autumn fruits and they contain fewer bad juices, especially when they are fully ripe. Those who guard the fruit on the vines provide the greatest proof of their nutrition, because throughout the two months that they keep watch they only eat figs and grapes – with perhaps a little bread as an accompaniment – yet they maintain a good weight. The flesh which results from them is not strong and dense, like that from meat, but rather spongy and flaccid, which is why it quickly reduces as soon as this food is stopped.

Grapes nourish less than figs, and the greatest advantage that they have is of passing through the body quickly. So if on any occasion they are held in the body, they are quite harmful, whilst figs when ripe do not possess this character. For even if they do not become noticeable by their passage through the body, yet they are digested well in the stomach and furnish nourishment to the body without any problems. Neither of these attributes is held by grapes, for they are not digested well when they are retained in the body; and in the course of their distribution to the liver and veins they produce a raw juice which is not easily converted into blood.

The reason is that the substance of the grapes is composed of what can be described as flesh and the moisture that is contained there, from which wine is made; and in addition the pips and the covering on the outside that is like a membrane surrounds all these things. But the substance of the pips is dry and somewhat astringent; it passes right through the intestines whilst undergoing no perceptible change in itself, just like the seeds in figs. There is a double correlation between the two fruits: firstly the seed provides the building block for the whole plant; and secondly it passes through the body without change, without being converted into juice and without being processed in the course of digestion.

There is also a connection with the skin that surrounds both fruits, since this fulfils the same function for them as the skin does for animals. The skin undergoes hardly any transformation in the stomach, and some people spit it out as useless, after sucking it and everything which is inside, together with the pips. Some people even try to spit out the pips, and particularly when the grapes are large; for with little grapes this is awkward to do.

The stomach clearly is especially loosed when just the flesh and juice of the grapes is drunk without the pips and the skin, but the effect is still more powerful when juice is drunk on its own. This juice is called 'must'. If the must does not find a swift exit, it fills the bowels with flatulence. Some nourishment for the body is derived from the must, although there is more nourishment in the fleshy part, which is why some grapes nourish more than they pass, whilst others pass more than they nourish. Therefore grapes in which there is little juice furnish more nutrition, whilst those which have more juice nourish less, but pass through the body more.

Grapes that are called 'noble' are those in which the pips contain a substance, which I call the flesh of the pip, that has little moisture but rather more solidity. These grapes are used during the course of the autumn, after being kept in different ways: for they are laid up in must, and also stored with seconds after being packed into clean jars.

By 'seconds' I mean the solid parts left behind when all the juice has been extracted from the grapes in the press. These solids are placed in containers, after being being compacted and squeezed very hard. The same product, which I call seconds, is also called 'lees'. The term for a mass of pressed grapes is in turn applied to the stalk of the grapes that grows from the branches. What the grapes hang from I myself call the 'peduncle'. Into this lees the new pots full of grapes are put, carefully covered with lids, so that nowhere is any air admitted, and pitch is plastered where the lids meet the jars, thereby stopping all evaporation. The pot itself should be made from fragrant clay and perfectly baked.

This type of grape strengthens a relaxed stomach, and stirs those who have lost their appetite to take food, but it does not pass down through the stomach and, if eaten to excess, affects the head. Much worse for headaches are grapes stored in must; but when hung up they do not harm the head so completely, check the stomach, or trigger its evacuation. They work in the same way with the appetite, since they neither awaken one that is weak, nor diminish one that is strong. More digestible than the other types of grape is that which I said people store in must and seconds for the whole of the following year up to the next vintage. When they have dried, those which are hung up become useless, some as soon as spring comes, the rest at any rate by the summer.

There is a considerable difference between the grapes in sweetness, astringency, sourness or absence of any pronounced quality. People call the last of these 'vinous'. Grapes that are sweet possess a hotter juice, and so cause thirst, whilst astringent and sour grapes are cooler. Vinous grapes lie midway between hot and cold. Sweet grapes relax the bowels, particularly when they are juicy, and, after these, juicy vinous grapes.

Sour and astringent grapes are useless not only for this purpose, but also for digestion in the stomach, assimilation and nutrition. In fact sour grapes, even if they are left to hang on the vine to ripen properly, do not turn sweet like this, although some astringent grapes change towards being sweeter when hung for a long time. As for acidic grapes, just as with sour grapes, even if they have hung for a long time, they cannot be made any sweeter, so it is right always to be cautious about eating them.

The safest use for all grapes is when they are naturally fleshy and ripe; they should be eaten in moderation, whether they are ripened to their fullest extent on the vine, or whether the rest of the ripening process follows from being hung up. After grapes that have been hung up come those that do not contain any astringent or acidic quality; these can be eaten in large quantities to move the stomach. Some people also drink must for the same purpose, particularly the sweetest must that is available, because it is extremely laxative, whilst must made from astringent or acidic grapes is perfectly useless in every respect.

I use those names which the people of today use, because I think it is better to put over the facts clearly than to speak in ancient Attic Greek. For anyone to whom the latter exercise is more valuable than a lucid explanation, the term 'refuse' is used for the solid parts of the grapes, when the must has been expressed, but for olives the term 'pressing' is used, when olive oil has been expressed; that which is left behind from wines, the majority of those who speak Attic Greek call 'lees'. So there is no general name among these people, as there is among all the other people who call the leftovers of crushed grapes 'lees'. In fact these three products are known by the Greeks of today under the name of 'lees'. The infusion from what is left after grapes have been crushed is called lees, which once again those speaking Attic Greek call 'seconds'. I personally call it 'pressings'.

After the remains of the crushed grapes have been put into small jars, water is poured over them until they are immersed, and when this seems to have been carried out satisfactorily, the hole at the base of the jar is opened so that the infusion can be drawn off. This is drunk instead of wine. Obviously the water is added by experience according to the quantity of crushed grapes, to ensure that the seconds are neither completely watery nor like neat wine. Then more water is again poured over the crushed grapes, although less than the first time, to make it acceptable to drink, which is why some of those who speak Attic Greek think it reasonable to call it 'seconds', which is not the same as what was described earlier.

Each type causes headache, unless they are drunk very watered, but it is the first variety that affects the head the most. What is good about this drink is that it quickly passes as urine, although it matters a great deal as to what sort of grapes were used to make the infusion. For when they are sweeter, the drink is far sweeter and is urinated more quickly, but when they are sour or sharp, the drink is far more unpleasant and less diuretic. The infusion becomes stronger and more like wine when the lees is kept until spring or summer; when used in the winter it is unlikely to affect the head and similarly it passes less in the urine.

Raisins

Raisins have the same relationship to grapes as dried figs do to fresh figs. There are many sweet varieties of raisins, but altogether few astringent varieties, most raisins being a mixture of sweet and harsh qualities. There is present in sweet raisins some indistinct harsh quality, whilst in sharp raisins there is present a hint of sweetness. Harsh raisins are colder in consistency, just as sweet raisins are warmer. Harsh raisins generally strengthen the stomach and block the bowels, but it is clear that astringent raisins do this even more than harsh raisins. Sweet raisins are midway in all of this, neither loosing the stomach strongly nor drawing on the bowels. The ability to temper the juices is always present in sweet raisins, as is the power to purge moderately, so that from a combination of these two effects they dull the biting pains in the mouth of the bowels, which is also called the stomach, and so there is a call for them as a reputable remedy for excessive biting pains.

Among the varieties of raisins the best are those that are oilier and have a thick skin. Some people make excellent raisins from large sweet grapes, for example the *scybelites*, but before they eat them they remove the pips. When they are old they have a hard and thick skin, so they must be soaked in water before eating, which also allows for the pips to be removed more readily. On the other hand, some grapes are harsh and small, but they have absolutely no pips. These are grown in Cilicia and are pale brown in colour, whilst those grown in Pamphylia, including the *scybelites*, are black in colour. As I have said, these are the largest varieties, whilst the smallest are the golden ones which are grown in Cilicia, and in fact other varieties are grown in Cilicia that are both sweet, black and medium in size, as they are in other areas, particularly in Libya.

Numerous varieties of grapes are grown in Asia: there can be found pale brown grapes, black grapes, sweet grapes and rather sour grapes. In cold localities, however, grapes do not fully ripen, nor do some of the raisins, which is why they are used in wines flavoured with resin to prevent them from acidifying quickly. The differences in the colour of raisins has nothing to do with their power, and the same is true for the differences in size. It is only the quality of taste that matters, and by paying attention to this you will ascertain, as I have already said, for what purpose and at what time the grapes should be used.

The nutrition from raisins is similarly distributed in the body as with grapes: a sweet quality from sweet grapes, harsh from harsh grapes, mixed from grapes with both qualities combined. In terms of quantity, there is more nourishment from oily and sweet raisins, and less from harsh raisins without any oiliness. If you compare an equal quantity of grapes with oily sweet raisins that have been stored, you will find the raisins to be more nourishing. These grapes have less of an aperient and purgative power than dried figs, but they are better for the stomach than dried figs.

Mulberries, which are also called morus

I have not written this book for those who choose to speak only Attic Greek – in any case they would probably not want to read it because they consider it far more important to pursue the health of the mind rather than the health of the body – but rather for doctors (who are not too bothered about whether Attic is used or not) and anyone else who lives logically (that is paying more attention to the body and soul than to honour, reputation, wealth and political power). I am fully aware that these individuals regard the Attic dialect naturally as being no finer than other dialects, but they do hold the health of the body to be the finest action in a life devoted to what is natural. On the basis that the clearest exposition will be of the greatest use to these people, I shall write the conventional modern nomenclature, even if what I set down was not the norm among the ancient Greeks.

The term mulberry is probably familiar to most people, if through nothing else than the medicine called moraceous that is made from the juice and which is good for the mouth. Recalling some of the autumn fruits which I mentioned earlier, many people today do not have a clue as to what Athenians six hundred years ago called them. Nowadays it can be observed that Athenians do not call each fruit anything different from other Greeks, but use the term 'mulberry' for 'morus' no less than mulberry itself, as well as applying the basic vocabulary for peaches, walnuts, apricots and other such fruits, following the common usage of other Greeks. Nobody can come to any harm if they are ignorant of the ancient nomenclature of fruits, but knowledgeable of their powers. Rather than being proficient in their nomenclature, it is better to know that, of the foods which are laxative, you should eat last those which pass slowly, whilst those which pass quickly should be eaten first, because such fruits rot in the stomach if they remain there for any length of time.

People in general do not appear to be completely unaware of the order in which you should eat food; in fact we can see them following this order in the case of most foods. They eat radishes before olives and fenugreek in fish-sauce, and after these mallows, beets and other such vegetables with olive oil and fish-sauce. Experience over time with foods prepared every day has taught them about their powers, if they have any sense, for everything which comes from long experience is only recorded and remembered by those who are attentive.

When mulberries reach an empty stomach after being eaten first, they pass through the bowels extremely quickly and prepare the way for other foods; but eaten second after other foods, or meeting with a bad juice in the stomach, causes them to rot quickly, because like gourds they posses an unusual capacity to rot that is difficult to describe. They may be the most harmless of the autumn fruits, but if they pass through the body without digestion they rot badly like melons, although they do not cause any great harm if they pass through the body quickly.

The correct time to use mulberries is the same as for melons, that is when the fabric of the stomach is dry and hot; this is also essential when the liver is like this. Mulberries and round gourds have nothing astringent about them, just like unripe gourds, cucumbers and melons; but this quality is plain in mulberries, especially when they are not yet properly ripe, and there is an even greater sharpness the more unripe they are. Some people, after picking them from the trees, dry them and store them, because they are a good medicine for dysentery and chronic diarrhoea.

But here is not the place to for me to discuss the power of medicines. Let me return instead to everything that mulberries can do as a food. I have already stated that they pass through the body easily, perhaps due to just the moistness and slipperiness of their flesh, but perhaps also due to some admixture of a harsher quality that encourages evacuation sufficiently, seeing that the astringent quality not only does nothing to assist the bowels to move, but can even constipate them. You have learnt in my book *On Simple Medicines* that quite a few things are composed of opposite qualities.

So I am showing that mulberries have just a little power on their own, compared with the great power that is present in purgative medicines, and as a result of this they both pass easily, but also rot if they stay in the stomach for any length of time. If they do not rot, they generally moisten, but they do not on the whole cool, unless they are eaten when cold. Like melons they supply hardly any nourishment to the body, but there is nothing in them that is emetic or bad for the stomach as there is in melons.

Cherries

Some cherries are like mulberries, although having less astringency; others are like blackberries, although they have a more pronounced astringency; and others are far more astringent than both these fruits. As regards the power in each of the varieties that I have just mentioned, refer in each case to mulberries and blackberries.

Blackberries

Some of those who live around me call the fruit of the bramble 'blackberry', just as they call the fruit of the mulberry tree 'mulberry' or 'morus'. Blackberries are rather astringent, and cause headaches if eaten in large quantities. Some blackberries also open the stomach. This fruit ought to be washed well before eating, something that should be done with mulberries too.

Blackberries do not relax the bowels, but instead check them, and if they are dried when still unripe and stored, they are even more liable to cause a stoppage. All medicines that are made with blackberry juice possess a more drastic power because of them.

Rose hips

The fruits of the wild rose are a little more astringent than blackberries, and thus are more costive too of the stomach. Peasants eat them, although they offer little nourishment to the body. They call these fruits 'rose hips'.

The fruit of the juniper tree

These fruits are called 'juniper berries'. They are fairly sharp, but contain some sweetness as well as some astringency. There is an aromatic hint about them too. Through their bitterness they are clearly heating, because it has been shown that everything bitter is heating, and also because of the aromatic smell and taste, since everything aromatic is hot. Juniper berries cleanse anything in the liver and kidneys, and they evidently thin any thick and viscous juices, and for this reason they are mixed in health medicines.

They contain a small amount of nutrition for the human body. If too many are eaten, they bite the stomach and heat the head, which is why they sometimes cause painful repletion. They neither check nor encourage the passage of foods through the bowels, but they are moderately diuretic.

123

The fruit of the Syrian cedar

The fruit of the Syrian cedar is called 'cedrelate seed'. It resembles the juniper in colour and shape – for it is yellowish and round – but it is distinguished by its bitterness. So it already seems that this fruit belongs to a medical catalogue, since it does not furnish the body with any nourishment, unless it is soaked in water. This is the common factor with all bitter foods: that after their bitterness has been removed they supply hardly any nourishment to the body. In addition the fruit of the Syrian cedar is harder and drier than juniper berries, so it is of course smaller and contain nothing as aromatic. It is therefore clear that it causes considerable biting pains in the stomach and triggers headaches, unless it is eaten in strict moderation.

Pine nuts

The pine nut has good thick juices and is nutritious, but it is not easy to digest. The Greeks today call them *strobiloi* rather than *konoi*.

Myrtle berries

The Greeks call this fruit the myrtle. Like the juniper berry it provides no nourishment, but its power is the complete opposite. For it is considerably astringent, and so it checks the bowels. In its power it is cooling, although not in proportion to its astringency, because it contains not only astringency, but also an admixture of some bitterness. It is a trait common to all foods with a marked medicinal quality that, when they lose this power through boiling, baking or soaking, they afford hardly any nourishment for the body, whereas to begin with they give absolutely no nourishment. The same thing happens with onions and leeks.

Apricots

Whether you want to call this fruit the Persian apple, or just 'apricot' as the Greeks do now, or whether you want to search for some other ancient name, is up to you when you have a free moment. Remember whichever name is most useful, and that the juice and flesh rot easily and are generally bad.

This means that you should not eat them, as some people do, after other foods, for they rot as they rest on top. It is essential to bear in mind these basic facts which are applicable to everything that is full of bad juices, moist, slippery and easy to pass: that because of these attributes they must be eaten before other foods, for then they pass through the body quickly, and lead the way for other foods; and that whatever is eaten last rots everything else.

Apricots and early ripeners

These belong to the peach family, although they differ by being slightly better, for they do not rot in the stomach as they do, nor do they acidify. To most people they seem sweeter, and hence better for the stomach, but in other respects they resemble peaches. This is the case with everything that is sweet, just as for things that are not sweet the stomach tends to be upset, troubled and roused to vomiting, straining to get rid of its pain very quickly. For everything that sinks down, it expels from itself, but anything that floats on the surface it removes by means of vomiting, and the same thing happens when bad juices run into it from the whole of the body. Everything that flows together into the upper part of the bowels is expelled through vomiting, whilst everything that flows into the lower part of the bowels causes diarrhoea.

That little nourishment is derived from all autumn fruits has been stated before. What are described as 'early ripeners' are better than apricots. All those who avoid the term 'early ripener' call both types of fruit apricot (*armeniaka*), but some people, rather than saying this five syllable word, use the word *armenia* with four syllables.

Apples

There is not a single type of apple, just as there is not a single type of pear or pomegranate, for some have a harsh juice, whilst others have a sharp or sweet juice. Some apples have a mixture of these qualities, so that they appear both sweet and astringent, whilst others clearly appear sharp but with an element of sweetness. In addition to these apples there are some that seem astringent, but with a touch of sharpness. You can find some apples that evidently share three qualities, so that they have sharpness, bitterness and a hint of astringency.

It is obvious that these three descriptions – astringency, harshness and bitterness – reveal one aspect of the juice. That sour foods differ from harsh foods by being more astringent, since the underlying aspect of these foods is astringency, is something which you have learnt in the fourth book of my work *On Simple Medicines*, where there is a discussion about the substance and power of the juices. The following facts should be remembered: that all apples are astringent, that they have a cold and earthy juice, that those which seem sharp are also cold and composed of fine particles, that sweet apples which have a moderate combination of these qualities tend to be rather hotter, just as those apples which are absolutely devoid of any quality and are watery tend to be colder.

So apples should be used according to the powers of the prevalent juices. Harsh apples can be employed when the stomach is weak because of hot bad temperament or excessive moistness, astringent apples can be administered when these two problems are exacerbated, sharp apples can be eaten when a thick fluid which is not completely cold can be assumed to have collected in the stomach. Which means that whatever is cold has no need of sharp apples, but of bitter apples: for sharp and bitter apples cut through the thickness of the fluids, although the method is different between apples that are cold and apples that are hot.

From what I have just said it is evident that astringent apples generally check evacuations, according to their degree of astringency, just as sharp apples, on meeting with a thick fluid in the stomach, cut through it and take it down with them, thereby hydrating the excrement, although if they encounter empty bowels they check them instead. Sweet juice is assimilated more, if it appears completely on its own without any bitterness or thickness, but if it contains some bitterness and thickness, more of it is evacuated.

There is another sort of juice which appears not just in apples, but also in everything else, and this juice is designated watery and inert, as I have mentioned before. It provides hardly anything that is good for the stomach, since it lies between the powers that I have just discussed, not unlike water itself. This is a fault in apples, because if they are being treated as food, these qualities are working either through pleasure or benefit. Whenever such apples are unpleasant to eat, fail to afford the sort of strength to the stomach that astringent apples give, and do not check a flowing stomach, they can without hesitation be despised, just like the apples (called 'platanes' because they look in many ways like the soft leaves of the plane tree) that are thrown to the pigs everywhere in Asia.

Before they ripen on the tree the best sort of apples ought to be regarded with caution, because they are difficult to digest, slow to pass and full of bad juices that can be, in addition, cold and slightly thick. Those apples that have been properly ripened are stored for the winter and the following spring, since they often come in useful for sick people, either when covered in spelt dough and baked gently under hot embers or cooked thoroughly in a bain-marie. You should serve them straight after a meal, sometimes accompanied also by bread to strengthen the stomach and bowels of those who have lost their appetite or are slow to digest their food, and of those who are suffering from vomiting, diarrhoea or dysentery.

Astringent apples are suitable for the same cases: for they are moderately astringent, when prepared as I have just suggested, whilst those that are somewhat harsh lose all their astringency when prepared like this, thus turning into a very close approximation of apples that are from the outset watery.

Since I have heard some people declare that their bowels are moved by eating astringent foods, I have considered it a good idea at this point to discuss at length for once what I have often come to realise through the process of logic and experiment.[4]

Once I heard a teacher from my home called Protus declare that his bowels had been relaxed after a meal of astringent pears and apples. I realised why this was happening and suggested that he try an experiment based on his experience. As a consequence of this experiment I have delved far deeper than anyone else has in the same situation. What I did was to ask this man to stay with me for a day so that I could observe when and how much he ate of these astringent fruits. My first instruction on inviting him was to live as he usually did and to omit absolutely nothing of his regular diet.

After his bath he did not drink much water, but ate for a starter fenu-greek, radishes and all the other foods that are eaten by most people. These he enjoyed before anything else, but at the the same time as he ate he drank a little sweet wine. His next course consisted of mallows in olive oil, fish-sauce and a dash of wine. Then he had some fish, pork and fowl. After a second drink he rested for a while, then ate some astringent pears. Following this meal we went out for a walk. We had not wandered far when his bowels performed in an absolutely commendable fashion. When I had observed this, I made an agreement with my friend, that on the following day he should once again entrust me with his dietary habits. He readily agreed to this. First of all after the bath I gave him some pears to eat, then some other things to follow, just as he usually did.

When he had done this, his stomach passed not just commendably, but also in considerable quantity. He was understandably surprised at what happened, and he asked me for an explanation; I went through with him what I am now going to describe.

'Since', I said, 'anything served with fish-sauce naturally relaxes the stomach when eaten at the start of a meal, astringent foods, when taken at the close of a meal, provide the cause for the evacuation, by strengthening the bowels and stimulating a downwards movement of whatever is contained in them. You would', I added, 'admit the truth of this more by eating on the next day astringent foods first of all, then something meaty, and as a finale dishes with olive oil and fish-sauce.'

'Certainly not', he answered, 'because I would immediately be sick, eating mallows in olive oil and fish-sauce as a desert.' 'What an excellent reply', I said, 'since mallows upset the belly and especially its mouth, which tends to be called the stomach by everyone now, whilst astringent foods brace and strengthen it. So if some other juice upsets it, as yellow bile has the habit of doing with some people when a lot of it collects, the person thus affected, if something astringent is eaten, at once expels downwards the troublesome juice.'

Then I pointed out to him a young man who, a few days before, had taken scammony juice to cleanse his system, but five hours after the dose no evacuation had taken place, and he complained that his stomach felt compressed, his belly was heavy and swollen, consequently he was pale and anxious, and he shared with me the symptoms that troubled him. 'As to how I cured the man, 'I said, 'let us listen to the young man himself'. I in fact introduced him to the teacher on the spot, and he explained how I instructed him to eat a little astringent apple, pomegranate or pear, and as soon as he had eaten, he was immediately rid of his discomfort, since his stomach passed a great deal all at once.

'You should understand', I said to the teacher, 'that this happened to you when you ate astringent things because of the weakness of your stomach and bowels as a whole.' 'What you say', he replied, 'is the truth and more. For my stomach is naturally like this, and it is easily upset by chance occurrences, and I eat something astringent after a meal the moment I sense my stomach to be sufficiently slack as to be close to feeling sick.' This story about the teacher should be adequate for an investigation into the emptying of the bowels in those who have a weak stomach, whenever they eat something astringent.

Large and small quinces

These fruits have something in them that other pomaceous fruits do not: which is that they possess a greater degree of astringency and a juice that will keep, provided what needs to be preserved is boiled with honey. The juice of other pomaceous fruits acidifies when stored since it contains an excess of cold moistness. Medicine made with the small quince is invaluable for those who have lost their appetites, and when it is not left by accident in the open I have found it to maintain its quality unchanged even after seven years.

It produces a thick crust around the mouth of the storage jar, just like the crust that appears quite often on honey and other similar things. This crust should not be disturbed, if the medicine or honey is to remain fresh for the longest possible time. Let me just say in passing that I give this reminder to ensure that the medicine stays fresh for a long time. Now I shall return to my discussion.

The juice of the small quince keeps, if it has been properly prepared, just like the juice of ordinary quinces, but it is less sweet and more astringent, so that it is employed for strengthening a particularly weak stomach. In Syria is made a quince-cake which lasts for such a long time that containers packed with it are exported to Rome. It is made from honey and the flesh of quinces that has been pulped and boiled with honey.

My medicine, which I make for those suffering from a loss of appetite, is made not only from honey and apple juice, but also contains a little white pepper, ginger and vinegar. But this is not the right moment to talk about it since I have discussed it at length elsewhere.[5]

Pears and pomegranates

By applying everything I said about apples to pears and pomegranates, I will not have to write a separate section on these fruits. Some of these fruits seem to be just astringent and harsh, others are sharp or sweet, and others are made up from a mixture of these qualities, whilst others have no absolute overriding quality and so are watery and harmless. Pears are used in very much the same way as apples.

Pomegranates are similar in some ways, but they differ in one respect, although not when baked with dough, boiled in water or cooked in steam: namely that they contain more juice than apples and pears, which in addition is sweeter in taste than the juice contained in the other two fruits. They are more useful than those fruits in some other ways. Hippocrates mentions them in the second book of his *Epidemics* as follows:

> A woman was troubled by heartburn which nothing could stop. So she sprinkled the finest barley flour over some pomegranate juice and satisfied her hunger, although she was eating only one meal a day. Also she did not vomit, which was what happened with Charion's son.[6]

So it is clear that when the bad fluids swamped the area around the mouth of the stomach (which is also called the cardiac region), the woman became nauseous and suffered from heartburn. For the word 'cardialgia' signifies nothing more than the symptom of feeling the stomach is being bitten.[7] The barley flour dried these fluids, whilst the pomegranate juice taken with it strengthened the bowels, so that the fluid in the bowel membranes could be rejected. Pomegranates provide hardly any nutrition for the body, so they are never needed for food, but only in the practice of medicine.

Pears (and particularly the large pears which the people who live round me call 'pounders') are quite nourishing. They chop them up and make wafer-thin cakes out of them which they dry and store for the winter. When there is shortage of food in the spring, they cook them in place of foods that afford little nourishment.

The Athenians pronounce the first syllable of *rhoia* (pomegranate) without an i, whereas the Ionians say it with an i. This has no relevance to life, just as it has no relevance to sorb apples, which all the modern Greeks call *oua*, but regarding which the Athenians beg to differ by omitting the u. So I shall leave to one side any speculation about names and return to the powers of fruits.

Medlars and sorb apples

To these fruits apply the same facts as to the fruits I described earlier: both are astringent, although medlars are far more so than sorb apples. This means that medlars are very well suited for a stomach that is in flux, but that sorb apples are more pleasant to eat, for at the beginning, unlike medlars, they do not possess any astringency, their juice being harsh instead of astringent.

Obviously it is best to eat only a few of these fruits, certainly not in large quantities as with figs and grapes, but rather as a medicine. This is much more important for you to know than that the first syllable of the word *oua* was written and pronounced by the ancient Athenians with the letter o alone.

Dates

It will neither harm anyone nor will it add any knowledge about its power, if you decide to call this fruit either 'the date' or – as is the custom among all the modern Greeks – 'the date palm' in homonymy with the tree.

There is a considerable difference between the different dates: some are dry and astringent like Egyptian dates, others are soft, moist and sweet like those that are called 'nob-dates', the best of which grow in Palestinian Syria around Jericho. In between these dates are all the other dates, some containing more, others less moisture, dryness, sweetness and astringency. But provided the extremes are well defined, the average is very easy to detect. In fact there are no dates that do not have an element of astringency and sweetness: nob-dates are a little astringent, Theban dates have a hint of sweetness. Sweet juice has been shown to be nourishing, whilst harsh juice is good for the stomach and for checking the bowels.

All dates are hard to digest and cause headaches if eaten to excess. Some dates also cause a biting sensation at the mouth of the bowels, and these tend to cause headaches. It is often remarked that doctors call the mouth of the bowels the stomach. The juice absorbed from them into the body is generally thick and has something viscous about it, particularly if the dates are oily like the nob-date, but whenever there is an admixture of sweetness with this juice, the liver is very quickly blocked and suffers harm through the inflammation and complete induration caused by this food. Following the liver the spleen is blocked and harmed.

Fresh dates are in all respects more harmful when a few too many are eaten. Sweet dates clearly have a hotter juice, whilst astringent dates have a colder juice. But fresh dates also fill the body with flatulence, just as figs do: for the correspondence between fresh and dried figs is the same as between fresh and dried dates. In areas that are not very hot, dates do not ripen properly, so they are useful for storing. Thus when people are forced to eat them when unripe they are filled with undigested juices, and seized by a shivering that is difficult to warm, and they suffer blockages in the liver.

Olives

Olives generally afford little nourishment for the body, particularly tree-ripened olives. The preferred way of eating these is with bread, but salty olives and pickled in brine olives are eaten without bread before meals with fish-sauce to loosen the bowels. Salty olives and swimming olives have as much astringent juice as tree-ripened olives have greasy juice, so they all strengthen the stomach and whet the appetite. The olives most suited to this task are those that are preserved in vinegar.

Chefs prepare olives in many ways. Indeed, I do not consider it right for a doctor to be completely ignorant of the art of cooking, because whatever tastes good is easier to digest than other dishes which may be equally as healthy. But this is not the right moment to consider either the art of cooking or the culinary profession. A special book will be assigned to this topic.

Nuts

Some people use the term 'royal nuts' for the nuts which everyone else today calls simply 'walnuts'. There are some other nuts called filberts that some people refer to as hazelnuts; they are far smaller than walnuts. Both sorts of nut possess a great deal that is useful, although they do not afford much by way of nourishment to the body, even if there is more nutrition in hazelnuts than in walnuts, since their substance is more compressed and less oily, whilst the walnut is spongier and has more oiliness in it.

For a short time it has a share of astringency, although as time passes this fades away as the whole of its substance changes to an oily juice, until eventually it becomes completely inedible as a result of its oiliness taking on a similar appearance to old olive oil. When green and moist, the walnut has no evident share of astringency or oiliness, but is perhaps rather inert, or what is usually termed watery as I have already said.

The walnut is more digestable than the hazelnut and is better for the stomach, especially when it is eaten with dried figs. Many doctors have written that if both these nuts are eaten with rue before any other food, no great harm will come from noxious drugs.

Clearly whatever is moist is more appropriate for evacuation, whilst whatever is dry is less appropriate. Quite a few people eat these nuts with fish-sauce to help relax their bowels. They are better for this purpose when green, as they then have less of a share of astringency, but when dried and then soaked beforehand in water, as some people do, the power is similar to those that are green.

Almonds

These nuts do not possess much by way of astringency. A cleansing and attenuating quality is prevalent in them, by means of which they purge the inwards and act towards the expectoration of moist matter from the lungs and chest. Some of them have such an overriding power of cutting through thick and viscous moisture that they cannot be eaten because of their bitterness.

They have an element of the fatty and oily quality, just like walnuts, so they too become oily, just like walnuts. This quality in them is less than that of walnuts, so it is only after a longer period of time that they seem to be as oily as walnuts. From these facts it is clear that they are not as useful for purging the stomach, and they afford little nourishment for the body. All nuts that contain a sufficient amount of that overpoweringly bitter quality are extremely useful for the spitting up of matter and of thick and viscous moisture from the lungs and chest.

Among those who do nothing useful in life, but call themselves speakers of Attic Greek, some think it is correct to call this nut feminine, whilst other reckon it is neuter, not realising, as they pit their energies against each other, that both words are written by the Athenians.

Pistachios

These grow in famed Alexandria, but much more so in Beroea in Syria. They do not contain much nourishment, but they are useful for strengthening the liver, as well as purging the juices that block its passages, for they have a quality that is simultaneously bitter, astringent and aromatic. I know that there are many other similar things besides that are good for the liver, as I have shown in my treatise *On Simple Medicines*. I must point out that they offer next to no help or harm to the stomach, just as they neither relax nor constipate the stomach.

Plums

When fully ripened this fruit is rarely found to be astringent, sharp or, in short, with any unpleasant quality. Before they reach this state, some display sharpness, others harshness, others bitterness.

The body derives very little nourishment from this fruit, but it is useful for anyone who chooses deliberately to cool and moisten the stomach to a moderate degree, for it relaxes (through being moist and sticky), just like some of the other items I have already mentioned. They can be used even when dried, like figs, and it is the general consensus that the best plums grow in Syria around Damascus; second to these are those that are grown in the Iberian peninsula, otherwise known as Spain. But the Spanish plums reveal no astringency, whilst some Damascus plums exhibit a lot.

The best plums are those that are moderately astringent, large and spongy; any that are small, hard and astringent are bad to eat and bad for the evacuation of the stomach, a characteristic especially of Spanish plums. Boiled in honeyed wine (use a lot of honey for this) they loose the bowels sufficiently, both if eaten on their own, and even more so if the honeyed wine is taken too. It is obvious that drinking sweet wine after eating plums contributes to the evacuation of the bowels, provided that an elapse of time is allowed and lunch is not taken immediately after them. This should be remembered as a basic rule with everything that relaxes the bowels, and just as with rules that are common to other ideas, it should be assumed that there is no need to hear a repeated explanation of them.

Jujubes

I do not have any information about jujubes that testifies either to their preserving health or to their curing diseases.[8] They are a food for women and little children, since they provide little nourishment, and are at the same time both hard to digest and not very good for the stomach. It is obvious that they furnish the body with hardly any nourishment.

Carobs

The carob (*ceration*), whose third syllable is spoken and written with the letter t, looks nothing like the cherry (*cerasia*) with an s, since it is a food that is woody and full of bad juices; consequently it is difficult to digest, for nothing that is woody is easy to digest. Since it does not pass through the body quickly, it is furnished with considerable bad qualities. So it would be better if these fruits were not exported from the areas in the east where they are grown.

Capers

These are shrubby plants that grow mainly in Cyprus. Their power is generally composed of fine particles, with the result that they afford hardly any nourishment to those who eat them, as is the case with all the other foods that are made up of fine particles. I use the fruit of these plants more as a medicine than as a food. These fruits are brought to where I live sprinkled with salt because they rot when left on their own.

So they evidently contain more nourishment when still green and not yet pickled, for in the pickling process they become completely neutralised and devoid of nutrition (unless the salt is rinsed off), but they do relax the bowels. When used as a food – after being washed and soaked until the salt has gone completely – they furnish very little nourishment; but as an accompaniment to bread and as a medicine they are ideal for whetting a jaded appetite, cleansing the stomach and bringing up phlegm, and for purging blockages of the spleen and liver.

In these instances they should be taken before all other foods, with vinegar and honey or oil and vinegar. The tender shoots of the caper plant are also eaten in the same way as terebinth shoots when still green, seasoned with vinegar and brine like terebinth shoots.

Sycamore-fig

In Alexandria I have seen the sycamore-fig tree and its fruit, which resembles a small pale fig. This fruit is not at all harsh, and at the same time, contains an element of sweetness. As it is somewhat moist and cooling in power, just like the mulberry, it can quite reasonably take its place between the mulberry and the fig. I think this is the reason that it was given its name.

I can only laugh at those who say that it is called a sycamore-fig because it looks like a fig or mulberry.[9] It is not produced in quite the same way as other fruits on trees, since it grows not from the branches and their twigs, but from the branches and the trunk.

Persea

I have seen this grow in Alexandria, since it is one of the great local trees. Allegedly its fruit is harmful in Persia, so that those eating it there die, but when it is transported to Egypt it becomes edible. It is eaten in the same way as pears and apples, whose size is much the same.

Citron

Those who deliberately choose to say meaningless things call it the 'medic apple', and yet they are clear and forceful in their words.[10] An investigation of the following matters is better: namely what powers the different parts of the citron possess, and how the citron can be used beneficially.

I will do this by stating that there are three parts to this fruit: the sharp centre, the fleshy pith and the outer skin. The skin is fragrant and aromatic, not just in smell but also in taste. It is naturally difficult to digest, as it is hard and knobbly. If it is used as a medicine, it helps somewhat with the digestion, just like many other things that have a harsh quality. By the same token when a little is eaten it strengthens the stomach, so that after being cut open and squeezed, its juice is combined with medicines taken in pill form that act as a laxative or purge the whole body.

Vinegar mixed with the inedible part of the fruit in which the pips are found is used for some other purposes, flat vinegar being made sharper through its addition. The middle of both the parts which give nourishment to the body, whilst containing neither harsh nor sharp qualities, are difficult to digest because of their hardness. Anyone who wants to liven up their dull taste, therefore, eats them with vinegar and fish-sauce. It is quickly found, either through experience or on the advice of a doctor, that they are digested better when taken like this.

Fruits of wild plants, including acorns

Plants are generally called wild if they grow in the ground without any agricultural care. For example, vines are called wild if no vine-dresser has
bothered to dig around them or prune them or remove young shoots or do
anything else to them. Among such plants are included the Valonia oak,
oak, ilex, cornelian cherry, strawberry tree and other similar trees; and also
of course certain bushes, such as blackberry, wild rose, wild pear, wild
plums (which those who live around me call prunes), and a bush which
bears a fruit resembling a medlar.

In Italy the fruit of this bush is called *unedo*; it is bad for the stomach,
causes headaches, and is rather sharp with only a little sweetness.
Cornelian cherries, blackberries, acorns and the fruit of the strawberry tree
are traditional foods among those who live in the country, whilst the fruits
of the other trees and bushes are not. When there are occasional food shortages where I live, the peasants store the abundant supplies of acorns and
medlars in pits instead of cereals, and so they keep them for the whole
winter and the first months of spring.

Such acorns were formerly forage for pigs, but then people stopped
feeding them in winter, as they had usually done up to that time, and
instead they slaughtered them at the beginning of winter and used them for
food. Later they opened their storage pits and ate the acorns, rendering
them suitable for food in one way or another. Sometimes they used to boil
them in water, and then bury them in hot ashes to bake them gently. Then
again they would grind them and make a thick soup with them. Sometimes
they used to soak them just in water, but add some seasoning: they would
pour a little honey over them, or cook them with milk. They provide an
abundant nutrition, unlike other things that have been described up to this
chapter of the present book. Acorns nourish like most of the foods
involving wheat, and in fact long ago, so it is said, people lived only on
acorns, and the Arcadians carried on doing this for a long time, although
all the other Greeks were using cereal crops.

The nourishment from acorns is slow to pass and thick of juice, so it
follows that they are hard to digest. The fruit of the strawberry tree is in
every respect worse than the acorn from the oak tree, and in the same way
the nutrition from what we call chestnuts, since these are the best of nuts
which some people describe as easily skinned. They alone of all the wild
fruits furnish a reasonable amount of nourishment for the body.

For cornelian cherries, wild plums, blackberries, rose hips, sloes, the
fruit of the strawberry tree, jujubes, the fruit of the nettle tree, winter cherries, the fruit of terebinth, wild pears and all other such foods possess little

that is nutritious, are full of bad juices, and are bad for the stomach and unpleasant to taste, since they are food rather for pigs – wild pigs, that is, which live in the mountains – because only wild pigs derive any nourishment from these fruits.

The nutrition from the plants mentioned above

We not only eat the seeds and fruits from these plants, but also the plants themselves, often whole, but often just their roots, or their twigs, or their fresh shoots, in accordance with the usage demanded on each occasion. In fact those who live round me tend to throw away the stem and leaves of the turnip, which they call French turnip, although they sometimes eat these when short of better foods. They do the same with radishes and that vegetable which is called 'charlock' in the local dialect where I live. This plant is, one could say, the wild radish.

When forced through shortage of food, people often boil and eat pellitory, water parsnip, alexanders, fennel, wild chervil, chicory, gum succory, daucus gingidium, wild carrot, and the tender shoots of most bushes and trees; some of these are even eaten when there is no shortage of food, like the top of the date palm which is called the heart.[11]

Why should I say anything more about soft shrubby plants? There are some plants that are eaten with vinegar and fish-sauce as a moderately nourishing dish when there are no food shortages. Other people add in addition olive oil, particularly when the plants are boiled first in water. For they can be used in two ways: the usual way is when they are raw, but sometimes they are boiled. By shrubby plants I am referring to: golden thistle, spindle thistle, eryngo, blessed thistle, spiny thistle, white thistle and one of the two varieties of pine thistle, which a few people pick from the fields, place in brine or vinegar, and store just like turnips, onions, wild leeks, pellitory and similar.

It is clear that, in addition to affording little nourishment for the body, all these things contain bad juices, and some of them are even injurious to the stomach, except, as I said, thistles freshly pulled from the ground. All of these plants are preserved in brine or vinegar, and stored for the whole of the subsequent year. Prepared like this they add a certain relish to food, if they are eaten in moderation, as do the shoots of the chaste tree and the terebinth.

So these are counted among the wild plants, and it is enough to know that in common with these plants they are all full of bad juices. There is no shared rationale for cultivated plants, but it is by far the best thing to know the power of each plant individually, particularly of those that are in constant use, which for this very reason are much sought after, since they have been proved through long experience to be better than the others. So I shall now say something about them in turn, beginning with the lettuce.

Lettuce

Many doctors judge this vegetable to be superior to all the others, just as the fig is among the autumn fruits; for it has better juice than them. But some people object to it receiving such high praise; even if there was any truth in this, compared with the vegetables and the most nourishing foods that contain the best juices it is second to none, for they say that it generates blood. Some people do not simply say blood but, while claiming that lettuces generate a lot of blood, add a great deal besides. Yet these people are in fact more deceived than anyone else, even if they were aiming sensible accusations at the lettuce; supposing it does generate a lot of blood, no one could reasonably censure it.

For it is clear that, of all the foods, this is the one with the best juices, and if in fact it does have in its nature to produce a lot of blood, it does not give rise to any other humours. If a considerable amount of blood is alleged to collect as a result of lettuces, and this is the reason why they are censured, it is extremely easy to correct the defect, since those who eat them can, first, engage in more exercise, and, second, serve fewer of them. These words should be enough to contradict those who incorrectly find fault with this vegetable.

It is important to realise that, whilst all vegetables produce a negligible amount of blood containing bad juices, the blood produced by lettuces is small in volume and without bad juices, although it is not wholly made up of good juices. Lettuce is eaten for the most part raw, but when in summer they start to go to seed, they are first boiled in sweet water and served with olive oil, fish-sauce and vinegar, or with one of the pickles, particularly those made with cheese. Many people also use them boiled in water before they begin to bolt, which is what I began to do when I had problems with my teeth.

For one of my colleagues saw that this vegetable had for a long time been a regular thing with me, but that now chewing was painful, so he introduced me to boiling lettuces. When I was young I used to use lettuce to refresh my upper bowel which was constantly filled with bile, but when I reached middle age this vegetable provided me with relief from insomnia, since I then yearned for sleep in contrast to when I was in my teens. For in my youth it was my habit to stay up willingly at night, but no sooner was I past my prime than this sleeplessness persisted, and I became bad tempered staying awake when this was not my intention. Lettuce taken in the evening was the only remedy for my insomnia.

I do not use the term 'lettuce' for anything other than what everyone today calls lettuce, since where I live the term lettuce is applied to another type of wild plant which grows beside the roads, on the banks of ditches, in pools of rain water and many uncultivated areas of land. This plant is small, in appearance like the cultivated lettuce when it has just started growing. It is distinguished by a small amount of bitterness, which increases as it gets bigger, whilst as soon as it has bolted this bitter juice is very firmly marked.

There is also a plant, similar to this sort of lettuce, which is called 'gum succory'. It is quick to bolt and has a pronounced bitterness. Its sap is sticky and white, like that of spurge, but it is not as pungent as the other two. I sometimes use it for sticking back the eyelashes. These vegetables are therefore called 'wild' to distinguish them from the cultivated varieties; I gave a general account of the latter a little before.

Picking up once again by way of summary on cultivated lettuce, which is customarily eaten by everyone and is called lettuce, I will say as a reminder that it has a juice that is moist and cold, although this juice is not in fact bad. Hence it is not digested in the same way as the other vegetables, nor does it check the bowels, just as it does not relax them. It reasonably follows that lettuce does not possess anything astringent or sour, by which the stomach is for the most part checked, nor does there fall to lettuce any of those qualities – such as saltiness, bitterness and anything mildly purgative – that positively encourages it to evacuate.

Endives

Whether the ancient Athenians called what is known only as 'chicory' among the Romans 'endives', or whether they were referring to some other type of wild lettuce, I cannot say for certain. Chicory possesses almost the same power as lettuce, although it is inferior in taste and in other areas that were discussed under the heading of lettuce.

Mallow

Wild mallow is different from cultivated mallow, just as wild lettuce is different from cultivated lettuce. The two types are distinguished, the wild by its dryness, the cultivated by its moistness. The mallow contains a degree of stickiness in its juice, whilst the lettuce does not, and it is clearly removed from any cooling property, as can be ascertained even before eating it by preparing a poultice for one of the hot diseases – for example erysipelas – with both types of vegetable in turn, just as many people do, by carefully mashing the soft parts of the leaves until they are smooth.

This vegetable passes through the body easily, not just because of its moistness, but also because of its stickiness, especially when it is swallowed with liberal quantities of olive oil and fish-sauce. It is average in the nutrition that it provides. If the juices of these three vegetables are compared, that of beet is composed of fine particles and is purgative, that of mallow is thicker and more viscous, whilst that of lettuce lies between the other two.

Beet

I said that, as with lettuce, there exists not only cultivated mallow, but also wild mallow; but there is no such thing as wild beet, unless you want to designate patience dock as such.

Beet juice seems to be moderately purgative, since it cause the bowels to evacuate and the stomach to suffer biting pains on occasion, especially for those people who are by nature sensitive, and so as a food it is bad for the stomach when eaten to excess.

There is little nourishment in beets, as is the case with other vegetables, but they are more appropriate than mallows for obstructions around the liver, and still more so when eaten with mustard or at least with vinegar. Eaten like this they are a good medicine for those with complaints of the spleen. In fact you could quite reasonably call beet a medicine rather than a food. I regard almost all these things as accompaniments for bread, if they are not eaten on their own as foods, just as sometimes leeks, pennyroyal, thyme, savory, oregano; and still more onions, garlic, nose-smart and the like.

Cabbage

Most people eat this vegetable as an accompaniment to bread, but doctors use it as a drying medicine. There is a discussion about it in my work *On Simple Medicines*, and in the book previous to this one, so I shall now summarise: its juice contains a purgative element, whilst its body contains more that is drying than that is productive for evacuation. So whenever I want whatever is in the stomach to be passed, it is essential to take the cabbage out of the three-legged casserole, in which it has been cooked with water, and put it at once into pots, in which olive oil has been blended together with fish-sauce. It does not make any difference if salt is used instead of fish-sauce.

But whenever I want to dry a moist stomach, I drain off the first lot of water, when the cabbage seems to have been partially cooked, put it in fresh hot water, and then boil the cabbage once again in this water until it is tender, but I do not cook the cabbage in this water when it is taken for clearing the bowels. For I do not want to get rid of all its special juice for this sort of use, but rather to reserve as much of it as possible, since nothing that has been cooked can really retain its own juice; instead it loses everything if it has been cooked for a long time.

But I said that lentils must be prepared in the same way as cabbage, since they have the power to do two things: that is both to evacuate and to constipate the bowels. Both cabbage and lentils prepared like this are called twice-cooked. Use the same method of preparation with onions, leeks (especially wild leeks) and garlic: in fact whatever else you want to change its original state to something opposite, bearing in mind the following before everything else, that anything cooked like this must not come into contact with either cold air or cold water, for then it will no longer be properly tender, not even if you boil it for longer. It is essential, as I have just said, to have hot water ready, so that when the cabbage is drawn from the first lot of water, it can be put into this hot water immediately.

Lentils and cabbage dry in almost the same way as each other, and for this reason they affect the eyesight, unless the eye as a whole ever happens to be moister than usual. But for the body, lentils afford considerable nourishment which is thick and full of black bile, whilst cabbage offers meagre nutrition which is wetter than that of lentils, as if this food was not solid but spongy. Cabbage is not a dish full of good juices, like lettuce, but has a wretched juice that smells unpleasant. I have to say that it clearly does nothing good or bad for urination.

Some people, who practise a pathetic form of pseudo-intellectualising, regard 'brassica' as the correct name for this vegetable, as the Athenians did six centuries ago, but not the Greeks of today, who are unanimous in their insistence of applying the term 'cabbage' to only this vegetable.

Orach and blite

These are extremely watery vegetables – without a quality, one might say – and certainly when they are cooked this is even more the case than with the large gourd, and definitely not less; otherwise among such plants only the lettuce is eaten. If you think about the sort of taste that belongs to orach and blite, and then bring to mind the taste of cabbage, you will conclude that lettuce occupies the midway point between these vegetables and cabbage, since cabbage is quite dry, but these others are complete wet. Hence they are not eaten with just olive oil and fish-sauce, but also vinegar is added, for otherwise they are injurious to the stomach.

It is said that these vegetables are perhaps inclined towards easy evacuation, especially if they combine slipperiness with wateriness, but in fact this inclination is not marked, but negligible, through there being nothing acidic or alkaline in them, qualities which encourage the bowels to evacuation. It is clear that even the nourishment they give to the body is very small.

Purslane

Some people use purslane as a food, but what little nutrition it does provide is watery, cold and viscous; as a medicine it cures sensitivity of the teeth through its lenitive viscosity, about which more is written in my book *On Simple Medicines*.[12]

Patience dock

This plant can, as I have said before, be called wild beet. It is similar not only in taste, but also in power, to cultivated beet. Since beet is more pleasant than patience dock, everyone eats it more, so I do not need a section about patience dock, since I have said everything that needs to be said about beet.

Curled dock

Even the name reveals the quality and power of this plant, for it is an acidic type of dock. Patience dock is not eaten raw, nor is beet, but curled dock is eaten raw in the countryside by pregnant women, and sometimes also by inquisitive children. It is obvious that curled dock is a far less nourishing vegetable than patience dock.

Black nightshade

I know of no vegetable that is as astringent as the black nightshade.[13] So understandably I rarely use it as a food, but frequently as a medicine. It is efficacious in every instance of astringent cooling, but it possesses hardly any nutrition.

Thorny plants

After these plants have been freshly pulled from the soil, and before their leaves have turned into thorns, they are eaten by the peasants not only raw, but also boiled in water. When raw they are dipped in vinegar and fish-sauce; when boiled they have olive oil poured over them. It has already been said that all vegetables contain very little nourishment, and even this is thin and watery, so shrubby plants are quite good for the stomach. Among such plants are golden thistle, spindle thistle, white thistle, teasel, blessed thistle, tragacanth, spiny thistle and artichoke, which is held in greater honour than it should.

Those who are always trying to be different spell it not with a k and an i in the first syllable (*kinara*), but with a k and a u (*kunara*). This food contains bad juices, particularly when it has already become rather hard, for then it holds a lot of bilious juice and its whole substance is rather woody, with the result that from its thin and bilious juice comes black bile. It is better then to eat it thoroughly boiled, served with olive oil, fish-sauce and wine, with the addition of some coriander; or without this sauce, if prepared in a skillet or frying pan. In the same way a lot of people eat these plant heads, which they call vertebrae.

Celery, alexanders, water parsnip and Cretan alexanders

All these things are diuretic, but the most suitable of them all is celery because it is more pleasant and better for the stomach.

Cretan alexanders are not unusual vegetables – in fact they are sold in large quantities in Rome – but they are more bitter and far hotter than celery, as well as possessing a certain aromatic quality. More diuretic than celery, alexanders and water parsnip, they also encourage menstruation in women. During the spring they put out shoots which can be eaten raw like the leaves. In winter the leaves are the only part of the plant to eat, there not being any shoots then, just as is the case with celery. After the shoots have been produced, the whole plant becomes more pleasant, both when eaten raw or cooked with a choice of olive oil and either fish-sauce, a dash of wine or some vinegar.

But alexanders and water parsnips are eaten cooked, for both of them seem unpleasant when raw. Some people serve celery and Cretan alexanders mixed with lettuce leaves, because lettuce – which is insipid and moreover contains a cold juice – becomes more pleasant and at the same time more useful if it takes on something of the bitter vegetables. This is in fact why some people also mix the leaves of rocket and leek with it, whilst others combine it with basil leaves as well.

In Rome the usual name for this vegetable is not Cretan alexanders (*smyrnion*) but black lovage (*holus atrum*). Perhaps at the outset it would be right not to number it among the foods, and similarly with the water parsnip and alexanders, for all such things serve as seasonings for foods, just like onions, garlic, wild and cultivated leeks, and in short everything that is bitter.

Among what is bitter can be listed rue, hyssop, oregano, fennel and coriander, all of which can be read about in cookery books, since they possess properties that are useful both to doctors and chefs, although each has a particular goal and aim, and I am surveying the uses of these foods, not the pleasure derived from them. But with some people the unpleasant-ness in a food contributes a great deal to indigestion, which is why it is better to season these foods in moderation. The common habit of chefs to use unsuitable seasonings in large quantities is such as to cause dyspepsia more than good digestion.

Rocket

This herb is definitely heating, so that it is not easy to eat on its own without mixing it with lettuce leaves. Its seed is believed to generate sperm and to arouse sexual urges. It causes headaches, and even more so if it is eaten on its own.

Stinging nettles, which are also called common nettles

This is one of the wild plants; its power is composed of fine particles. So understandably no one uses it as a food unless under the pressure of great shortage. It is useful as an accompaniment to bread and as a medicine for relaxing the stomach.

Daucus gingidium and wild chervil

Daucus grows for the most part in Syria and is eaten like wild chervil by those living where I do. Generally it is good for the stomach, whether one prefers to eat it raw or boiled. It cannot withstand prolonged cooking.

Some people serve it with olive oil and fish-sauce, whilst others toss it also in wine or vinegar; it is much better for the stomach and whets an weakened appetite when eaten with vinegar. But it is evident that this plant is more medicinal than culinary, because it has a considerable share of astringency and bitterness.

Basil

The majority of people use this as an accompaniment to bread, eaten with olive oil and fish-sauce, but it contains bad juices, and for this reason its unsatisfactory qualities are exaggerated, some people alleging that, if mashed up and put in a new pot, it quickly produces scorpions in a matter of a few days, especially when the pot is warmed by the sun each day. But whilst this is rubbish, one can say in all honesty that this herb is full of bad juices, injurious to the stomach and difficult to digest.[14]

Fennel

This plant sometimes grows of its own accord, rather like dill, but it is also sown in gardens. Dill is invariably employed in seasonings, fennel as an accompaniment to bread. Around where I live it is stored, following almost the same method as with pellitory and terebinth, so that is can be used for the whole year, as are onions, turnips and other similar things, some laid up in just vinegar, others in vinegar mixed with brine.

Asparagus

It is not the present intention to look at whether you should pronounce the second syllable of asparagus with a p, as everyone does now, or with a ph, because I am writing for those who want to maintain their health, not those who make efforts to speak in Attic Greek, even if they know this about Plato, yet have no idea about his writings or thought.[15] Since therefore almost all Greeks call those soft stems, at the moment of bursting into fruit and seed, asparagus with a p, I will explain their power and leave those who use them to call them what they want.

Many vegetables and plants in general in the course of nature produce shoots like this, but not all of them are eaten. So my appraisal will be about everyday usage, just as I have said before.

Cabbage shoots, which some people call sprouts (*cyma*) – through synaeresis, it seems to me, of the three syllables of the word used for cabbage (*crambe*) – are no less drying than cabbage, although cabbage is drier in constituency than the leaves of other vegetables, especially when it is close to coming into fruit. By other vegetables I mean lettuce, orach, blite, beet and mallow; the reverse is true for radish, asparagus, turnip, mustard, nose-smart, pellitory and almost all the other things which, although bitter and hot, tend to be moister.

Hyacinth, celery, water parsnip, rocket, basil, curled dock, patience dock and all the other pot herbs produce some shoots like this before they go to seed. When they have seeded they dry out and become useless as food. All these plants are boiled in water and served with olive oil, fish-sauce and a dash of vinegar. In this way they become more pleasant and better for the stomach, although they furnish the body with nourishment that is negligible and without good juices.

There is another type of asparagus which grows in the shrubby plants called sweet broom, periwinkle and fiery thorn. There are two subdivisions of these plants, firstly royal and secondly meadow, just as one sort of bryony is different from the other. All these plants are good for the stomach, diuretic and contain little nutrition. However, if they are digested properly, they are more nourishing than the vegetable type of asparagus, to the same degree that they are drier. What is the similarity between the shoots on bushes and the shoots on trees? There is no precise identification, even though the shoots on trees are woodier, so a discussion is needed next on their individual characteristics.

Shoots

The shoots of trees and bushes have the same relationship as asparagus does with vegetables, because these are also new sprouts which appear when the plant is about to fruit. The difference is that the trunk of a tree is permanent, the trunk being the equivalent of the stalk of vegetables and herbs which lasts only for a year.

The shoots of all trees and bushes can be eaten if they are boiled in water, except for some that are either unpleasant in taste or medicinal which nobody eats in times of plenty, since everything else is so much better. Yet in times of shortage they are used out of necessity as food, for they perhaps provide some nourishment if properly digested. But better than these are the shoots of terebinth, chaste tree, vine, mastich, bramble and wild rose. Where I live terebinth shoots are put in vinegar or vinegar mixed with brine for storing.

The difference between the parts of edible plants

I would have hoped that what Mnesitheus wrote in his book *On Foods* was true. General statements, if they are true, explain much in a few words, just as they inflict great damage, if they are not true. This is what Mnesitheus said in general about the parts of plants:

> Firstly all roots are difficult to digest and do not agree with the stomach. I give, by way of example, radishes, garlic, onions, turnips and all other similar things. For in the case of all these plants the root, and whatever is edible that grows under the ground, is as difficult to digest, the reason being that nutriments are carried from the roots to all the parts of the plant. So the roots convey a lot of moisture to these parts, but retain most of the moisture that is difficult to digest, since it is impossible for all this moisture to be digested.
>
> Whatever is digested appears to be brought to perfection, whilst the moisture in the roots, after being distributed to the parts of the plant elsewhere, must have undertaken the final part of the digestion, since everything is fed from the root. So it is inevitable that undigested moisture exists in the root. After collecting in this place, it awaits the completion of the digestion above.

That is what Mnesitheus states for you. As a speech it is believable, but practical investigation shows him to be deceived. The roots of radishes are in fact much more bitter than their stalk and the leaves. This is also the case with onions, wild and cultivated leeks, and garlic. But if you want to compare the roots of beet, mallow and turnip with their leaves, you will find that the power of their roots is stronger. This is the case with the root of marsh mallow, which appears to be some sort of wild mallow. It is evident that the root, just like beetroot, disperses many types of inflammations, but that the leaves are incapable of doing the same.

And yet all the medicinal plants, whose roots resemble those already described, have leaves that are weaker than their roots, as for example cyclamen, squill, cuckoo-pint, edder-wort and very many others. With other plants most of the substance is in the stems and the trunks, but with these it is in the root, and nature expands and nourishes this part of them, diverting whatever has not been properly worked up in them to the leaves and stalks. These plants therefore have a large root even in winter, whilst the stem grows in spring, at which point it starts to fruit.

With creatures, nature sometimes appears to apply the waste from the general substance of the animal to the creation of certain superfluous parts – something Aristotle also said – as in the case of deer with their horns, and other animals with the amount and size of their prickles or hair. So it is safer to examine each of the parts in plants by itself, tasting and smelling first, then also testing through eating. For smell and taste, by giving information about the sort of juice and savour the part of the plant possesses, also immediately indicate their whole constitution.

Through experiment their power can be accurately ascertained, if of course one conducts these experiments by means of a suitable application of logic, since in these experiments both the consistency of the plant and its attendant juice are sometimes made known.

For some plants have moist watery juice, whilst others have thick viscous juice, which you should personally taste again, because some of these are sharp, acidic, or bitter, whilst others are salty and briny, just as others are astringent, sour, watery or sweet. It is therefore important not to rely on Mnesitheus, although his general argument is sound, but rather to test each of the parts of plants for themselves.

Turnip

You can call this plant turnip or kohlrabi. The part that grows out of the ground is like a vegetable, whilst the root that is in the earth is hard and inedible before it has been cooked, but once boiled in water it would be surprising if it furnished any less nutrition than related plants. There are so many different recipes for it that it is stored in brine or vinegar so it can be available for use throughout the whole year.

It provides the body with a juice that is thicker than the average, which means that if too much is eaten, particularly if it is not sufficiently digested in the stomach, the humour described as raw collects. No one appears to contradict or support that it relaxes the bowels, especially when it has been well cooked. It calls for lengthy cooking, and it is best when boiled twice, as was said before on the subject of this cooking method. If it is served rather underdone, it is more difficult to digest, causes flatulence and is injurious to the stomach; sometimes it even causes biting pains in the bowels.

Cuckoo-pint

The root of this plant is eaten in the same way as the root of the turnip, although in some places it grows rather more bitter, so that it is closer to the root of edder-wort. After the first lot of water has been drained off, it must be put into fresh hot water for boiling, as was described for cabbage and lentils. In Cyrene the plant is completely different from the one which grows around my home. For the cuckoo-pint in this locality has hardly anything bitter or medicinal about it, so it is more useful than turnips. So the root is exported to Italy, because it can keep for a long time without rotting or sprouting. Clearly such a vegetable is nutritionally superior, whilst if expectoration is intended from the chest and lungs of any collected thick and viscous matter, the variety that is more bitter and medicinal is better.

It is boiled in water with mustard or vinegar, and eaten with olive oil and fish-sauce, and also with pickles, both those made with salt and those made with cheese. It is not a secret that the juice (by which life is nurtured) distributed from cuckoo-pint to the liver and the whole body is somehow rather thick, as was said about turnips, particularly when the roots are without medicinal properties, like those which come from Cyrene. For near me in Asia many of the cuckoo-pint plants are very bitter and possess medicinal power.

Edder-wort

I sometimes offer the root of this plant to eat, like the root too of cuck-oopint, after boiling it two or three times to remove its medicinal quality, when the viscous and thick matter surrounding the chest and lungs requires a stronger power. You should bear in mind a factor common to all foods: that whatever is sour and bitter furnishes little nourishment for the body, whilst whatever is flavourless, and even more so whatever is sweet, provides a lot of nourishment. This is still more pronounced if the foods have a compact substance, and are neither moist, thick or spongy in their consistency.

It is vital always to remember this advice and to ascertain whether each of the foods being tested loses during boiling or baking or frying its strong qualities, for then there will be no need to listen to me discussing each item in turn, but instead I will provide a continuous commentary on what is edible, as I have been doing with all the other items.

Asphodel

The root of asphodel is somewhat similar to the root of squill in size, shape and bitterness. However, when it is prepared like lupins it loses most of its bitterness, and in this respect it differs from squill, for the quality of this plant is quite difficult to wash away. Hesiod seems to praise asphodel in these words: 'nor how great an advantage there is in mallow and asphodel'.

I myself know that in times of shortage some peasants struggle to make it edible with lots of boiling and soaking in sweet water. Certainly its root has an aperient and thinning power, just like the root of edder-wort. Hence some people administer its shoots as a superb remedy for jaundice.

Hyacinth

Hyacinths belong to the same category as the plants just mentioned. Their root is eaten without the leaves, but sometimes in spring their shoots are eaten. They have a pronounced bitter and astringent power, which is why they somehow whet the appetite in the case of a relaxed stomach. They are not denied to those requiring an expectoration of something from the chest and lungs, even though the substance of their body is rather thick and viscous. Yet their bitterness counteracts their thickness, allowing them to cut through thick and viscous matter, as has been stated in my book *On Simple Medicines*.

So if they are boiled twice, they are more nutritious, but they do not agree with those who need to expectorate, as they lose all their bitterness. When prepared like this it is better to eat them in vinegar blended with olive oil and fish-sauce, since they then become more pleasant, more nourishing, less flatulent and easier to digest. Some men who fill up on their food feel quite clearly that they hold their semen and are keener for sex.

There are many different recipes for them: they can be boiled in water, as I have said, elaborately seasoned dishes can be made with them, they can be served fried, and they are popularly baked in the ashes. However, they do not withstand prolonged boiling, but suffice with an extremely brief time in the water. Some people do not boil them at all beforehand, preferring instead to keep their bitterness and astringency, since this provides greater encouragement for eating.

If they are used for this purpose, there is something beneficial in them, provided this happens over the course of two or three days; but if they exceed this limit when prepared like this, particularly when they are eaten, as usually happens, when still quite raw, they conversely remain undigested. Some indeed cause both flatulence and colic if they are not properly digested. The food that comes from them being eaten like this does not contain good juices; whereas from those which are cooked thoroughly or even twice, as has been explained, the juice is thicker, but otherwise better and more nutritious.

Carrot, wild carrot and caraway

The roots of these plants are eaten, but these provide less nutrition than turnips and less in fact than the taro from Cyrene. They are clearly heating and display a certain aromatic quality. As with other roots they are difficult to digest. They are diuretic and, if used excessively, supply an average amount of bad juice. Caraway root contains better juices than the carrot.

Some people call the wild carrot daucus, since it is more diuretic, of greater medicinal value and in need of lengthy cooking, if it is intended to be eaten.

Truffles

These should be classified among the roots or bulbs, since they have no pronounced quality. Chefs use them as a vehicle for seasonings, just as they do with all the other foods that are called flavourless, harmless and watery in taste. What all these foods have in common is that the nutrition they distribute to the body holds no particular power, but is rather cold, whilst in terms of thickness – of whatever sort is present in what has been eaten – it is thicker from truffles, but moister and thinner from large gourds, and in proportion from the other foods.

Fungi

Of the fungi, mushrooms boiled well in water come close to being a flavourless food.[16] But they are used not just in this way, but also prepared and seasoned in many other ways, like all the other foods that have no particular quality. The nourishment that they provide is full of phlegm and clearly cold as well; it is injurious to the stomach if too many are eaten.

After mushrooms come amanitae. It is generally safer not to touch the other fungi, for they have been the cause of many deaths. I know of one person who ate lots of a particular mushroom which is thought to be harmless; these mushrooms had not been properly cooked. The entrance to his bowels was constricted, felt heavy and was cramped; his respiration was difficult; he fainted; his sweat was cold. He was only just saved by dosing with whatever disperses thick juices, such as vinegar mixed with honey, on its own or with hyssop and oregano gently boiled in it. He took this from someone sprinkled with sodium carbonate, and with their help he vomited the mushrooms which he had eaten, which already were changing into phlegm that was very cold and thick.

Radishes

Those who live in the cities, for the most part, only eat these raw as a starter with fish-sauce to relax the bowels, but some people pour vinegar over them. Those who live in the country often serve them with bread, rather like the other natural accompaniments, among which are fresh oregano, nose-smart, thyme, savory, pennyroyal, serpyllum, green mint, catmint, pellitory and rocket. All of these accompaniments to bread are edible when green. They are eaten with foods, and as plants are classed as herbs.

The stalk and leaves of the radish are eaten, but more out of necessity than from choice. The root however is constantly eaten, but as an accompaniment more than a food, since its power is attenuating and obviously heating. Its bitter quality is predominant. In spring it has the tendency to produce a stalk that grows tall, just like everything else which runs to stalk. This stalk is boiled and eaten with olive oil, fish-sauce and vinegar, just as is the case with turnip, mustard and lettuce.

Obviously this stalk nourishes more than the raw radish, as the bitterness is deposited in the water, yet it contains hardly any nutrition. Some people eat the stalk and the radish itself boiled like a turnip. What is surprising about all those doctors and lay people who eat them raw after dinner to aid the digestion is that they claim what they do has been sufficiently tested, yet everyone else who copies them is harmed.

Onions, garlic, leeks and leeks, both cultivated and wild

People frequently eat the roots of these plants, but rarely the stalks and leaves. Through their considerably harsh power, they heat the body, as well as both thinning the thick juices and cutting through the viscous juices in it. However, by boiling them two or three times you can take away their harshness, although they nevertheless still cause thinning and furnish an extremely meagre degree of nourishment to the body. On the whole they should not be served until they have been cooked.

But garlic is eaten not just as an accompaniment to bread, but also as a medicine for the health, because it contains aperient and discutient powers. If it is boiled briefly to remove its bitterness, it is less efficacious, but it does not still retain its bad juices, in the same way as when leeks and onions are boiled twice.

Wild leeks differ from cultivated leeks in the same way as all similar species of wild plants are different from their cultivated types. Some people store them in vinegar for a whole year, just like onions. You can do the same for wild leeks, and this improves them as a food and removes some bad juices.

But avoid continual use of all bitter foods, especially when the person eating them is by nature rather bilious. For such foods are suitable only for those who collect either phlegmatic juice or juice that is raw, thick and viscous.

9

ON THE POWERS OF FOODS
Book 3

Food from animals

There remains to discuss the food derived from animals, since there is no small distinction between the powers in their parts and whatever is encompassed in or generated by them. Among the latter are eggs, milk, blood, cheese and butter. Not all the parts of animals possess the same power, but some meats, when they are properly cooked, produce excellent blood. This is particularly the case with wholesome animals, such as pigs, although the sinewy parts produce blood that is more phlegmatic.

Of all foods, therefore, pork is the most nutritious. Athletes display the most striking proof of this fact, for if one day they eat an equal weight of some other food when training for their exercises, on the next day they grow weaker; if they continue this over several days, they not only grow weaker, but also clearly show signs of malnutrition. Similar proof of this theory is given when boys are working out in the gym and when others undertake some tough and strenuous activity, such as digging for example.

Beef furnishes nourishment which is substantial and not easily digested, although it generates thicker blood than is suitable. If anyone more inclined by temperament to melancholy should eat their fill of this food, they will be overtaken by a melancholy disease. These diseases are cancer, elephantiasis, scabies, leprosy, quartan fever and whatever is detailed under the heading melancholia. With some people the spleen increases in volume through the action of this humour, as a result of which cachexy and dropsies ensue.

In the thickness of its substance, beef exceeds pork to the same degree as pork exceeds beef in its viscosity. As regards the digestion, pork is far better, both for those in the prime of life, the strong and people who pursue the activities of those in their prime, and also for anyone else who is still growing. Pigs at the peak of their life are suitable for healthy adolescents,

154

just as cows should be before their peak, because beef is far drier in temperament than pork, as an adult male compared to a boy.

It is therefore understandable that all animals naturally in possession of a drier temperament are more moderate when young, whereas the nature of the moister animals moves in time towards a more balanced temperament as they age. So not only do calves have flesh that is better for the digestion than fully grown cows, but kids are better than goats, because goat is by temperament less dry than beef, but when they are compared there is great deal of difference between man and pig.

The similarity between the flesh of man and pig in taste and smell has been observed when certain people have eaten unawares human meat instead of pork. Such incidents perpetrated by unscrupulous restaurateurs and other such people have been witnessed in the past. Sucking pigs furnish nourishment that is excrementitious to the same degree as sucking pigs are moister than fully gown pigs. Understandably they are less nutritious, because moister food is both distributed and excreted quickly.

Lambs have moist and phlegmatic flesh. The flesh of sheep, on the other hand, is even more excrementitious and unwholesome. The flesh of nanny-goats combines unwholesomeness with bitterness. He-goats are worst for wholesomeness and digestion; next in order come rams, then bulls. With all these animals, however, those that have been castrated are better. Old animals are worst for the digestion, wholesomeness and nutrition, this being the case even with pigs, for although they are moist by temperament, those that have grown old sometimes have flesh that is dry and difficult to digest.

Hares have flesh that generates thicker blood, although as regards wholesomeness it is better than beef and lamb. Venison is no less unwholesome than these and difficult to digest.

Wild asses come close to these, provided they are young and in good condition. Although some people serve the flesh of domestic asses when they have grown old, they are extremely unwholesome, very difficult to digest, bad for the stomach and in addition are unpleasant to eat, just like horses and camels, which people eat who resemble asses and camels in mind and body.

Some people even serve bears, although they are much worse than lions and leopards, but they only eat them once or twice.[1] As previously stated, it is important to boil anything like this twice.

As for dogs, what can I say? In some countries they are often eaten when young and plump, and particularly after they have been castrated. Moving on from these animals, not a few people eat panthers, in the same way as asses, that is when they are in good condition, like wild asses. Some doctors not only eat these animals, but also recommend them. When it is autumn, the hunters around me serve fox, because they are fattened by the grapes.

All other animals, when the have their own particular food in abundance, become far better for eating, just as they are worse when the opposite is true. Every animal that feeds off grass sprouting from the ground or the branches and shoots of trees, in the season when their growth is luxuriant, grows more healthily, fattens up and is very suitable to eat.

For the same reason those animals which must feed on an abundant supply of grass become thin and full of bad juices in the winter and the early and middle part part of spring – for example cattle – but with the passage of time they clearly become full of good juices and more plump as the grass grows, thickens and progresses towards seeding. But any animal that can be fed on little is better at the beginning and middle of spring – for example sheep – whilst goats are better at the start and in the middle of summer, when the bushes (their usual food) are full of shoots.

Once you have heard me comparing the species of animal with each other, review, assess and investigate my argument by testing it, not comparing an animal that is well fed and fat with one that is lean and badly fed, nor a young animal with one that has grown old – for that is a pointless and unfair assessment – but compare what in each type or species (or however you want to call them) is best.

I will then have no need of lengthy passages for the discussion of all the animals that belong to each country, such as the little animal in Spain that looks like a hare (which people call a rabbit), the creature in Lucania in Italy that is someway between a bear and a pig, or like the animal midway between the field mouse and the so-called dormouse that is eaten both in that region of Italy and in many other places.

All these animals are nourishing and clearly fat. Test this out by trying them. Listen and learn about the ways of preparing them, something which each of the locals has discovered through experience. What is the power of each of them, you can now find out from me too. Everything that is eaten after roasting or frying furnishes the body with a drier food, whilst everything boiled beforehand in water provides a moister food, whereas everything seasoned in a casserole falls between these.

There is also a considerable difference in the method of seasoning. Whatever is full of wine and fish-sauce is drier than when they are omitted; whatever lacks these, but contains either a lot of new wine boiled down, which some people name reduced wine, or is boiled in what is called simple, plain and white sauce, is far moister than what has been mentioned before. But everything cooked only in water is even moister than these.

The greatest difference in preparation lies in the power of whatever is added to them, since these are all drying, although some more, others less so. They include the seeds of dill, celery, caraway, bastard lovage, cumin and some other seeds like them, whilst of the plants they include leeks, onions, dill, thyme, savory, pennyroyal, sweet mint, marjoram and everything else belonging to the business of cooking, which for the moment is not going to be discussed.

As I stated before, the comparison between the differences in animals must be done with those that are in the best condition, as should also be the case now with whatever recipes are best. You have heard enough about the flesh of quadrupeds, so the next step is the other parts that contain some power, after the following note about snails.

Snails

It is perfectly obvious that this creature should not be listed under fowl or fish. But unless I mention it with the land animals, I really will say nothing about the nutrition from the snail. It would be unreasonable to omit it, unlike the grubs found in wood, vipers and other snakes, and all the various things that are eaten in Egypt and some other countries. Anyone reading these words – and I include myself – would never eat the foods that derive from them. But the Greeks all eat snails on a regular basis. The snails have hard flesh and because of this are difficult to digest, but they are extremely nutritious if they are digested.

Like testaceans, they contain a juice that relaxes the stomach, and so some people, after seasoning them with olive oil, fish-sauce and wine, use the resulting stock as a laxative for the bowels. If you want to use the flesh of this creature only as a food, first boil it in water before transferring it to fresh water, then boil it once again in this water, season it and boil it a third time until the flesh becomes really soft. Prepared like this it will check the stomach, yet still furnish the body with sufficient nourishment.

The extremities of animals

People eat the extremities of quadrupeds – such as trotters, snouts and ears – generally after boiling them in water and serving them with vinegar and fish-sauce (occasionally with mustard too), whilst others serve them with oil and fish-sauce, pouring over wine as well; some again serve them with vegetables, either boiled in water or seasoned in casserole.

Piglet's trotters are the most suitable when added to cooked barley, because this makes them superior and they become more tender, which

157

means that they are better for working up in the mouth and the stomach.

There is a considerable difference too with the method of preparation, not only for the extremities of animals, but also for all their parts, which I stress is more to do with cooking. Whilst on the subject, in this work only the general differences in their use will be shown, since they will be compared with one another as if they were prepared in the same way, as was said earlier. Such a comparison is fair.

The extremities of the body contain the smallest amount of soft fat and are by nature the least fleshy, whilst whatever is sinewy and skinny predominates, although not like the sinew and skin that the body has as a whole, for in the extremities they are exercised far more. This is why they are rather glutinous. In fact it is to this state that all sinew and skin comes when boiled. It is therefore natural that they afford less nourishment for the body, because they pass through the stomach easily as a result of their glutinosity.

Pig's trotters are better than their noses, just as noses are better than the ears, for the latter comprises just cartilage and skin. Cartilage from fully grown animals is completely indigestible, whilst cartilage from animals that are still growing – provided it is chewed properly in the mouth – supplies a little nourishment to the body when it is digested. Note that the relationship between what I am saying here with the rest of the animals is the same, because the gap in excellence between the food from the extremities and the meat of pigs, mirrors the gap between the extremities of pigs and the corresponding parts of other animals.

It is clear that I give the sinewy parts in the trotters their name because of their similarity to what is strictly called sinew, something which takes its origin from the brain and spinal marrow. The sinewy bodies in the extremities are thus called through this resemblance, although they are in fact the unnoticed bonds of the bones and the particular tendons within them.

Tongues of quadrupeds

A peculiarity of the substance of this part is its rather spongy flesh that is filled with blood. Flesh is actually a muscle, particularly in its central part. At its extremities most flesh finishes up as important sinews, which the majority of doctors call the termination of the muscles. The muscles which extend to the ends of the limbs bring about the largest of these sinews. Some of the muscles, however, have extremities that are sinewy.

Chefs choose the tongues of pigs for their recipes. The flesh of the tongue possesses a body that is, as has been said, characteristically spongy. But chefs do not pick the tongue out on its own, nor do they cook just the tongue, but they add the muscles that are imbedded in it, as frequently the epiglottis and larynx, then the glands peculiar to the tongue which produce saliva, and those parts which belong to the tonsils and the larynx.

The flesh of the arteries, veins and nerves of the tongue are linked with the rest of the flesh, and they are eaten with it, except that in this constituent part the three sorts of vessel are proportionately greater and larger. Pay attention next to what the power of food is from glandular bodies.

Glands

The substance of the glands is as far removed from the substance of the tongue, as the substance of the tongue is removed from the flesh.[2] They are not all precisely separated to an equal degree, but instead by lying adjacent and touching this substance they are perhaps similar to the glands in the udders when they are not yet full of milk. The glands in the udders do not work at their allotted task continually, like almost all the other glands do, such as the ones around the tongue which are naturally ready for the production of saliva, for those in the udders become looser, more spongy and full of milk following conception, whilst at other times they do not contain any milk. When they are contracted and compacted, they are as different from one another as soaked sponges are from those which have dried up. This is the name given to the glands which squeeze out all the moisture and grip and contract the whole body, enclosing it in bonds.

Some of these types of glands exist both in the pharynx and larynx, just as also in the membrane to which the intestines are attached, but the latter are small and consequently escape the notice of a lot of people, whilst those in the fauces and the larynx are obvious and large. There are, as well, other small glands in many parts of the body which support cleavages of vessels. The gland called the thymus is by no means small, but in newly born animals it is absolutely huge, although as they grow up it decreases in size.

A common attribute of all these glands is that they appear pleasant and friable as food. The glands in udders, whenever they contain milk, exhibit some of the sweetness of milk. This is why these glands – and particularly those from pigs – are much sought after by gourmets as a food when full of milk by gourmets. If they are digested properly in the stomach, the nourishment they furnish is similar to that from meat, although as they are somewhat inferior when they are being digested, they create raw or phlegmatic humour – the moister glands the more phlegmatic humour, the harder the glands the raw humour – about which there has been discussion earlier.

Testicles may be classed as glands, although their flavour is not so good as udders because they also contain something that smells, thereby revealing the nature of the semen which they generate, just as kidneys smell of urine. Moreover the testicles of quadrupeds are much less easily digested, but the testicles of fattened cockerels are very pleasant and give the body excellent nourishment. The glands lying to the back of the bladder are quite close in nature to the testicles.

Some people even reckon the kidneys among the glands, for they seem to be rather like glands. But kidneys are quite unwholesome and difficult to digest, as are the testicles of older animals, whenever they cut them off and eat them. Better, of course, are the testicles of younger animals. Kidneys from bulls, goats and rams are unpleasant, difficult to digest and full of bad juices.

Testicles

The people around me cut the testicles off young pigs and bulls, although not for the same reason: with pigs it is because they are going to be eaten, for the flesh of castrated pigs is sweeter, more nourishing and more easily digested, whilst with bulls it is for their agricultural use, since uncastrated bulls do not readily obey commands. On the other hand they cut the testicles off goats and sheep for both these reasons.

All the animals just mentioned have testicles that are difficult to digest and unwholesome, although when cooked properly they are nourishing. The degree to which their testicles are more or less nourishing depends on what was said about their meat. Pork is superior to the other meats, just as the testicles of pigs are superior to other testicles. Only the testicles of cockerels are in every respect the best, particularly those from cockerels that have been fattened on grain.

Brain

Every brain is a very phlegmatic and unwholesome food, being both slow to pass, difficult to digest and bad, too, not least for the stomach. Some doctors are taken in by its soft texture and offer it to their patients, although among other things it causes nausea. So whenever an emetic is desired after a meal, a portion of brain should be served in an oily sauce with the last course. Care should be taken over those with no appetite who were labelled 'food aversive' in antiquity. One should therefore quite understandably desist from eating brain after other foods because everyone knows from experience that it causes nausea.

It is on good grounds that many people serve it with marjoram, just as some serve it with subtly seasoned salt, for since it is full of thick juices and surplus matter, it is better to bring up the whole lot after preparing it with hot and cutting ingredients. If, however, it is properly digested, it furnishes the body with a fair amount of nourishment.

Bone marrow

Bone marrow is sweeter, more pleasant and greasier than brain, so that, if you compare tastes, it seems that brain has a hint of harshness about it. Marrow induces nausea if eaten in large quantities, as does brain, but if you cook it well it is nutritious.

Spinal marrow

Spinal marrow shares the same characteristics as brain, but it is a misnomer to call it marrow: for marrow is moister, softer and greasier not only than spinal marrow, but also than brain. But since it is enclosed by the bones of the spine, and since it is similar in colour to marrow, it is called marrow, just as some people call the brain 'marrow'.

Spinal marrow is connected with the brain and has the same nature, but it is a little harder, especially towards the end of the spine. In fact, the further away it is from the brain, the more it is hardened. It only has a small amount of greasiness, so it escapes from causing nausea, and if it is properly cooked, it affords a considerable amount of nourishment for the body.

Lard and suet

Both of these are oily, but they differ from each other in moistness and dryness. Lard is a moist substance which, like oil, thickens over a long course of time. Suet is far drier than lard and so, even if it is poured out when hot, it solidifies easily and hardens. Both hold little nutrition and serve more as accompaniments to meat than as foods in their own right.

Offal from animals

The liver of every animal is full of thick juices, difficult to digest and slow to pass. The best sort of liver, not only for pleasure but also for other reasons, is that which is called 'fig-forced', a name derived from the feeding of lots of ordinary dried figs to the animal that is being prepared for slaughter. This is done particularly with pigs because the offal of this animal is by nature sweeter than the offal of other animals. Yet even these are improved when the animal eats lots of special dried figs, although it does not seem sensible for people to pass over what is naturally better and turn to inferior things.

Turning to the other bits of offal, the spleen is not quite so sweet to the taste – for it exhibits a certain amount of astringency – and so understandably it is believed to be unwholesome and productive of melancholy blood. In so far as their texture is thinner, lungs are easier to digest than both the liver and the spleen, although they are far less nutritious than the liver, and what nutrition they do afford the body is rather more full of phlegm.

The heart is, in substance, a fibrous and hard piece of flesh, and for this reason it is difficult to digest and slow to pass. But if it is digested well, it furnishes the body with a considerable amount of nutrition that is not full of bad juices. On the subject of kidneys – for some people list these too with offal – there has been a discussion earlier.

Belly, womb and intestines from animals

These parts are harder than the flesh; which is why they generate, even if they are digested properly, a juice that is not like genuine blood and irreproachable, but instead rather cold and raw. They therefore need first and foremost a considerable amount of time to be digested properly and to produce good blood.

The differences between domestic and wild animals

The temperament of domestic animals is wetter than that of wild animals, because of the moisture of the air in which they live and their easy life. Wild animals struggle to live in the mountains, often exhaust themselves and spend their time in drier air. This is why their flesh is harder and contains absolutely no fat, or at least very little.

So they keep without deteriorating for many more days than domestic animals that lead a lazy life. Obviously the food from them contains nothing excrementitious, whilst the food from lazy domestic animals is excrementitious. It is therefore a foregone conclusion that such food is more nourishing and supplies far better juices than the other.

Milk

This is also one of the foods that derives from animals, differing to a considerable degree according to the time of year, but still more according to the animals. Cow's milk is thickest and oiliest, whilst camel's milk is extremely watery and the least oily, and after these come horse's milk and then ass's milk. Goat's milk is average in consistency, but sheep's milk is thicker.

As for the season of the year, milk is most watery after parturition, and it always grows thicker as the passage of time passes. In the middle of summer it attains its own natural mean. After this it gradually thickens until lactation stops. It is as liquid in spring as it is plentiful.

That milk differs, as has been said, according to the type of animal is immediately apparent to anyone who looks, but it is clearer still from the making of cheese with each sort of milk. The most watery milk holds the greatest amount of whey, but makes by far the densest cheese. Naturally the most watery milk relaxes the stomach more, whilst the thickest milk does this less. On the other hand the thickest milk is more nutritious, whilst the thinnest milk is not so nutritious.

If someone first boils the milk and then consumes the whey, the bowels will not be completely opened. But when pebbles heated in the fire have been dropped in the milk and all the whey is consumed, the stomach is no longer opened if it is prepared like this, and in fact the opposite is achieved. I administer this to people suffering biting pains in the stomach because of acidic secretions. Dropping in red-hot disks of iron achieves not less, but even more than pebbles.

Milk when prepared like this curdles easily in the stomach, so it is mixed too with honey and salt, but it is safer to pour in some water, just as is done by not a few doctors. Do not be surprised if those who consume the whey also pour in some water, for they are not recoiling from the wetness of the whey, but its sourness, through which all milk relaxes the stomach, since it is made up of a combination of opposite substances, namely the whey and the cheese.

Besides these it has a share of a third substance, an oily juice, cow's milk having the most of this, as has been said. So people make from it what is called butter, in which can be clearly discerned through taste and observation alone how much oiliness it possesses. If you smear it on any part of the body and rub it in, you can see that the skin is oiled just as if with olive oil. If you spread it on the dry skin of a dead animal, you can observe its action. Moreover, people in many of the cold countries where there is no olive oil use butter when bathing. It is apparent that if you pour it over burning charcoal, it makes a flame just like fat does. I often use it too where suet is employed, mixing it in poultices and other medicines.

Cow's milk, as I said, is the oiliest. Sheep and goat's milk possess some degree of oiliness, but much less than cow's, whilst ass's milk contains the least amount of this oiliness. That is why is rarely curdles in the stomach when drunk warm as soon as it runs out from the udders. If one takes it with some salt and honey, it cannot thicken and curdle in the stomach. For this same reason its laxative effect becomes greater, since it contains a lot of whey, from which all milk derives a loosening power in proportion to the constipating effect it holds because of its cheesy substance.

As much as the whey is inferior in taste to the other substance in milk, so it has an advantage over everything else which empties the stomach. The ancients therefore seem to me to have used it as a drink for relaxing the stomach. Enough superior honey should be added to sweeten it without upsetting the stomach; by the same token, enough salt should be added without damaging the taste. If you should really want it to relax more, add as much salt as possible.

This topic has now been discussed at greater length than the present description demands, for the intention was to run through all those factors which are agreed to be good in milk as a food. When the argument is combined with the evacuation of the stomach, it digresses through parallel association. I am therefore returning to my original intention and will speak about what has not yet been stated for the power in milk, one idea standing out in particular, that of everything we eat, milk has almost the best taste. But there should be no misunderstanding of what I have just argued, because I am not saying that milk is simply the best in taste, but merely among the best.

For milk which does not taste good is of no help to a healthy state of the humours, with the result that it makes those who use it full of bad juices. This is clear from a baby who, after its first wet-nurse had died, was covered all over its body with sores because another wet-nurse provided it with milk containing bad juices. This second wet-nurse lived on a diet of wild vegetables from the countryside, for it was spring time and a food shortage was pressing. So she was also full of these sores, as were some other people in the same area who were living on a similar diet. I noticed this with lots of other women who were feeding their babies at that same time. In fact if anyone drinks the milk of a goat or another animal that grazes on scammony or spurge as part of its fodder, the stomach will generally run.

You must pay as much attention to the powers in milk as to the powers in all the other foods, not merely to what has been discussed, but only to what is best. As much as something in each category falls short of being the best, so it falls short of helping us.

So milk that has the most whey is the least dangerous, even if you use it all the time, although since it contains only a little of this liquid, but a considerable amount of thick cheesy substance, it is not safe for everyone who takes their fill of it, because it harms the kidneys of all those who are inclined to form stones, and it creates blockages in the livers of those who are prone to this. Such people include those in whom the ends of the vessels which transfer the food from the bottom of the inward parts to the protuberances are narrow.

All milk is good for the areas around the chest and lungs, but it is not suitable for the head, unless you have a particularly strong head, just as it is unsuitable for the parts below the cartilage of the breastbone that are easily filled with flatulence. For it turns to wind in the stomachs of most people, and there are very few who avoid this. If foods containing thick juices are boiled for a long time, then the flatulent effect is dissipated, but instead they cause more obstructions in the liver and stones in the kidneys. Such foods have been listed in the first book of this work: starch, fine flour, groats, processed wheat grains, rice, pasta, honey cakes, and breads that are not properly baked, sufficiently kneaded, adequately salted or including the correct proportion of yeast.[3]

Just as in the case of these foods, so with all the other foods that some people eat after combining them with milk, the power of what is mixed in either increases or decreases the powers of milk. Let me now define the power of milk and say it is wholesome and nutritious, even though it is composed of contradictory substances and powers, namely laxative and costive, and the cause of obstructions and attenuation. Whatever is serous in milk, dilutes the thickness of the juices and relaxes the stomach, whilst whatever resembles cheese, checks the stomach and thickens the juices by which, as I have said, blockages are caused in the liver and stones in the kidneys.

Its continuous use is harmful to the teeth and the surrounding flesh (which people refer to as the gums) because it makes the flesh flabby and the teeth liable to decay and easily corroded. After taking milk, dilute wine should be used for rinsing the mouth, and it is better if you also add some honey to the wine, because it cleans away thoroughly everything that resembling cheese in the milk sticks to the teeth and the gums.[4]

But if you are someone who does not suffer a headache after using wine without the addition of water to rinse out your mouth, this practice is better for the teeth and the gums. Of course the addition of honey makes the mixture better for both. The best procedure with the safety of the teeth in mind – in other words so they are not harmed by the milk – is to wash the mouth out after drinking milk first with honeyed wine and then with astringent wine.

Sour milk

Sour milk (as it is called) does not affect the teeth of anyone who is in good health, but those who are colder than they should be – either because of some innate bad temperament or an acquired condition – are affected by it. Sometimes these people experience the symptom of having their teeth set on edge. This is caused by acid food or vomit, the same as usually happens with unripe mulberries and everything else that is astringent and sharp.

Obviously the stomach that is colder for whatever reason does not digest sour milk well, whilst the average stomach finds it difficult to digest, although not wholly indigestible. All stomachs that are warmer than the norm, whether at the beginning or through some subsequent cause, are brought to this sort of temperament, and as well as not being harmed, derive something good from such food. People take it when previously heated and then put around with snow, as they do too with many other similar foods and obviously water as well when prepared in the same way.

This is why there occurs to me a sense of amazement when so many doctors make statements about each food, that some are beneficial, others harmful, easy and difficult to digest, containing healthy and harmful juices, with or without nutritional value, bad and good for the stomach, laxative or costive of the bowels, or with some other excellence or fault. In the case of some foods it is possible to demonstrate that one particular food is unwholesome for everyone, or hard to digest or bad for the stomach, but for the majority of foods the truth cannot be given in a single statement without equivocation.

Since, however, my complete work is necessarily long, because I am setting down for each food the distinctiveness which comes from their natural temperament and the states that they subsequently acquire, it would appear better to have defined in general terms at the outset the method of my instruction, as I did in the first book of this work, and also to recall to mind particularly the foods which are not naturally simple, a prime example being milk, because it is composed of opposing substances and powers, although to the senses it appears to be made up of homogenous particles.

It therefore happens that, even when it is excellent, it sometimes acidifies because of the difference in bowels, sending back up again fatty belching, even if it is composed of opposite substances, through which anything that remains undigested in the stomach becomes acidic and fatty. Lack of heat is the cause of acidification, excess heat the cause of gas. Both of these exist in milk, because it contains within itself not only a serous nature, but also a fatty and a cheesy nature.

This is why sour milk never becomes fatty when it remains undigested, even if it should encounter bowels that are extremely bilious or inflamed, for it does not still keep its hot and bitter quality and power, which milk possesses in its whey, nor does it cling to the fatty and moderately heating power because of the fattiness in it. The only thing that is left behind when this is made is the cheesy quality, although not even this has the same nature as it had at the beginning, but is changed to something colder.

So with curds, it is enough to say that they are cold and full of thick juices. Digestion that is not easy follows from the temperament of the body being average. Throughout my books, whenever I explain something simply, I have often been of the opinion that the discussion leads to this. And yet what goes under the name of raw juice, whose nature I have discussed earlier and explained elsewhere in a previous book, is understandably generated in large quantities from this type of food. Not without reason is it good for inflamed bowels, since it is in complete contrast to what is very cold.

It is important not to write about each food, but to recall only some, such as the sort of juice that occurs in curds, cheese and everything with thick juices, which has the habit of generating stones in the kidneys when they are hotter than normal – either through a natural bad temperament or through some other condition that occurs afterwards – but do not have passages wide enough for the heat.

The constitutions of bodies that are most prone to disease are made up of parts that differ in their temperament, as is the case, for example, with a stomach that is quite hot, but a brain that is cold, and similarly lungs and chest that are sometimes completely cold when the stomach is hot. The reverse often happens when everything else is hotter than normal and just the stomach is colder, and the same is true for the other parts of the body when the liver is hotter.

This is why I pointed out from the start that, when it comes to the powers of foods, the most valuable teaching is an explanation of the difference in moisture, dryness, heat and cold, as well as how viscous or thick the substance is, and in addition how homogenous it is, and whether it is composed (like milk) of contradictory temperaments. I said that I would act as a guide to the discerning of these factors from smell, taste and other supplementary indications which I discussed at the beginning of this book. This is what I have done in the present instance of milk, by revealing its nature from those indications inherent in it, either when it is heated, curdled with rennet, or separated into its constituent parts by some other process.

For what is designated as curdling is carried out without rennet whenever the milk is sufficiently heated and then drizzled with cold honeyed vinegar. The same can also be done with honeyed wine. Sometimes curdling can be achieved even without this ingredient, by pouring the milk into a pot containing extremely cold water. Milk that is expressed after birth congeals at once when heated over a hot fire for a short time. The ancient comic poets used to call milk that has congealed like this 'beestings pudding' (*pyriaston*), whilst everyone who lives like me in Asia Minor calls it 'beestings pie' (*pyriephthon*). This is, strictly speaking, milk without another ingredient.

When, after being mixed with honey, it is curdled with rennet, its thin and watery part is separated off by this process, and some people serve it on its own when curdled like this, since it is made up both of the cheesy element in the milk, the hot and fiery element in the power of the rennet, and the honey that is combined with them. But some people drink the whey with the curds, either in similar proportions or more of one than the other. It is clearly the case that it relaxes the stomach for some people more than others, depending on the quantity of serous liquid.

Obviously it nourishes the whole body more for those who eat only what has curdled, but less for those who take it also with some of the serous liquid, and even less for everyone who takes a little of the curds and a lot of whey. Similarly there is a considerable difference with the milk that, whether with or without honey, curdles after birth. When honey is not added, this milk becomes rather less digestible, full of thicker juices and even slower at being evacuated. The nutrition for the whole body from both of these types of milk is none the less plentiful.

That is enough information about the power of milk for the present discussion. All its uses for sick people, either for those wasting away for whatever reason, or for those with festering soreness in the lung, are appropriate to *The Therapeutic Method*.

Cheese

I have already discussed the power of cheese in the section on milk, but now is the right time to assign a particular section to it. Through the addition of rennet it absorbs during its preparation an element of harshness, and it becomes wholly removed from moistness, particularly when it has matured. This is when it becomes harsher, definitely hotter and more heating, as a result of which it generate more thirst, becomes harder to digest and contains bad juices.

So for these reasons no benefit accrues from combining foods which are thick with harsh and cutting powers, since there is some harm lurking in whatever is good. There is greater harm from inherent unwholesomeness and heating warmth than from the dilution of what is thick. Such juice causes problems, particularly with the formation of kidney stones. It has been shown that kidney stones are produced in those bodies where the thickness of the juices is combined with a fiery heat. You should therefore take special care to avoid this sort of cheese, since it is no good for digestion, assimilation, urination, evacuation of the stomach, or for the healthy state of the humours.

Although the next worse cheese is that which is not old or harsh, you can hold it as being less bad that what has just been described. Of all the cheeses, the best is freshly produced, such as the sort that is made in my home town of Pergamum and in the surrounding area of Mysia which the locals call *oxygalaktinos*. This is an extremely pleasant cheese for eating and causes no harm to the stomach. It is the least problematic to digest and excrete of all the cheeses. In fact it does not have any bad juices, nor does it have excessively thick juices, a common defect of all other cheeses. Among the wealthy inhabitants of Rome the best and most popular cheese is called *vatusicum*, but there are some cheeses from other places, too, that are good.

Since there are a great many individual differences in the nature of the animals and the methods of preparation, and since there is also the age of the cheese to take into consideration, I will try here to define the power of each cheese with a few observations by which you will be able, if you pay attention to these matters, to recognise the better and the worse cheeses with ease. There are two points to make about the type of cheese: the first concerns the consistency of the cheese, that is whether it is softer or harder, denser or more porous, more glutinous or rather crumbling; and the second is connected with the quality of its taste, that is whether sharpness predominates, or bitterness, or greasiness, or sweetness, and if so, whether the quality exists on its own or in roughly equal combination.

As regards the differences in variety of the types I have just mentioned, the softer is better than the harder, whilst the loose-textured and porous is better than what is altogether dense and compressed. Cheeses which are very glutinous or are crumbling almost to the point of roughness are bad; those cheeses which are in between are better.

The best distinguishing factor in taste lies in a cheese that exhibits no pronounced quality, but possesses a little more sweetness than any of the other qualities. Sweet cheese is better than cheese without sweetness, and cheese that has a moderate amount of salt in it is better than cheese that contains a lot of salt or no salt at all. After eating a cheese that you have checked like this, it is possible to ascertain further through belching whether it is a better or worse sort of cheese. Better cheeses gradually lose their quality, whilst worse cheeses maintain their quality. It is clear from this that worse cheeses are hard to alter and change, so that they are difficult to digest; for change inevitably follows on the digestion of all the foods whose qualities I have described earlier.

Blood from quadrupeds

Blood is difficult to digest, especially if it is thick and full of black bile, as is the blood of oxen. The blood of hares is celebrated as being the sweetest, and most people usually cook it with the liver, but others cook it too with the rest of the inwards. Some also eat the blood of young pigs, just as others eat the blood of bigger pigs when they have been castrated. But they do not sample the blood of boars, since it is at the same time unpleasant and difficult to digest. Even Homer knew that the blood of goats is pleasant to eat.

Food from fowl

Although the ancients all called winged creatures with two feet by the name of birds, it is now usual for the Greeks to refer only to chickens like this, including the males or cockerels too.

All birds are less nutritious compared to animals, particularly pigs, in comparison with which you can find nothing more nutritious. However, the flesh of birds is more easily digested, particularly that of partridges, francolins, pigeons, cocks and chickens.

Harder than these is the flesh of thrushes, blackbirds and small sparrows (including those that live in towers); harder still than these is the flesh of turtle-doves, ducks and ringdoves. The flesh of pheasants is like that of chickens when it comes to digestion and nourishment, but it is superior in terms of enjoyment in eating. The flesh of peacocks is even harder, more difficult to digest and more fibrous than these.

It is vital to know a fact common to all birds, as indeed to all quadrupeds: that is the flesh of birds that are still growing is better than those past their prime, whilst the median point between these two parameters is when they are in their prime, for the flesh of whatever is very young is bad, but in a completely different way to those that have grown old; for the flesh belonging to the latter category is hard, dry and sinewy, and therefore difficult to digest and affording little nourishment to the body, whilst the bodies of very young creatures are slimy, moist and consequently excrementitious and easily passed through the stomach. Let me remind you of these facts which concern all creatures in general; for these facts apply to all of them in the same way as regards the differences in age.

There is a standard method of preparation with an eye to health which I have discussed already, but which I shall repeat briefly. Keep in mind just the powers: whatever is baked or fried is drier, whilst whatever is boiled in fresh water gives a moister nourishment to the body. I have said enough before about dishes in white sauce or complex seasonings, and about the domesticated and the wild.

There is a considerable difference between animals that live in lakes, marshes and swamps; and those that live in mountains and dry areas. The flesh of animals is analogous to these places: either dry, devoid of excrementitious matter and easy to digest; or moist, excrementitious and difficult to digest.

Goose and ostrich

The term goose was familiar even to the ancients, but ostrich was not, for they called them giant sparrows. When I was still in my teens I once heard a teacher posing the following conundrum: that these creatures are, when one tries to argue and prove one way or the other, in some respects birds, but in other respects not. It is better not to puzzle over this, but rather what sort of power is derived from these birds as food. Once you have heard this from me, you can learn in your own time from someone else whether these creatures should be called birds.

Their meat is excrementitious and much more difficult to digest than the meat of the birds previously mentioned, although their wings are no worse than the others.

For in the case of many birds, particularly all those that are small and with tough meat, the nature of the wings is fibrous and hard. Some birds have meat that is wholly like this, as for example the meat from cranes which some people eat after first hanging for several days. Perhaps midway between cranes and geese is the meat of what are called bustards (*outis*) or bistards (*otis*): for people say and write the first syllable both ways, that is with the letters ou and o.

Differences between the parts of animals

The inwards of birds share similarities with the flesh, something that is supposed to happen as well with quadrupeds, although the inwards of all of these are completely inedible. What is not analogous are the stomachs, for they are edible and nourishing. Some of them are even pleasant, for example those of geese, and then in turn those of chickens that have been fed on wheat.

As with pigs, the livers of other animals are fattened beforehand through a diet of dried figs, whilst with geese food is used that has been soaked in whey, not just so that the liver may become very pleasant to eat, but also so that it might be extremely nourishing, full of good juices and ready to pass without any difficulty. In the same way it is good for the digestion in the stomach.

The wings too of geese are suitable for the digestion and nourishment, but even more so the wings of chickens. Since there is a considerable difference between the flesh of old creatures and the flesh of the plainly young, there is also a great difference between the wings, and similarly between the dry and the fat; the best wings are those of birds that are well fed and young, whilst the worst belong to dry old birds.

The feet of virtually all birds are inedible.

There is no approval nor any castigation of the crests and combs of cocks.

The testicles are best, especially of cocks fed on grain and even more so of all cocks that eat their food in milk whey, because they are wholesome, nutritious and easily digested. They do not, however, encourage or check evacuation.

Birds have small brains, yet these are much better than those from quadrupeds to the extent that they are harder. The brains of birds from the hills are better than those from the marshes, as are all the other parts of their bodies.

Some people mistakenly swear by ostrich gut as a digestive medicine, whilst others go more for the gut of the shearwater. Yet they are not easily digested, nor is there a digestive medicine among the other birds, like ginger and pepper, and in another way wine and vinegar. If I should try to pronounce on the tongues or beaks of birds – which everyone knows about – I would be suspected quite rightly of waffling.

Eggs

Eggs are food from birds which differ from one another in three respects: first, in the substance peculiar to each one, for chicken eggs are superior to pheasant eggs, but inferior to geese and ostrich eggs; second, in some eggs being laid after a longer period of time, whilst others in a short time; and third, in some eggs being boiled for a long time, others until moderately hard, whilst others are just warmed through. It is as a result of these differences that they are called hard boiled, soft boiled and suckable.

The best for food are soft boiled eggs, suckable eggs being less nutritious but passing through the body more easily and soothing a rough throat. Hard boiled eggs are difficult to digest, slow to pass and furnish the body with a heavy food. Eggs baked under hot ashes are even slower to pass and more unwholesome. Eggs cooked in a frying pan – because of this they are called fried eggs – have the worst nourishment in every way, because as they are cooked they become greasy, and besides producing a thick juice they also contain something bad and excrementitious.

Better than boiled and baked eggs are those called poached. The recipe for them is as follows. Drizzle them with oil, fish-sauce and a little wine, put hot water into the large basin containing their pot, then cover the whole lot completely with a lid. Put over a flame until the eggs are of a moderately firm consistency. If they have become too firm, they turn out like boiled and baked eggs, but if they are average in firmness they are better digested than hard eggs and furnish the body with finer food.

So for a moderate consistency you should aim for eggs that can be poured over the plate, not leaving them to thicken completely, but removing the pot from the fire while they are still runny.

Fresh eggs hold a considerable superiority over old eggs, for the freshest are the best, the oldest are the worst, whilst those that are midway differ with each other in excellence or badness according to the distance that separates them from the extremes.

Blood from birds

Some people feed off the blood of chickens and pigeons, particularly those fed on wheat, since it is no worse than the blood of pigs, with reference both to gastronomy and digestion, although it is altogether inferior to the blood of hares. All blood is hard to digest and excrementitious, however it is prepared.

Food from animals that live in water

There are many species of animal that live in the water and even among these there exist different types. But now, like I did in the previous chapters, there will be set down the similarities in these animals that are useful for medicine. It makes no difference in the present instance to say medicine or healthy living. Just as in the other books, so I will talk about everything that people always eat.

Mullet

The mullet is a type of scaly fish that lives not only in the sea, but also in lakes and rivers. There is, consequently, a substantial difference between mullets as a whole, so that mullets in the sea appear to belong to a different species than mullets in lakes, rivers, meads or channels that flush the lavatories in the cities.

For the flesh of mullets which live in water that is muddy and dirty is excrementitious and rather slimy, whilst the flesh of mullets that live in the clear sea is excellent, particularly when the sea is whipped up by the wind. On the subject of calm and waveless sea, the less fish are exercised, the worse their flesh, so they are inferior when they live in what are called lagoons, and still worse when they are in lakes; and if these happen also to be small and without big rivers, springs and strong currents, they are indeed much worse. When there is absolutely no current and the water is standing for long enough, they are at their worst.

I spoke at the beginning about those that live in marshes, water-meadows and similar sorts of places, for they have wretched flesh living in such localities. Better are all those fish that grow up in river and similar sorts of places where the flow of the water is swift, but those living in marshy lakes are not good.

Fish become better and worse according to their diet. Some thrive on weeds and lots of excellent roots which makes them superior, whilst others eat slimy weeds and unwholesome roots. Others again which live in rivers that flow through a big city, feeding off human sewage and similarly unpleasant food, are the worst of all, as I have said, so that, if they are left out dead for a short time, they immediately putrefy and smell disgusting. They are altogether unpleasant to eat and digest, and contain a paucity of good food, but an excess of excrementitious matter. It is therefore hardly surprising if bad juice collects in the bodies of those who eat them every day.

Since these are the worst, the best are the complete opposite, their habitat – as I was saying – being the cleanest sea, especially where there are no shores fringed with earth or without any rocks, but rather sandy or rocky coasts. If the shores also face northerly winds, they are even better, for because exercise suited to every creature contributes considerably to their wholesomeness, the purity of the wind mixed with the water adds still more to the excellence of their substance.

It is evident from what has been said that some seas are better in this respect to others, either because they are absolutely clean, or because they are fed by lots of large rivers. The Black Sea is an example of the latter, for the fish there are as superior to fish in lakes as they are inferior to fish which live in clean sea.

There are also a few fish living in lakes which are like this, and where a large river creates a lake that joins on to the sea, people call some of them 'lagoon-fish'. If the river does not form a lake, then it is mixed with the sea, and the water turns into a combination of salt and fresh, and the flesh of the fish that live there become midway between river and sea fish.

This should be your common denominator for all the other fish that live in rivers, lakes and seas. The great majority of them do not share the properties of both, since fish from the sea avoid river water, whilst fish in rivers and lakes avoid the sea. But of all the fish, the mullet especially uses both types of water and has a tendency to swim up against the stream of the river and go as far as it can from the sea. This mullet does not have many small bones, in the same way as none of the other sea fish have any.

Like related species, mullet entering the sea from rivers or lakes are full of such bones, because the flesh of nearly all fish born in lakes and rivers are found to be full of tiny bones, whilst fish from the sea do not have any. At the point where the mouth of a large river joins the sea, a few river fish are caught in the sea and a few sea fish are caught in the river, as is witnessed by the presence of the bones that have just been mentioned, either when there are a lot or absolutely none. Thus a few river fish enter the sea, but all sea fish like rivers.

The taste also serves as an immediate indication to anyone eating the better mullet, because the flesh is more full of flavour, pleasant and without any oiliness. Oily foods that are bland in taste are not only worse to eat, but are also more difficult to digest as they are bad for the stomach and unwholesome. This is why these foods are prepared with marjoram.

Some of the people where I live call the fish that is born in a river 'white mullet', assuming them to be another type of mullet. Otherwise this fish is similar in every way to the other fish, although it is a little more pale, has a smaller head and is more pronounced in flavour. The power of this food, as I have said before, is the same as that of mullets which live in rivers. As for the name, there is no dispute about this. I will now say what is particularly useful to know about this fish.

It is one of those fish that can be pickled, and the mullet that lives in lakes is far better when prepared like this, because everything that is slimy and smelly in its flavour is removed. Whatever is freshly pickled is better than anything pickled over a long period of time. But a general statement about pickled fish will be made a little later, and also about fish preserved in ice.

Bass

I have not noticed this fish living in fresh waters, but I have seen it moving up from the sea to rivers or lakes. This explains why when small it is rarely caught, just as the mullet is often caught at this stage. Although it belongs to the open sea, it does not shun lagoons and the mouths of rivers, for it derives its appellation from those fish that withdraw to the deep.

The food from this and from other fish is generative of blood, although thinner in consistency than that from quadrupeds, so that they do not furnish abundant nutrition and pass through the body quickly. But since we sometimes use the shorter name for two contrasting things, and at other times without any contrast, it should be understood that the contrast (to put it simply) is in blood midway between the extremes.

At its worst it is thick in consistency, just like liquid pitch, but alternatively it is serous to the extent that after it has been drained out of the vein to congeal it exhibits a lot of watery moisture floating on the surface. The best blood is perfectly balanced between these extremes, such as is made from the very finest bread, about which there is a discussion in the first book, and from the fowl which have been described, namely partridge and other similar birds. Fish from the deep are similar to these foods and to sea fish.

Red mullet

This also belongs to the deep-sea fish. It is praised by people since it excels the other foods in the pleasure it gives when eaten. Its flesh is harder than almost all of them, and is quite friable, which shows that there is nothing sticky or oily about it. This makes it more nutritious, when digested properly, than all the other fish.

It has been stated before that its food is rather hard, composed of denser particles (so to speak) and, being more earthy, more effectively nourishing than moister and softer foods, since it moreover clearly has the substance necessary for supplying the body with nourishment. This can be judged from its flavour. For with all foods that are by their whole nature different from the animals that feed off them, either the animals do not eat them completely or they eat them without enjoyment. With those that are similar, the moister they are, the less nutrition they provide, so they are digested and distributed more easily.

The flesh of the red mullet is therefore pleasant since its nourishment is suitable for human nature, but being harder than the other fish it can nevertheless be eaten every day, since it is friable, lean and with a degree of bitterness. Things that are both oily and sticky from the outset fill us up quickly and ruin the appetite, while we cannot bear eating them for many days in a row.

Gourmets rate the liver of red mullet highly for its taste, but some of them do not consider it right to eat the liver on its own, but prepare in a jar a mixture of olive oil and fish-sauce with a little wine, cut up the inward into this so the liver and the sauce prepared earlier make a single juice which to the senses is uniformly blended, and eat the flesh of the red mullet dipped in this sauce.

But I do not believe that the taste or benefit it gives to the body can support this level of praise, and the same is true for its head, although gourmets delight over even this, and say that it should be placed second only to the liver. I am, however, unable to understand why so many people buy the largest red mullets, because they do not have tastier flesh than the smaller fish, nor are they easy to digest, since they have hard flesh. That is why I ask any of the people who buy big red mullets for large sums of money what the reason is for their enthusiasm towards them. Their reply to me is that they buy such large fish primarily because of their liver, but subsequently also for their head. But that is enough talk about red mullets at this point in the discussion about their relationship to what is useful.

The best red mullets live in clean sea, like all the other fish too, not least because of their food. In fact those that feed off hermit-crabs smell bad, and are unpleasant, difficult to digest and unwholesome. Cutting open their stomach is the test of this before eating them, but their immediate smell and taste is the test when eating them.

Rock fish

Parrot-wrasse, blackbird-wrasse, tordo-wrasse, rainbow-wrasse, cook-wrasse and perco are all called rockfish after the places in which they are found living, because they lie hidden and breed not on smooth, sandy or earthy coasts, but where there are rocks and cliffs.[5]

Of these the best in flavour is held to be the parrot-wrasse, then the blackbird-wrasse and the tordo-wrasse, and following these the rainbow-wrasse, cook-wrasse and perco. The food from them is not only easy to digest, but also extremely healthy for the human body, since it generates blood that is of average consistency. What I mean by average is blood which is not too thin and watery, yet not particularly thick. This average spans a considerable range, the limits of which have been discussed in an earlier section.

Gudgeon

This fish lives by the shore. It is also one of the fish that always remains small. The best for both flavour and digestion, and also distribution and wholesomeness, are those which live by sandy shores or rocky cliffs. Those that live at the mouths of rivers, or in lakes or lagoons, are not as wholesome or digestible. If the water is in addition muddy, or the river carries away the waste of a city, the gudgeon there will be worse, just like all the other fish that live in these waters.

So it is understandable that there is no clear difference between related fish which always live in the cleanest sea, and shun the freshest water and water that is a mixture of this and the sea. The same is true for the sea fish that come second after these, for they do not show as great a difference between each other as those which live in both types of water. The best of this sort live in the cleanest sea, whilst the worst of all these live in the rivers which carry away the waste of the cities. Those that lie midway are average. These matters have been discussed in the previous sections where I was writing the piece about mullet.

Just as the flesh of the gudgeon is harder than that of rockfish, so it is also softer than that of the red mullet. Thus the bodies of those who eat it are nourished accordingly.

Fish with soft flesh and a recipe for white sauce

In the third book of his work *On Food*, Philotimus wrote as follows about fish with soft flesh in these words: 'Gobies, cook-wrasses, rainbow-wrasses, perci, murries, tordo-wrasses, blackbird-wrasses, horse-mackerel, and then hake, and additionally bonito, flounder, haddock, skate, maigre and the whole genus of fish with soft flesh are more easily digested than other fish'.

This is why it is right to wonder how he omitted the parrot-wrasse, since this holds the leading place among the rockfish, all of which have flesh that is extremely friable and soft compared with other fish. Some of these have soft flesh, but are not friable, since they contain a glutinous and oily juice, and although in this respect they are similar to rockfish, they differ in the hardness of their flesh.

Almost all the deep-sea fish are therefore like this, except if some of them ruin their flesh through inappropriate nourishment, like the red mullet eating hermit-crabs. The latter are little creatures that resemble tiny crabs and are yellow in colour. But rockfish have no use for a varied diet, different localities or fresh water, and so they are always without reproach.

What Philotimus called hake, but other people label as poutassou, possesses flesh that can rival the rockfish by relying on appropriate food and clean sea water. Yet when it uses inappropriate food, and if it spends time in mixed waters, and especially those that are bad, they do not shed the softness of their flesh, but instead acquire oiliness and viscosity, because of which they not only fail to remain as pleasant but they also distribute excrementitious nourishment from themselves.

As I have said, it is important to bear in mind with all fish the following common denominator: that the worst fish are nurtured at the mouths of every river that flushes toilets, kitchens, baths, the dirt of clothes and linen, and everything else that is to do with the city that they run through which must be washed away, and especially when the city is densely populated.

The flesh of the murry that lives in such water is found to be extremely bad, although it is impossible to find it either entering rivers or breeding in lakes. But nevertheless the very worst is found at the mouths of these rivers, like the one which flows through Rome, which is why this fish alone is the cheapest of all those from the sea are sold in this city, on a par with the fish which breed in the river itself. Some people call these fish Tiberine, since they have a distinct appearance that does not look anything like those which live in the sea.

Because the combination of whatever flows from the city makes them particularly wretched, one can understand from this how those which are born in the river are better before they reach the city. There is also another river called the Nar which, joining the Tiber about forty-four miles from the city, contains much better fish than those living in the Tiber, since it is both sizeable right from its source and remains clean, maintaining a swift downward stream as far as the Tiber and nowhere – even for a little while – forming a lake.

So everyone who by habit has experience of the local fish does not need the signs that have just been delineated for their discernment; but everyone who is inexperienced, whether as a local or coming from another city, should check all these things right from the start, before arriving through their own testing at an understanding of the nature of each of these fish.

It was therefore important for Philotimus not simply to mention all of the fish with soft flesh together by including them indiscriminately with the other rockfish. For rockfish are universally the best, not the capelan, murry nor similarly the goby. Some of these live in rivers and lakes, others in the sea, others in what are called lagoons, others wholly in mixed water where the mouth of a big river joins up with the sea.

These in turn differ radically among themselves, like of course the grey mullet and the murry. The capelans vary less than these, although they vary quite a lot between each other. Gobies do not have as soft flesh as capelans and rockfish, nor do the umbrina or ombrina, for they are called both names. But I am completely puzzled by Philotimus on the subject of the skate, because the turbot (which it resembles) has softer flesh than it, although it is considerably inferior to the capelan.

You should therefore understand that the fish called the haddock, and all the others that Philotimus lumped with the rockfish and the capelan, must be placed in between fish with hard and fish with soft flesh. For they are not quite fish with hard flesh, but they fall short of fish that have genuinely soft flesh.

In this category Philotimus also omitted the sole, just with the rockfish he omitted the parrot wrasse, unless of course he was applying the word 'flatfish' to the sole as well, for they are in some ways similar, although the sole and the flatfish do not exactly belong to the same species. The sole is also softer, more tasty and in every way superior to the flatfish. Yet maybe the horse-mackerel lies midway between fish with soft and fish with hard flesh. However, none of the fish that have been mentioned require vinegar, mustard or marjoram, unlike the fish that are oily, viscous and hard. Some people eat them cooked in a frying-pan, others bake them, others prepare them in casserole, such as turbot and skate.

But the recipes that chefs devise for casseroles are generally the cause of indigestion, whilst the recipes which are best for the digestion are made with white sauce. This is how it is made: pour in plenty of water and sufficient olive oil, together with a little dill and leek. Then reduce the sauce by a half and stir in sufficient salt as not to make the whole sauce too salty.

This recipe is also suitable for those who are ill, whilst fried fish are fine for those who are in perfect health, followed in order by fish baked over a fire. But this recipe requires olive oil and fish-sauce with a little wine, whilst for fried fish it is better to have proportionately more wine and fish-sauce, and just a drizzle of olive oil. For those who immediately suffer from an upset stomach because of this, a little vinegar with some fish-sauce and pepper in it should be prepared, because by changing this food containing the above seasonings, they both have a better digestion and are not troubled when evacuating, which is why some people particularly eat fried foods with wine and fish-sauce, the majority sprinkling on some pepper, a few some olive oil.

Whenever some of the described fish have been fried, they are digested better and are more wholesome than every other recipe. Of all the fish that have been mentioned, this is the finest food for those who do no exercise and for the elderly, the weak and the sick, although those who work out need more nutritious foods, about which there has been an earlier discussion. But it has already been stated on several occasion that soft and friable food is best for the maintenance of health, because it is the most wholesome of all. For guaranteed health, there is no better way than through wholesomeness.

Fish with hard flesh

Philotimus wrote about these fish, too, in the second book of his work *On Food* as follows and in these exact words:

> Weavers, gurnards, squali, bullheads, sea-breams, and in addition to these scads and red mullets, and then also sea-perches, sharks, parrot-wrasses, dog-fish, conger eels, large sharks, hammerheaded sharks, and all fish with hard flesh are difficult to digest and distribute thick and salty juices to the body.

That is what Philotimus says. But let me examine each of his statements in turn starting from the beginning.

Weavers and gurnards clearly appear, to those who eat them, to have hard flesh. There is not, however, just one type of squali, because among the Romans there is a fish that is highly prized called a lamprey, and this is a type of squali (*galeoi*) which does not seem to live in the Aegean Sea, and this explains why Philotimus appears to have no knowledge of it. Yet this word is written in the texts under two spellings, some having *galeoi* with three syllables and others having *galeonymoi* with five syllables. Obviously the lamprey that is famous among the Romans belongs to the fish with soft flesh, whilst the other squali are endowed more with hard flesh.

Philotimus then correctly lists bullheads, scads, red mullets, sea-perches and sharks among the fish with hard flesh. But he makes a mistake by including the parrot-wrasse among these fish, since they belong to the rock-fish. Next he wrote about dogfish, which ought to be numbered among the cetaceous creatures, since they have hard and excrementitious flesh, which is why when cut up and salted they are used as food only by the occasional person, because they are unpleasant and slimy. So they eat them with mustard, olive oil and vinegar and sauces that are similarly sharp.

In this category are whales, dolphins and seals. Close to them come the large tunnies, although in the flavour of their food they are not like those that have been mentioned earlier, for they are unpleasant, too, especially when fresh, but get better when pickled. The flesh of tunnies less in age and size is not so hard and is obviously more easily digestable. Still better than these are the small tunnies, which are unrivalled by the best pickled fish when salted.

Most of these are exported from the Black Sea, being inferior only to those from Sardinia and Spain. Pickled fish is most prized because of its flavour and the tenderness of the flesh, and it is the custom now for such pickled fish to be universally called a sardine. After sardines and small tunnies the grey mullet which is exported from the Black Sea is particularly valued, and after them the corb. The following things should therefore be said about pickled fish by way of an appendix.

Philotimus properly mentioned the hammerheaded shark among the creatures with hard flesh, but he ought to have mentioned as well their unpleasantness, just as in fact the unpleasantness of the other creatures which he passed over completely. But he stated correctly that conger eels, sea-breams, large sharks and eagle rays have hard flesh. Some of the others too, as he himself says, belong to the fish with hard flesh, although he does not give their names, because they are not used much by people. So it is better to examine their powers, whilst leaving aside their names.

Philotimus stated correctly that whatever has hard flesh is more diffi-cult to digest than whatever has soft flesh, because the digestion in the stomach and the assimilation into each of the parts of the body that is being nourished is easier in the case of softer things, but more difficult in the case of harder things. These belong to what is altered, because softer things are altered more easily since they undergo modification more readily. Modification is the alteration of whatever is being changed. So he was correct when he said that fish with hard flesh are difficult to digest, and correct too when he said that they produce thick juice, for harder food possesses a thicker substance, whilst softer food has a thinner substance.

But if hard food makes salty juices, this ought to be investigated in turn. For Philotimus, just like his teacher Praxagoras, stated that salty juice comes from whatever has been cooked for too long. I think that this statement should not be set down as plain fact, but rather given some refinement. But since there is a common thread running through all hard foods, I will assign them a special section and examine them next.

Whether everything that is hard produces salty juices during cooking

As regards hard things – not just fish with hard flesh, but also all other foods – Praxagoras and Philotimus thought that salty juice came from prolonged boiling. They called this juice not only salty or briny, but also nitrous.

I also notice that when most things are reduced (or if you wish when everything is reduced), the longer they are boiled, the saltier they always become, then a little later, as they themselves want, they also turn bitter. On the other hand a solid body, when boiled in water, releases into it that quality it had at the start, so that after a while it becomes inert (so to speak) and watery, exhibiting neither any saltiness, bitterness, sharpness or astringency. You can see how true this is more clearly if you boil whatever you want after changing the water, for you will find that whatever is being boiled has lost its particular quality since the water has absorbed it.

So lupins, being one of the cereals, make the water bitter, because they naturally possess a bitter quality themselves. This is the case too with bitter vetch, wormwood, southernwood, hulwort and everything else that is bitter: the solid body that has been boiled down appears to be less bitter. But if, after changing the water, you boil it once again in a fresh lot of water as I have just said, you will find that even more bitterness is lost than before, and if you change the water a third or fourth time, even more is lost than before, so that in time it loses all its bitterness.

In the same way everything that is harsh (for example garlic, onions and leeks) gives the water which has been used for boiling a definite harshness, although its own innate harshness is reduced; if you change the water, they lose their bitterness completely. In fact the longer apples, medlars and wild pears are boiled, the sweeter they become, although the water they are cooked in becomes astringent. If you boil only their juice, first it becomes more salty, but then it grows more bitter.

So regarding juices there must be agreement, as has been said, with what Praxagoras and Philotimus understood, but about solid bodies it must be accepted that things are otherwise. For if, as I said a little earlier, you transferred these foods from the first lot of water to the second, and then again to a third or even a fourth, you would find that they had at the outset shed their juice immediately so that they appeared watery and flavourless to the taste. If they are not transferred to a change of water, the water they are boiled in will necessarily first become saltier, then bitter.

I think it was sauce in particular that deceived the followers of Praxagoras by turning saltier as it was being boiled, for they did not realise that, since salt or fish-sauce had been added at the beginning as seasoning to the water, it was inevitable as the boiling proceeded for its own juice to become saltier, just as you might, without adding anything else, mix in the smallest amount of salt with the cleanest and sweetest water. For when it is heated it becomes saltier. Why is this surprising? Even the best water when boiled too much takes on a salty quality after a time.

Testaceans

Since the covering, as it were, surrounding each particular body as a whole is called a skin, the covering for whelks, purple shellfish, oysters, clams and all other similar creatures stands in relation to skin, which is why they are called testaceans. So the shell which surrounds them clearly resembles a piece of pot or a stone. It is a common feature of all of these creatures to contain a salty juice in their flesh which is laxative for the stomach, whilst it is a distinctive feature of each one to contain more or less juice according to their quality and quantity.

Oysters have the softest flesh of all the testaceans, whilst small clams, red thorny oysters, razor-shells, murex, whelks, and everything that is similar has hard flesh. Understandably these relax the stomach more, but furnish the body with less nutrition, whilst whatever has harder flesh is more difficult to digest, but nourishes better. All the other testaceans are cooked, but oysters are eaten without being cooked, although some people fry them in a pan.

Just as it is difficult to digest the flesh of testaceans, so it is difficult to break them up. It is for this reason that I often decide to serve them to those people who corrupt food in their stomach through unpleasant juices, whether these flow from the liver into the stomach or are held in its membranes. They may contain everything, as I said, but whatever has hard flesh contains less salty juice, which is laxative for the stomach, than oysters. I therefore serve them to those who corrupt their food, after boiling them two or three times in the best water, transferring them to fresh water as soon as the previous lot of water seems salty.

From them comes a large amount of what is called raw juice, whilst phlegm comes from whatever has soft flesh. Just as their flesh becomes difficult to digest and constipates the stomach, after their salty juice is taken away, so the stomach is completely relaxed and the body receives no nourishment if the juice which is produced when they are seasoned with salt and fish-sauce is drunk, which is also the usual recipe with clams.

Crustaceans

Lobsters, crabs, common crabs, crawfish, prawns, crayfish and other such animals have a thin shell surrounding them, similar in hardness to testaceans, but containing less salty juice, although they do nevertheless contain a considerable amount. Their flesh is hard throughout, and because of this they are both difficult to digest and nutritious, provided of course that they boiled beforehand in fresh water.

Their flesh, like that of oysters too, checks the stomach when they have deposited their salty juice in the water after being boiled first, as I said. Just like the hard flesh of testaceans, their flesh does not spoil easily.

Cephalopod molluscs

They are called molluscs because they do not have any scales, rough skin or shell, but are soft like humans. Included among them are octopus, cuttlefish, squid and everything else that resembles these.

When touched, therefore, they appear soft, because they do not have a covering that is scaly, rough or shell-like, although their flesh is hard, difficult to digest and contains a small amount of salty juice. If, however, the flesh is digested, it furnishes the body with a considerable amount of nourishment, but for the most part it produces raw humour.

Cartilaginous fish

The skin of these creatures is rough and shines in the dark, which is why some people say they are called cartilaginous (*selachia*) because they possess this light (*selas*). Among them the torpedo and the sting-ray have flesh that is soft, just as it is also full of flavour, passing down quite well through the stomach and being digested without difficulty. But it is also moderately nourishing, like of course everything else that has soft flesh.

Common to all these is the fact that the parts next to the tail are far more fleshy than the middle parts. This is especially true for the torpedo, for it seems that the middle of these creatures has a peculiar sort of fragile cartilage. Rays, skates, monk-fish and everything else like that are harder, more difficult to digest and provide greater nourishment to the body than torpedoes and sting-rays.

Cetaceous creatures

There has already been a discussion of the cetaceous creatures which live in the sea, among which are seals, whales, dolphins, sharks and the biggest of the tuna, as well as dog-fish and everything similar, so now I must say in summary that they all have hard flesh which is excrementitious and full of bad juices.

This is why they are generally first pickled before they are used, because it renders the food that they distribute to the body composed of finer particles, and so it can be digested more quickly and converted better into blood. The fresh flesh, whenever it is not properly digested, collects an excessive amount of raw humour in the veins.

Sea urchins

People eat these with honeyed wine and with fish-sauce for clearing the stomach. They also make dish with them, adding eggs, pepper and honey. They are a food of little nutritional value and their power lies midway between thinning and thickening the humours.

Honey

Up to now all the foodstuffs have fallen into two categories, the one from plants, the other from animals. But honey is separate from both of these categories. It appears on the leaves of plants, although it is not their sap, fruit, or constituent part, but rather it resembles the dew, although it is not as regular or as plentiful as that.

I know that sometimes in the summer so much of it has been found on the trees, bushes and leaves of some plants that the farmers say jokingly that Zeus has rained honey. The preceding night was pleasantly cool, as it is in summer – for it was summer at that time – whilst the day before the air was a mixture of hot and dry. It appears to those who are experts in nature that vapour from the earth and sea is carefully rarefied and cooked by the heat of the sun, then collected by the ensuing coolness in the night and condensed. Where I live this phenomenon rarely occurs, whilst on Mount Libanus it happens often each year, so that the people there spread skins out over the ground and shake the trees, catching whatever runs off them and filling pots and jars with honey.[6] They call this honey-dew and air-honey.

Clearly the substance in the making of the honey has some resemblance to dew, although it appears in both excellence and worthlessness to have some connection with the plants on whose leaves it collects. So it is best where there is a lot of thyme and other plants and shrubs that are by temperament hot and dry. For the honey with the finest particles is produced in these plants, and because of this it turns to bile easily in a hot body. It is more suited to a cold body, whether it is so disposed through age, illness or nature. If it has been turned into blood, it can nourish a cold body, although it sooner turns to bile in a hot body than into blood.

Being composed of fine particles means it necessarily contains something bitter too, which is why it stirs the stomach to evacuation. If we take this element from it, we make it much more suitable for assimilation and digestion. This is the best method of removal: first mix it with a lot of water, then boil it until it stops foaming. It is clearly important all the time to skim off the foam as soon as it is formed, for through this preparation the bitterness disappears and the honey is quickly assimilated since it no longer causes the bowels to defecate.

Honey and water which has been boiled either for a short time or not properly tends to pass through the body before it can be digested, assimilated and nourish the body. The difference between them lies in the honey which has not been properly boiled causing some flatulence in the bowels and intestines, whilst the honey which during boiling has had all its foam removed does not cause flatulence and is diuretic. If you lick honey on its own without the addition of water, it is less nourishing, but passes better through the stomach. If you eat too much honey, it tends to excite the upper part of the bowels to vomit, but when boiled without water, it is not such an emetic, nor does it act as aperient on the bowels, but is instead assimilated and more nutritious. If it is boiled with water it is less diuretic.

When it does nourish, it furnishes the body with considerable food, so that it has seemed to some people to be wholly nourishing. But on this subject enough has been said in the third book of the work *On Diet in Acute Diseases* by Hippocrates, which some people subtitle *Against the Cnidian Opinions*, others *On Barley Soup*, although both are mistaken, as has been shown in my commentaries on this work. For the moment it is better to say about it everything which has been said. By way of a summary, it is suitable for old people and those whose bodily temperament is completely cold, whilst for those of us who are in the prime of life, and when hot convert it into bile, it provides little nourishment, unless its change into bile can be avoided because, if that happens to it, it cannot then nourish properly.

It is clear that I am talking about pale-yellow and yellow bile being produced by it, not black bile. I have frequently stated in numerous places that it is the habit of doctors to call this simply bile without any reference to colour, but to describe all the other biles by the name of their colour. But all the others are seen evacuated when the body is seriously ill, except for greenish bile. Yellow, pale-yellow and leek-green bile are vomited and often passed even when there is no illness.

Wine

Everyone agrees that wine is among that which nourishes; and if everything nourishing is a food, it must be said that wine too should be classed as a food. Some doctors, however, state that there is no need to call wine a food; certainly drink, which also goes under the name of beverage, is distinguished logically in speech from food, just as food is also called victuals, provender and edibles. These are therefore the reasons why they do not think it correct to call wine a food, although they do agree that it is nutritious, which is all I need at the moment.

If they believe that certain other substances are nourishing, but refuse to call them foods, I could summarise all their learning in just one book. But as it is only wine that they are unhappy about calling a food, although it is nutritious, they allow me to add to this work on foods a brief note about wines, because those powers that Hippocrates mentioned in his book *Diet in Acute Diseases* belong to medicine rather than food.[7] I in fact explained those powers in the third part of my commentary on that book and in my *On the Therapeutic Method* and *Hygiene*. In this present work I am going to talk about the differences in their nutrition, beginning as follows.

Of all the wines the red and thick are most suited for the production of blood, because they require little change before turning into it, whilst after these come wines that are dark, sweet and thick, then those that are red and dark in colour, but thick in consistency and containing something of an astringent quality. White wines that are at the same time thick and astringent are less able to nourish than these. The least nourishing of all are wines that are white in colour, but thin in consistency and almost resembling the water that is needed for what is called honey-water.

That thick wines are more nutritious than thin wines is revealed by their natural quality and reinforced through experience of them. Sweet wines are digested more easily in the stomach and are better assimilated than harsh wines because they are hotter in power. Thick wines are digested very much more slowly, and the same is true for their assimilation, but if they meet with a stomach strong enough to digest them properly, they furnish the body with plenty of nourishment. It is obvious that their superiority in nutrition over thinner wines is matched by their inferiority in micturition.

Pickled foods omitted from the previous book

I have put off talking about pickled and average foods until the end of this book. So in case these should be omitted, it is the right moment now to run through each of their powers.

Animal carcasses are suitable for pickling, provided they have hard, and at the same time excrementitious, flesh. What I mean by 'excrementitious' is, as I said in the previous book, flesh that has phlegmatic moisture diffused in it. The greater the quantity and thickness of this moisture, the better the flesh becomes when pickled.

Anything which has a constitution that is either completely soft or is absolutely dry and without superfluity is not suitable for pickling. For the power of salt, as has been shown in my treatise *On Simple Medicines*, is such as to dissipate, through attenuation and absorption, excessive moisture in those bodies with which it has contact. Whilst nitron-foam and porous sodium-carbonate have the ability to attenuate and disperse, they are unable to draw together or make firm.

So all bodies that are naturally dry become inedible when sprinkled with salt for preserving. Anyone can test this by pickling hare and producing what looks like preserved weasel. The flesh of plump pigs in their prime is ideal for pickling, but two extremes should be avoided, namely the dryness of old pigs and the excessive moistness of sucking pigs; for just as dry bodies become like leather when pickled, so the opposite is true, that when too much moisture is flowing, the meat dissolves and resembles salt.

It is for this reason, then, that all fish with soft flesh and without anything excrementitious – such as those called rock fish and the poutassou from a clean sea – are suitable for pickling. Corb, grey mullet and tuna, as well as pilchard, sardine and what are called Spanish mackerel are suitable for pickling. Sea creatures like whales are better for pickling since they have excrementitious flesh. The worst for pickling are red mullets because their flesh is dry without anything superfluous.

It is clear from this that anything hard, sinewy, resembling skin and leathery is very difficult to digest when pickled. Whatever possesses the opposite composition is made up of fine parts and thins thick and glutinous juices. The best of these in my experience are the pickled fish which were called Sardinian by doctors in the past, but which people now call 'sardine', and grey mullets which are exported from the Black Sea. In second place after these come corb, tuna and Spanish mackerel.

Average foods

In each of the categories of foods that I have said exist, there are some foods that are average. For among those that have hard flesh and those that have soft flesh one can find some midway between those that have neither soft nor hard flesh, and the same is true for foods which are thinning and fattening, heating and cooling and drying and moistening.

Foods that are suitable for animals to eat to maintain their natural temperament without any problem are all those which match their constitution, whilst useful nutrition for animals with a bad temperament either at the outset or from subsequent acquisition, is not what matches their temperament, but what is contrary to their temperament. For whatever is by nature faultless is safeguarded by what is like, whilst whatever is poorly composed is led to its proper state by what is opposite. So there will be a special balance in the nature of every animal, for example one for humans, one for dogs and one for each of the other animals. For humans there is, in turn, a particular balance according to the time of life and another – especially with the contrasts in the way of life – according to race and the place where they have for most part lived.

GLOSSARY OF PLANT NAMES

This list is not intended to be exhaustive, but to serve merely as a guide to avoid confusion over some of the stranger or more problematic plants.

English	Greek	Botanical
Alexanders	hipposelinon	Smyrnium olusatrum
Apricot	praikokkion	Prunus armeniaca
Asphodel	asphodelos	Asphodelus ramosus
Axeweed	pelekinos	Securigera coronilla
Barley	krithe	Hordeum vulgare
Bean	kuamos	Vicia faba
Beet	teutlon	Beta maritima
Birds' peas	okhros	Lathyrus ochrus
Bitter aloes	aloe	Aloe vera
Bitter vetch	orobos	Vicia ervilia
Blackberry	batinon	Rubus fructicosus
Black nightshade	strukhnon	Solanun nigrum
Blite	bliton	Amaranthus blitum
Cabbage	krambe	Brassica cretica
Calavance	phaselos	Vigna sinensis
Carob	keration	Jacaranda procera
Chaste-tree	agnos	Vitex agnus-castus
Cherry	kerasion	Prunus cerasus
Chickling	lathuros	Euphorbia lathyris
Chickpea	erebinthos	Cicer arietinum
Cleavers	aparine	Galium aparine
Cretan alexanders	smurnion	Smyrnium perfoliatum
Cuckoo-pint	aron	Arum italicum
Cucumber	sikuon	Cucumis sativa

191

English	Greek	Botanical
Curled dock	oxulapathon	Rumex crispus
Darnel	aira	Lolium temulentum
Daucus	giggidion	Daucus gingidium
Dill	anethon	Anethum graveolens
Dodder	orobagkhe	Cuscuta europaea
Edder-wort	drakontion	Dracunculus vulgaris
Einkorn, one-seeded wheat	tiphe	Triticum monococcum
Emmer	olura	Triticum dicoccum
Fenugreek	telis	Trigonella foenum-graecum
Fig	sukon	Ficus carica
Haver-grass	aigilops	Aegilops ovata
Hedge-mustard	erusimon	Sisymbrium polyceratium
Hellebore	helleboros	Helleborus orientalis
Hemp	kannabis	Cannabis sativa
Hyacinth	bolbos	Hyacinthus orientalis
Italian millet, panic	meline	Setaria italica
Jujube	serikon	Zizyphus vulgaris
Large gourd, bottle gourd	kolokuntha	Lagenaria siceraria
Leek	prason	Allium porrum
Lentil	phakos	Ervum lens
Linseed	linon	Linum usitatissimum
Lupin	thermos	Lupinus albus
Mallow	malakhe	Malva silvestris
Medlar	mespilon	Mespilus germanica
Melon	melopepon	Cucumis melo
Millet	kegkhros	Panicum miliaceum
Mulberry	moron	Morus nigra
Myrtle	murton	Myrtus communis
Nose-smart	kardamon	Lepidium sativum
Oats	bromos	Avena sativa
One-seeded wheat, einkorn	zea	Triticum monococcum
Onion	krommuon	Allium cepa
Orach	atraphaxus	Atriplex rosea
Ordinary wheat	puros	Triticum vulgare
Panic, Italian millet	meline	Setaria italica
Patience dock	lapathon	Rumex patientia

English	Greek	Botanical
Pea	pisos	Pisum sativum
Peach	persikon	Prunus persica
Pellitory	purethron	Anacyclus pyrethrum
Pennyroyal	glekhon	Mentha pulegium
Persea	persion	Mimusops schimperi
Poppy	mekon	Papaver somniferum
Purslane	andrakhne	Portulaca oleracea
Quince	melon kudonion	Pyrus cydonia
Red-topped sage	horminon	Salvia horminum
Rice	oruza	Oryza sativa
Rice-wheat	zeia	Triticum monococcum
Rocket	euzomon	Eruca sativa
Rose hip (fruit of the wild rose)	kunosbaton	Rosa canina
Round gourd, bottle gourd	kolokunthe	Lagenaria siceraria
Rye	briza	Secale cereale
Savory	thumbra	Satureia thymbra
Scammony	skammonia	Convolvulus scammonia
Sesame	sesamon	Sesamum indicum
Serpyllum, wild thyme	herpullos	Thymus serpyllum
Sorb apple	oua, oa	Sorbus domestica
Sycamore fig	sukomoron	Ficus sycamorus
Syrian cedar	kedron	Juniperus excelsa
Tare	aphake	Vicia angustifolia
Taro	aron	Colocasia antiquorum
Vetch	bikon	Vicia sativa
Watermelon	pepon	Citrullus lanatus
Water parsnip	sion	Sium angustifolium
Wild carrot	daukon	Daucus carota
Wild chervil	skandix	Scandix pecten-veneris
Wild chickling	arakos	Lathyrus annuus

NOTES

The aim of these notes is to expand the brief references that Galen makes
to other medical texts, comment briefly on some of the more unusual ideas
and suggest further reading. A thorough examination of foodstuffs can be
found in André (1981), whilst ancient views on the nutritional properties
of breads, vegetables and nuts are set out in Grant (1997).

1 INTRODUCTION

1 There is an excellent account of Galen's life in his own words translated into
   French by Moraux 1985. The chronological table (33–4) is particularly useful.
2 It was partly the uncertainty of the outcome and fear of pain from treatment by
   scientific doctors that fostered these temple healings. In addition the gods were so
   interwoven into everyday life of the majority of people that the concept of divine
   intervention was wholly natural (Jackson 1988: 138–69). It may be that doctors
   welcomed particular cults like that of Asclepius because they permitted the referral
   of patients for whom medicine was of no avail (Temkin 1991: 85).
3 *Hp.Aer.*3 and Edelstein 1967: 323–4.
4 Gal.*Alim.fac.*1.25.2=6.539K.
5 D. Gourevitch ('Les voies de la connaissance: la médicine dans le monde
   romain' in Grmek 1995: 95–108) describes the basic tenets of the Dogmatists,
   Empiricists, Methodics, Asclepiodists and Pneumatists. Edelstein (1967:
   349–66) examines the relationship between ancient philosophy and medicine.
6 Gladiators (Gal.*Alim.fac.* 1.19.1=6.529K) were both attractive – physically
   and sexually – and repellent – threatening and declassé (Weidemann 1992: 26-
   30). Barton (1993: 59–60) stresses the Roman paradox of this terrible suffering
   which furnished such pleasure, eroticism and self-indulgence meeting in the
   descriptions of death and the gladiator.
7 Weidemann 1992: 120.
8 This travelling is represented in the dietetic works, e.g. Cyprus
   (Gal.*Alim.fac.*1.11.2=6.507K) and Alexandria (Gal.*Alim.fac.*2.36=6.617K).
9 Translated by Singer 1997a: 3–22.
10 See G. Marasco 'L'introduction de la médicine grecque à Rome' in van der Eijk
   et al. 1995, vol.1: 35-48.
11 Scarborough 1969: 109 and 137.
12 Smith 1979: 227.

13 'Les démonstrations d'anatomie étaient la répétition, sous la forme d'un spectacle destiné au grand public cultivé, des dissections et vivisections animales qui faisaient partie de l'apprentissage médical.' (A. Debru, 'Les démonstrations médicales à Rome au temps de Galien' in van de Eijk *et al.* 1995, vol.1: 73).

14 Smith 1979: 227.

15 V. Nutton, 'The medical meeting place', in van der Eijk 1995, vol.1: 10 and H. W. Pleket, 'The social status of physicians in the Graeco-Roman world', in van der Eijk *et al.* 1995, vol.1: 32.

16 Nutton 1979: 157-8.

17 V. Nutton, 'The medical meeting place', in van der Eijk *et al.* 1995, vol.1: 9.

18 Smith 1979: 100.

19 Smith 1979: 72–4 and 122. G. E. R. Lloyd ('Galen on Hellenistics and Hippocrateans: contemporary battles and past authorities' in Kollesch and Nickel 1993: 145–63) explores the reasons for Galen choosing Hippocrates as his authority.

20 Temkin 1991: 51–75.

21 Smith 1979: 77 and P. J. van der Eijk, 'Historical awareness, historiography and doxography in Greek and Roman medicine' in van der Eijk (1999): 8–9.

22 'it is hard to condemn Galen in his age and circumstances for lack of surgical boldness in his recommendations' (Phillips 1973: 180).

23 Scarborough 1969: 125–6.

24 Sen.*Ben*.6.16.2, see Scarborough 1969: 114 and H. W. Pleket 'The social status of physicians in the Graeco-Roman world', in van der Eijk *et al.* 1995, vol.1: 33. L. G. Ballester ('Galen as a medical practitioner: problems in diagnosis', in Nutton 1981: 13–46) focuses on the way in which Galen made his diagnoses and shared them, wherever possible, with his patients.

25 For medicine as a craft see Temkin 1991: 216–7. For the gradual change in attitude towards doctors, particularly in the eastern part of the empire, see V. Nutton, 'The medical meeting place', in van der Eijk *et al.* 1995, vol.1: 32.

26 H. F. J. Horstmanshoff, 'Galen and his patients', in van der Eijk *et al.* 1995, vol.1: 90–1.

27 Temkin 1991: 219.

28 Temkin 1973: 154, Phillips 1973: 173, Edelstein 1967: 390 and Temkin 1991: 47. How Galen regarded Stoic beliefs is examined by P. Manuli ('Galen and Stoicism', in Kollesch and Nickel 1993: 53-61).

29 P. J. van der Eijk, 'Galen's use of the concept of "qualified experience" in his dietetic and pharmacological works', in Debru 1997: 39.

30 Langholf 1990: 88–90.

31 Temkin 1973: 155–6. A useful discussion of the philosophical arguments underlying ancient theories about the digestion, and how Galen came to think about this bodily process, can be found in Tieleman 1996: 66–105.

32 Brain 1986: 9–14.

33 Brunt (1994: 52) mentions Galen's implication that scientific progress required the backing of patronage. Indeed some doctors looked more to the wealth accruing from their patrons than to intellectual questioning of medical principles.

34 H. von Staden ('Galen and the "Second Sophistic"', in Sorabji 1997: 47–51) examines Galen's public performances with the caveat that much of the enthusiasm may be self-advertisement. Two examples of Galen's wit are a joke involving suspense (Gal.*Alim.fac*.2.29.3=6.612K) and an allusion to flying snails (Gal.*Alim.fac*. 3.2.1=6.668K).

35 M. Kobayashi, 'The social status of doctors in the early Roman Empire', in Yuge and Doi 1988: 416–9.

36 Von Staden 1975: 186.

37 P. J. van der Eijk, 'Galen's use of the concept of "qualified experience" in his dietetic and pharmacological works', in Debru 1997: 35–57.

38 Singer (1997a: xxiii-xxxix) examines this problem thoroughly. By way of conclusion he argues that an explanation for disease based on the body was intended to support the higher philosophical theories, although the exact relationship between the two sides of the argument was frequently passed over. This may suggest that Galen himself was hesitant about linking all his ideas into a single interlocking system.

39 Smith 1979: 116. See Singer (1997a: li) on the dating on *On the Powers of Foods*.

40 V. Nutton ('Galen and the traveller's fare', in Wilkins *et al.* 1995: 363) comments on the wide scope of Galen's observations.

41 Gal.*Alim.fac.*2.27.2=6.609K, and, for modern versions of these recipes, Grant 1999: 136, 139–40 and 148. A contrast can be made between the chef, who aims mainly at pleasure, and the doctor, who can show scientifically how some foods are of greater benefit than others (Plastira-Valkanou 1998).

42 See Hankinson 1991: xxxiv on the dating of *On the Therapeutic Method*.

43 V. Nutton ('Galen in Egypt' in Kollesch and Nickel 1993: 11–31) examines what we know of Galen's period of almost four years in Alexandria which ended in AD157. Since Alexandria was regarded as one of the chief centres of medical learning, it may be that Galen made frequent reference to his sojourn there in order to prove his academic credentials and reinforce his image as the learned and independent physician.

44 Kühn's edition is often given a lukewarm reception by scholars: Furley and Wilkie (1984, v) describe it as 'very imperfect' and Brain (1986, ix) says that the 'text is corrupt in many places'. From a textual point of view these assertions are probably true, but on a practical level what Kühn produced is quite serviceable, as Singer (1956: xx) states: 'Despite the many aspersions on Kühn's text, I have found very few misprints and no large number of passages either grammatically or anatomically unintelligible.'

2 ON THE HUMOURS (19.485-496K)

Schmidt 1964 gives a detailed commentary on this work. The author, he suggests, does not stray from the Hippocratic view of the humours. It is therefore reasonable to include the treatise as representing what Galen thought overall about the humours.

1 That old people were prone to excess phlegm was proposed from the time of Hippocrates: see Byl 1996: 265–70.

2 Hp.*Epid.*6.2.1=5.276L.

3 Hp.*Hum.*1=5.476–8L The suggestion is that, like flowers, each humour has its own particular colour or that the skin, if the humours have left its surface, looks wizened and colourless.

4 Philiscus is mentioned in Hp.*Epid.*3.1.4=3.44–6L, although Hippocrates actually names him Philistes. Minor errors of this type are a typical result of referring to texts by memory rather than opening a book, a consequence partly of the Roman educational system that stressed learning and partly of cumbersome papyrus rolls that deterred speedy referencing.

5 The case of the woman who gave birth to twins is described in Hp.*Epid.*3.17.14=3.140–2L, Pithion (or Python) in Hp.*Epid.*3.1.1=3.24–6L, Silenus in Hp.*Epid.*1.8=2642–4L, cf.1.2=2.608L.

6 Hp.*Aph.*3.21=4.494–6L .

3 ON BLACK BILE (5.104-148K)

1 As Langholf (1990: 46–9) points out, black bile does not exist *per se*, although the other three humours are clearly evident from wounds (blood), the throat (phlegm) and urine (yellow bile). The closest to an manifestation of black bile was the dark urine caused by malaria – otherwise known as blackwater fever – which was spreading in Greece during the time of Hippocrates (see Grmek 1983: 409–436). It may be that the concept of black bile originated from the metaphorical use of black meaning bad or malignant rather than from any physical symptoms.

2 Erasistratus of Ceos lived in the early third century BC. He appears to have developed many of the ideas inherent in Hippocratic medicine by using a system of logical medical procedure (see Smith 1982). He probably worked in Alexandria and may have carried out dissections on the human body (Lloyd 1975). It may be that Galen attacked the Erasistrateans precisely because they were so close to what he was doing with the legacy of Hippocrates and he needed to stake out his own claims to uniqueness.

3 Plistonicus was a doctor of the dogmatic school and lived in the third century BC. Philotimus (or Phylotimus) was a doctor of the early Hellenistic period. Praxagoras of Cos, a dogmatist of the fourth century BC, wrote on anatomy, diseases, physics and the humours.

4 Rufus of Ephesus wrote on dietetics and pathology in the early second century AD. Some of his works have been translated into English: *On the Interogation of the Patient* and *Anatomical Nomenclature* (see Brock 1929: 112–29).

5 Cf. Hp.*Hum*.14=5.496L 'For the humours vary in strength according to the season and district, summer, for example, being the cause of bile, spring the cause of blood, and the same in each of the other cases.'

6 Cf. Hp.*Hum*.20=5.502L 'In some instances bloodletting at a seasonable moment is possible, but at other times bloodletting is not just unsuitable but a disadvantage.'

7 *On Elements: A Work in Two Books*, 1.413–508K.

8 Hp.*Nat.Hom*.4=6.38-40L. Jouanna (1975: 256) believes that the idea of humours separating was very much part of the new medical vocabulary coming into being in the fifth century BC. Galen comments on this passage elsewhere in more depth (see Mewaldt 1914: 32–4).

9 Hp.*Aph*.4.24=4.510L.

10 cf. Hp.*Hum*.13=5.494L 'If the summer happens to be bilious, and if the increase in bile is left unattended, then there will also be diseases of the spleen.'

11 Proetus had three daughters. When they reached puberty they went mad. Melampus promised to cure them, provided that Proetus ceded some of his kingdom and handed over one of his daughters in marriage. The cure was a thorough purging with white hellebore' (see Grant, forthcoming).

12 *On the Natural Faculties*: 2.1–214K, translated by Brock 1916.

13 Hp.*Prog*.12=2.138-142L.

4 ON UNEVEN BAD TEMPERAMENT (7.733-752K)

1 *On Temperaments*: 1.509-649K, translated by Singer 1997a: 202–89.

2 *On Anatomical Proceedures,* translated by Singer 1956.

3 Hp.*Loc.Hom*.42=6.334L. 'Pain happens as a result of both cold and heat, and as a result of excess and deficiency.' Anything normally hot that is chilled, or

normally cold that is heated, suffers pain. Such use of allopathy and homeopathy are discussed by Craik 1998: 203–5.

4 Hp.*Loc.Hom.*36=6.329L. 'Maladies which take the form of sores rising over the surface of the body should be treated by drugs in conjunction with fasting.' The text of Hippocrates is garbled. Presumably purging drugs and fasting (i.e. reducing) are being prescribed (Craik 1998: 193).

5 *On the Causes of Symptoms*: 7.42–272K.

6 *On the Causes of Disease*: 7.1–41K, translated in this present volume.

7 *On Simple Medicines*: 11.379–892K and 12.1–377K. *On the Therapeutic Method*: 10.1–1021K, translated by Hankinson 1991: 3–78.

5 ON THE CAUSES OF DISEASE (7.1-41K)

1 *On the Use of Pulsations*: 5.149-180K, translated by Furley and Wilkie 1984:195–227.

2 *On the Use of Respiration*: 4.470-511K, translated by Furley and Wilkie 1984.

3 *On Unequal Bad Temperament* (7.733-752K), translated in this present volume.

4 *On the Differences between Diseases*: 6.836-880K.

5 *Nat.fac.* (2.1-214K).

6 The human body was considered as malleable in its early days (see Holman 1997). Soranus, who practised medicine under the emperors Trajan (AD 98–117) and Hadrian (AD 117–138), described in his *Gynaecology* (2.14–15) how the swaddling bands should be applied to the baby: the bands had to mould every part according to its natural shape or used to bring each part into its natural shape. A general account of the raising of children is given in Bertier 1972: 87–143. Midwives were ideally supposed to be literate, have a good memory, enjoy their work and act honestly (see Phillips 1973: 165–6).

6 ON BARLEY SOUP (6.816-831K)

1 Galen often sets himself up as the only person (apart from Hippocrates of course) who actually understands medicine. This stance is in part an attempt to lend scientific authority to his own writings. He also argues that doctors make mistakes because of faulty texts, incorrect measurements, misunderstood words and the problems of correctly analyzing the powers of drugs and foods. See H. von Staden, 'Inefficacy, error and failure: Galen on *dokima pharmaka aprakta*', in Debru 1997: 59–83.

2 Hp.*Vict.*2.40=6.536–8L.

3 Hp.*Epid.*2.11=5.88L.

4 Hp.*Acut.*4=2.244L.

7 ON THE POWERS OF FOODS: BOOK 1 (6.453–553K)

1 The founder of the Empiricists was Philinus of Cos (third century BC). They believed that it was impossible to understand nature and thus futile to investigate what cannot be seen. Instead, the practical side of medicine was emphasised. Diocles of Carystus supposedly set up the Dogmatist school of medicine in the fourth century BC. Anatomical knowledge was regarded as a necessity, but unseen causes were held to be behind disease. In many ways the Dogmatists were a combination of the sceptical views of the Empiricists and

the philosophical ideas of the Pneumatists (see Grmek 1995: 97–100).

2 *Epid*.2.2.11=5.88L, 6.6.2=5.324L.

3 Foods were considered to be at one end of a spectrum of medicinal substances, the other end being occupied by drugs.

4 There are difficulties with the terms mentioned here, as Galen acknowledges, for the Greek words *koilia*, *entera* and *stomachon* could be used technically for bowels, intestines and stomach respectively, or generally to mean just guts or insides.

5 Scammony: Otherwise known as Syrian bindweed (*Convolvulus scammonia*), the resin obtained from the root of this plant acts as a drastic cathartic.

Hellebore: Two types of hellebore were used in antiquity, white (*Veratrum album*) and black (*Helleborus niger*). Both are purgative, although black has a more narcotic effect (see Grieve 1931: 388–9 and 391). Ctesias (quoted by Orib.8.8) remarked on the improvements in the contemporary understanding of hellebore dosages compared with the knowledge of his father and grandfather about such matters. Smith (1979: 179) cites this as an indication of medical progress.

6 Hp.*Alim* 19=9.104L.

7 Each age had a particular predominance of humours, old age being burdened with cold phlegm, youth with hot blood. An individual temperament could therefore shift in its focus during the course of a lifetime. See Byl 1996: 265–70.

8 Philistion of Locri (c. 427–347 BC) wrote a book on dietetics that was famous throughout antiquity. Ariston (fifth century BC) also wrote on diet. Euryphon of Cnidus (fifth century BC) researched veins, diseases and diet. Of Philetas nothing more is known apart from this reference to him. Galen talks elsewhere of problems over putting the name of an author to a particular work: 'in a book on a healthy diet, which some people ascribe to Hippocrates, others to Ariston, others to Philistion, some to Pherecydes' (Hp.*Aph.Comm*.1=18A.8–9K).

9 The leaves of Aloes (*Aloe vera*), a succulent plant belonging to the lily family, can be used as a gently purgative (Grieve 1931: 26–29). With the various forms of copper, 'descriptions are as vague as nard and equally confusing to modern interpreters (Nutton 1985: 143). Copper compounds were used to help with healing wounds (Gal.*Simpl.Med*.9.35–7=12.241–2K).

10 Heraclides of Tarentum (first century BC) worked on pharmacology, therapeutics and dietetics. He leaned towards the Empiricists.

11 Athenaeus frequently quotes from the work of Mnesitheus *On Foods*, for example when discussing the digesting of chestnuts (Ath.2.54b) and pine kernels (Ath.2.57b–d). He lived in the fourth or possibly third century BC (see Bertier 1972: 1–10).

12 A commentary on this passage about breads can be found in Grant 1997: 120–4.

13 Refined bread: the Greek term means washed bread. The opposite to this sort of bread is full of bran, otherwise known as dirty bread (see Baldwin 1996).

14 Galen's fascination with sociology gives us a rare vignette of peasant women at work. Women are hardly ever recorded by Roman writers as farm hands – the ideal is to represent them spinning wool and looking after the home – and yet they must have been employed, not only to make bread, but also to sow and harvest the wheat itself (Scheidel 1995).

15 Metal horseshoes were rarely employed in antiquity, so hipposandals made of broom were fastened around hooves for journeys over rough ground (Grant 1997: 262–3 and M. Mingaud, '*Spartum*' in Amouretti and Comet 1993: 45–69).

16 The evidence for Praxagoras of Cos (latter part of fourth century BC) is scanty,

but he seems to have been interested in the humours as the cause of disease and in understanding the arterial pulse. See Furley and Wilkie 1984: 22–6.

17 'Scientific medicine had quite a pronounced philological character' (I. Sluiter, 'The embarrassment of imperfection: Galen's assessment of Hippocrates' linguistic merits' in van de Eijk 1995, vol.2: 519–35). Philology was an obvious way in which to study Hippocrates.

18 Hom.*Od*.4.604.

19 Thphr.*HP* 8.9.2.

20 Actually Hdt.3.36.2. Galen wrote quickly from one end of a papyrus roll to the other. He could not refer quickly, if at all, to other texts because of the cumbersome nature of the papyrus roll. Mistakes or erroneous attributions are therefore not uncommon (see Smith 1979: 159–60).

21 Dsc.2.89–90.

22 A recipe in Apicius (Apic.2.2.10 and André 1974: 148) includes boiled wheat, pine nuts, almonds, raisins, reduced wine and pepper.

23 Hom.*Il*.8.188.

24 Millet swells up more than any other cereal when made into a porridge, so it would have been especially good for satisfying the hunger (see Spurr 1986: 89–102).

25 Rice was imported from Egypt and India. The water in which rice had cooked is mentioned by Apicius (Apic.2.2.8) in passing as a thickening agent, which suggests that it was not an exotic item on the table.

26 The term 'elephantiasis' does not appear in the surviving medical sources before the first century BC, although by the first century AD it is remarked upon frequently. The detailed description by Rufus of Ephesus (quoted by Orib.45.28) shows it to be a form of leprosy (see Grmek 1983: 249–60).

27 André (1981, 39) argues for this bean being indentified with *Dolichos sinensis L.*

28 Hp.*Alim.* 2.45=6.524L. This is the sole reference in the Hippocratic corpus to calavances or *dolichoi* (see Joly 1984: 269).

29 Hippocrates recommended relaxing walks after meals and avoiding exposure to extremes of temperature if headaches were to be avoided. Foods which were emolient, light, easily digested and quick to pass were ideal. Wine and other heating foods (such as hemp seed) were troublesome. See Calogiuri 1997.

30 There has been a recent revival of interest in the extract of this seed for use in the alleviation of the discomfort suffered by some women during menstruation. The plant itself (*Vitex agnus castus*) grows in the Mediterranean area as a shrub or small tree of no more than three metres in height. Modern scientific research has shown that chaste tree seed possesses mild contraceptive properties and, although it appears not to damp the libido, it does allow for chasteness in the sense of not being pregnant (Riddle 1992: 31 and 35–6). For this very reason the women of Athens used to put sprays of chaste tree under their beds during the festival of the Thesmophoria (Riddle 1992: 61 and von Staden 1992: 36–40).

8 ON THE POWERS OF FOODS: BOOK 2 (6.554–659K)

1 By AD 100 the Dog Star (or Sirius) was rising at the end of July (Grant 1997: 157-8). This was the hottest part of the year. Alcaeus (quoted by Ath.1.22e–f) wrote: 'Wet your lungs with wine, because the Dog Star is rising, a tough time, everything parched with the burning heat.'

2 *On the Temperaments*: See Singer 1997a: 202–89, especially 283ff: 'one should constantly bear in mind that each body possesses some peculiarity of mixture

which belongs to its own specific nature but differs from any other specific nature.'

3 The history of the large gourd, watermelon and melon proper is described by Sallares 1991: 483. Probably to begin with domesticated melons were green-fruited and so were inferior to modern melons in taste and texture.

4 In many ways this story shows how Galen's view of the correct method of medical inquiry was 'demonstrative', proceeding as it were from first principles which required no demonstration, to conclusions which correspond to reality (see Brunt 1994: 51). Thus fish-sauce is assumed 'naturally' to relax the stomach when taken at the start of a meal, although no test is set up to verify this assertion. Expanding on this theme, von Staden (1975: 192) argued that ancient scientific inquiry moved towards experimental passivity, that is a random trying out of similars without any attempt at understanding why or how similar things either have similar effects or are affected similarly.

5 Gal.*San.Tuend.*6.15 =6.450-1K 'after taking two Roman pints of apple juice, you must mix with this an equal quantity of the finest possible honey and one and a half pints of vinegar; simmer gently over hot coals and, after skimming, mix in three ounces of ginger, two of white pepper and simmer once again until the consistency of honey.'

6 Hp.*Epid.*2.2=5.84L.

7 For the word cardialgia: the upper entrance to the stomach still bears the name 'cardia' because of the difficulty in differentiating between pain of the heart and pain at the end of the stomach.

8 *Zizyphus vulgaris* Lmk.=*Zizyphus jujuba* arrived in Syria from Japan via Persia in the early first century AD. In taste the fruit resembles a date.

9 The fruit does not have any seeds inside and the tree resembles a mulberry in foliage, size and appearance.

10 Citron was the only citrus fruit in the ancient world; it resembles a large knobbly lemon and is still grown in the Mediterranean for candying (see Grant 1997: 193–7).

11 When forced through shortage of food: food supplies could be erratic, especially for those in the countryside who often had no recourse to the stockpiles of wheat maintained in the cities. See Garnsey 1988, especially 8–16 on the frequency of food crises and 43–86 on the relationship between peasant and urban communities.

12 Purslane (*Portulaca sativa*) can be used for external application in inflammation and sores (Grieve 1931: 660–1).

13 The whole plant (*Solanum nigrum L*) can be gathered in early autumn and dried. In some countries the fresh leaves are eaten in place of spinach. The berries sometimes have bad effects on children (Grieve 1931: 582–3).

14 This is a rare mention of what is now one of the standard Mediterranean herbs. In antiquity, however, it was thought to nurture scorpions (Grant 1999: 103).

15 Even if they understand this about Plato: Galen ranked Plato as second only to Hippocrates, although he held that those who called themselves Platonists did not understand Plato's view of the relation of the soul and the body. Galen in fact went further than this and stated that Plato lifted his most important ideas from Hippocrates (De Lacy 1972 and Smith 1979: 86).

16 The Romans were usually wary of mushrooms. Numerous stories were told of people dying from unintentionally eating poisonous varieties (Plin.*Nat.* 22.92–99, Juv.5.146-8, Sen.77.18 'You are frightened of death – but how can you be frightened of it in the middle of a "fungifest"?'

9 ON THE POWERS OF FOODS: BOOK 3 (6.660–748K)

1 Cf. Petr.66.6 where Scintilla, on tasting bear meat, almost vomited up her own guts.

2 Galen used the term glands generically to describe various anatomical structures which both appear and feel spongy. He classified the glands under four headings: unifunctional (e.g. salivary, intestinal, thyroid and seminal), dual mechanical in that support and protection are offered (e.g. pancreas), trifunctional with nourishing, protecting and supporting processes (e.g. mesenteric lymph nodes and thymus) and finally a type of glandular body that occurred in groups to which he gave no name (today these are called lymph glands). See Marmelzat 1991. A culinary translation would give 'sweetbreads', but the English term seems too specialised in this context.

3 Roman pasta was fried and then added to a sauce. It was in medieval Italian cooking that pasta first came to be cooked directly in a stock or sauce (Grant 1999: 95).

4 Dilute wine should be used for rinsing the mouth: the astringency of the wine was presumably thought to counteract the oiliness of the milk. A similar principle is seen at work with a toothpaste formula given by Galen (*Comp.Med.Sec.Loc.5.5*=12.884–6K) where the hard and dry ingredients act sympathetically on hard and dry teeth (see P. T. Keyser, 'Science and magic in Galen's recipes (sympathy and efficacy)', in Debru 1997: 194).

5 The soft flesh of rock fish enabled them to be digested easily and for their substance to disappear in sweat without harming the kidneys (Diphilus of Siphnos quoted by Ath. 8.355a-357a, Gal.*Meth.Med.* 8.2=10.537K).

6 Mount Libanus: a mountain range to the east of Beirut. V. Nutton ('Galen and the traveller's fare', in Wilkins *et al.* 1995: 365) mentions the honeydew that was reported to collect there, but does not give an explanation for the phenomenon. Amyntas (quoted by Ath. 11.500d) relates how honeydew was exuded from the leaves of certain oak trees. These leaves were collected and pressed together into balls. Wine could be sweetened by maturing such a ball of leaves in it before drinking. Zeus was connected with honey, for he was given the epithet 'Meilichios' ('meli' meaning 'honey' in Greek) and as such was worshipped by the Athenians at the festival of Diasia (Thuc.1.126.6).

7 On wine in Greek medicine see Jouanna 1996.

EDITIONS AND
TRANSLATIONS OF
ANCIENT AUTHORS

All references to ancient authors have been made according to the standard abbreviations as listed in Lewis and Short's *Latin Dictionary* and Liddell and Scott's *Greek Lexicon*. For the guidance of readers these abbreviations are cited below in square brackets. When referring to works by Galen and Hippocrates, the usual convention has been followed of listing the volume and page numbers of the Kühn (denoted by K) and Littre (denoted by L) editions respectively.

[Apic.] Apicius, *The Roman Cookery Book*, edited and translated by B. Flower and E. Rosenbaum (1958), London: Harrap.

[Ath.] Athenaeus, *The Deipnosophists*, translated by C. B. Gulick (1927–41), Cambridge, Mass./London: Loeb Classical Library.

[Cic.ND] Cicero, *On the Nature of the Gods*, translated by H. Rackham (1933), Cambridge, Mass./London: Loeb Classical Library.

[Dsc.] Dioscorides, *De Materia Medica*, edited by M. Wellmann (1906–14), Berlin: Weidmann.

[Gal.] Galen, *Opera Omnia*, edited by C. G. Kühn (1965 reprint of 1823 edition), Hildesheim: Georg Olms:
[AA] *On Anatomical Procedures* (see under C. Singer in main bibliography).
[Alim.fac.] *On the Powers of Foods*, 6.453–748K (translated in this volume).
[Atr.Bil.] *On Black Bile*, 5.104–48K (translated in this volume).
[Caus.Morb.] *On the Causes of Disease*, 7.1–41K (translated in this volume).
[Caus.Symp.] *On the Causes of Symptoms*, 7.85–272K.
[Comp.Med.Sec.Loc.] *Medical Compounds according to Places*, 12.378–1003K and 13.1–361K.
[Elem.] *On Elements*, 1.413–508K.
[Hp.Aph.Comm.] *Commentary on Hippocrates' Aphorisms*, 17B.345–887K.
[Inaeq.Int.] *On Uneven Bad Temperament*, 7.733–752K (translated in this volume).
[Lib.Prop.] *On my own Books*, 19.8–48K.

[*Meth.Med.*] *On the Healing Method*, 10.1–1021K.

[*Nat.fac.*] *On the Natural Faculties*, 2.1–204K (see under A.J. Brock in main bibliography).

[*Praen.*] *On Prognosis*, 14.599–673K (see under V. Nutton in main bibliography).

[*Ptis.*] *On Barley Soup*, 6.816–31K (translated in this volume).

[*San.Tuend.*] *On the Preservation of Health*, 6.1–452K.

[*Simpl.Med.*] *On Simple Medicines*, 11.359–892K and 12.1.377K.

[*Us.Part.*] *On the Use of the Parts*, 3.1–933K.

—— *De Ptisana, De Alimentorum Facultatibus*, edited by K. Koch, G. Helmreich, C. Karbfleisch and O. Hartlich (1923), Corpus Medicorum Graecorum 5.4.2, Leipzig: Teubner.

[Hdt.] Herodotus, *Historiae*, edited by C. Hude (1916), Oxford: Oxford University Press.

—— *Histories*, translated by A. de Selincourt and revised by A. R. Burn (1972), Harmondsworth: Penguin.

[Hes.*Op.*] Hesiod, *Works and Days*, edited by M. L. West (1978), Oxford: Oxford University Press.

—— *Hesiod and Theognis*, translated by D. Wender, (1973), Harmondsworth: Penguin.

[Hp.] Hippocrates, translated by W. H. S. Jones, E. T. Withington and P. Potter (1923–88), Cambridge, Mass./London: Loeb Classical Library:

[*Acut.*] *Diet in Acute Diseases*, vol. 2: 63–125.

[*Aer.*] *Airs, Waters, Places*, vol. 1: 71–137.

[*Alim.*] *Food*, vol. 1: 343–361.

[*Aph.*] *Aphorisms*, vol. 4: 99–221.

[*Epid.*] *Epidemics*, vol. 1: 147–287.

[*Hum.*] *Humours*, vol. 4: 63–95.

[*Loc.Hom.*] *Places in Man*, see edition by E. M. Craik in main bibliography.

[*Nat.Hom.*] *Nature of Man*, vol. 4: 3–41.

[*Prog.*] *Prognosis*, vol. 2: 7–55.

[*Vict.*] *Diet*, vol. 4: 225–447.

—— *Oeuvres Complètes d'Hippocrate*, edited by E. Littre (1839), Paris: Baille.

[Hom.*Od.*] Homer, *Odyssea*, edited by T. W. Allen (1908), Oxford: Oxford University Press.

—— *Odyssey*, translated by W. Shewring (1980), Oxford: Oxford University Press.

[Hom.*Il.*] Homer, *Ilias*, edited by T. W. Allen (1902), Oxford: Oxford University Press.

—— *Iliad*, translated by E. V. Rieu (1950), Harmondsworth: Penguin.

[Juv.] Juvenal, *The Satires*, edited by J. Ferguson (1979), Walton-on-Thames: Nelson.

[Orib.] Oribasius, *Collectionum Medicarum Reliquiae*, edited by J. Raeder (1928–1933), Corpus Medicorum Graecorum 6.2.1–2, Leipzig: Teubner.

[Petr.] Petronius, *Satyricon*, translated by M. Heseltine and W. H. D. Rouse (1969), revised edition, Cambridge, Mass./London: Loeb Classical Library.

[Plin.*Nat.*] Pliny, *Natural History*, translated by H. Rackham, W. H. S. Jones and D. E. Eichholz (1938–1962), Cambridge, Mass./London: Loeb Classical Library.

[Plu.*Mor.*] Plutarch, *Moralia*, translated by E. L. Minar, W. C. Helmbold, P. A. Clement and H. B. Hoffleit (1961–69), especially 'Table Talk' in vol. 8 (612b–697c) and vol. 9 (697c–748d), Cambridge, Mass./London: Loeb Classical Library.

[Scrib.Larg.] Scribonius Largus, *Compositiones*, edited by S. Sconocchia (1983), Leipzig: Teubner.

[Sen.*Ben.*] Seneca, *On Benefits*, translated by J. W. Basore (1935), Cambridge, Mass./London: Loeb Classical Library.

[Sen.*Ep.*] Seneca, *Letters*, translated by R. M. Gummere (1917–25), Cambridge, Mass./London: Loeb Classical Library.

[Sor.] Soranus, *Gynaecology*, translated by O. Temkin (1956), Baltimore: Johns Hopkins University Press.

[Thphr.*HP*] Theophrastus, *Enquiry into Plants*, translated by A. Holt (1908), Cambridge, Mass./London 1916.

[Thuc.] Thucydides, *History of the Peloponnesian War*, translated by C. F. Smith (1919–23), Cambridge, Mass./London: Loeb Classical Library.

BIBLIOGRAPHY

Amouretti, M-C. and Comet, G. (eds) (1993) *Des Hommes et des Plantes: Plantes Méditerranéennes, Vocabulaire et Usages Anciens*, Aix-en-Provence: Université de Provence.

André, J. (1974) *Apicius: L'Art Culinaire*, Paris: Les Belles Lettres.

—— (1981) *L'Alimentation et la Cuisine à Rome*, 2nd edn, Paris: Les Belles Lettres.

Baldwin, B. (1996) 'Sordid bread: more food for thought', *Hermes* 124: 127–9.

Barton, C. A. (1993) *The Sorrows of the Ancient Romans: The Gladiator and the Monster*, Princeton: Princeton University Press.

Bertier, J. (1972) *Mnésithée et Dieuchès*, Leiden: Brill.

Bio, A. M. I. (1987) *De Bonis Malisque Sucis*, Radici 8, Napoli: D'Auria.

Boulogne, J. (1997) 'L'apport de Galien à la méthode médicale', *Revue des Études Grecques* 110: 126–42.

Boys-Stones, G. (1997) 'Plutarch on the probable principle of cold: epistemology and the *De Primo Frigido*', *Classical Quarterly* 47: 227–38.

Brain, P. (1986) *Galen On Bloodletting: A Study of the Origins, Development and Validity of His Opinions, with a Translation of the Three Works*, Cambridge: Cambridge University Press.

Brock, A. J. (1916) *Galen On the Natural Faculties*, Cambridge, Mass.: Harvard University Press.

—— (1929) *Greek Medicine*, London: Dent.

Brunt, P. A. (1994) 'The bubble of the Second Sophistic', *Bulletin of the Institute of Classical Studies* 31: 25–52.

Byl, S. (1996) 'Vieillir et être vieux dans l'Antiquité', *Les Études Classiques* 64: 261–71.

Calderini, I. G. G. (1986) *Nobilità delle Arti*, Radici 6, Napoli: D'Auria

Calogiuri, P. (1997) 'Il mal di testa nel *Corpus Hippocraticum*', *Rudiae* 9: 77–88.

Craik, E. M. (1998) *Hippocrates: Places in Man, Edited and Translated with Introduction and Commentary*, Oxford: Clarendon.

Dalby, A. (1996) *Siren Feasts: A History of Food and Gastronomy in Greece*, London: Routledge.

De Lacy, P. (1972) 'Galen's Platonism', *American Journal of Philology* 93: 27–39.

Debru, A. (ed.) (1997) *Galen on Pharmacology: Philosophy, History, Medicine*, Proceedings of the Fifth International Galen Colloquium, Leiden: Brill.

Durling, R. J. (1993) *A Dictionary of Medical Terms in Galen*, Leiden: Brill.

Edelstein, L. (1967) *Ancient Medicine*, Baltimore: Johns Hopkins University Press.

Edlow, R. E. (1977) *Galen on Language and Ambiguity: An English Translation of Galen's 'De Captionibus (On Fallacies)' with Introduction, Text and Commentary*, Leiden: Brill.

Furley, D. J. and Wilkie, J. S. (1984) *Galen On Respiration and the Arteries: An Edition with English Translation and Commentary of De Usu Respirationis, An in Arteriis Natura Sanguis Contineatur, De Usu Pulsuum, and De Causis Respirationis*, Princeton: Princeton University Press.

Garnsey, P. (1988) *Famine and Food Supply in the Graeco-Roman World: Responses to Risk and Crisis*, Cambridge: Cambridge University Press.

Garofalo, I. (1997) *Anonymi Medici De Morbis Acutis et Chroniis*, Leiden: Brill.

Grant, M. D. (1996) *Anthimus: On the Observance of Food*, Totnes: Prospect.

—— (1997) *Dieting for an Emperor: A Translation of Books 1 and 4 of Oribasius' Medical Compilations with an Introduction and Commentary*, Leiden: Brill.

—— (1999) *Roman Cookery: Ancient Recipes for Modern Kitchens*, London: Serif.

—— (forthcoming) 'Dietetic responses in Galen to madness', *Classical Bulletin*.

Grieve, M. (1931) *A Modern Herbal: The Medicinal, Culinary, Cosmetic and Economic Properties, Cultivation and Folklore of Herbs, Grasses, Fungi, Shrubs and Trees with all their Modern Scientific Uses*, London: Cape (reprinted 1976, Harmondsworth: Penguin).

Grmek, M. D. (1983) *Les Maladies à l'Aube de la Civilisation Occidentale: Recherches sur la Réalité Pathologique dans le Monde Grec Préhistorique, Archaïque et Classique*, Paris: Payot.

—— (ed.) (1995) *Histoire de la Pensée Médicale en Occident: Antiquité et Moyen Age*, Paris: Seuil.

Hankinson, R. J. (1991) *Galen On the Therapeutic Method Books I and II*, Oxford: Clarendon.

—— (1998) *Galen On Antecedent Causes*, Cambridge: Cambridge University Press.

Holman, S. R. (1997) 'Moulded as wax: formation and feeding of the ancient newborn', *Helios* 24: 77–95.

Jackson, R. (1988) *Doctors and Diseases in the Roman Empire*, London: British Museum.

Joly, R. and Byl, S. (1984) *Hippocrate Du Regime*, Berlin: Akademie-Verlag.

Jouanna, J. (1975) *Hippocrate: La Nature de l'Homme*, Berlin: Akademie-Verlag.

—— (1996) 'Le vin et la médicine dans la Grèce ancienne', *Revue des Études Grecques* 109: 410–34.

Kagan, J. (1994) *Galen's Prophecy: Temperament in Human Nature*, New York: Westview.

Kollesch, J. and Nickel, D. (eds) (1993) *Galen und das Hellenistische Erbe*, Stuttgart: Franz Steiner.

Langholf, V. (1990) *Medical Theories in Hippocrates: Early Texts and the 'Epidemics'*, Berlin/New York: de Gruyter.

Lascaratos, J. and Marketos, S. (1997) 'The fatal disease of the Byzantine Emperor Andronicus III Palaeologus (1328–1341)', *Journal of the Royal Society of Medicine* 90: 106–9.

Lloyd, G. E. R. (1975) 'A note on Erasistratus of Ceos', *Journal of Hellenic Studies* 95: 172–5.

Marmelzat, W. L. (1991) 'Galen on "glands" and "spongy flesh": with special reference to an ancient mechanico-biophysical theory for superficial lymph node function', *Journal of the History of Medicine and Allied Sciences* 46: 419–39.

Mazzini, I. (1997) *La Medicina dei Greci e dei Romani: Letteratura, Lingua, Scienza*, Rome: Jouvence.

Mewaldt, J. (1914) *Galeni In Hippocratis de Natura Hominis Commentaria Tria*, Corpus Medicorum Graecorum 5.9.1, Leipzig: Teubner.

Moraux, P. (1985) *Galien de Pergame: Souvenirs d'un Médicin*, Paris: Les Belles Lettres.

Nutton, V. (1979) *Galen On Prognosis*, Berlin: Akademie-Verlag.

—— (ed.) (1981) *Galen: Problems and Prospects*, London: Wellcome Institute.

—— (1985) 'The drug trade in antiquity', *Journal of the Royal Society of Medicine* 73: 138–45.

Phillips, E. D. (1973) *Greek Medicine*, London: Thames and Hudson.

Plastira-Valkanou, M. (1998) 'Medicine and fine cuisine in Plato's *Gorgias*', *L'Antiquité Classique* 67: 195–201.

Riddle, J. M. (1985) *Dioscorides On Pharmacy and Medicine*, Austin: University of Texas Press.

—— (1992) *Contraception and Abortion from the Ancient World to the Renaissance*, Cambridge, Mass.: Harvard University Press.

Roques, D. (1993) 'Médecine et botanique: le siphion dans l'oeuvre d'Oribase', *Revue des Études Grecques* 106: 380–99.

Rundin, J. (1998) 'The vegetarianism of Empedocles in its historical context', *The Ancient World* 29: 19–36.

Sallares, R. (1991) *The Ecology of the Ancient Greek World*, Ithaca: Cornell University Press.

Scarborough, J. (1969) *Roman Medicine*, Ithaca: Cornell University Press.

Scheidel, W. (1995) 'The most silent women of Greece and Rome: rural labour and women's life in the ancient world', *Greece and Rome* 42: 202–17.

Schmidt, A. (1964) *Ps.-Galeni Liber de Humoribus Critice Editus, Adnotationibus Instructus,* unpublished Ph.D. thesis, Gottingen.

Siegel, R.E. (1968) *Galen's System of Physiology and Medicine*, Basle: Karger.

—— (1976) *Galen On the Affected Parts*, Basle: Karger.

Singer, C. (1956) *Galen On Anatomical Procedures*, Oxford: Oxford University Press.

Singer, P. N. (1997a) *Galen: Selected Works*, Oxford: Oxford University Press.

—— (1997b) 'Levels of explanation in Galen', *Classical Quarterly* 47: 525–542

Smith, W. D. (1979) *The Hippocratic Tradition*, Ithaca: Cornell University Press.

—— (1982) 'Erasistratus's dietetic medicine', *Bulletin of the History of Medicine* 56: 398–409.

Sorabji, R. (ed.) (1997) *Aristotle and After,* Bulletin of the Institute of Classical Studies Supplement 68, London: Institute of Classical Studies.

Spurr, M. S. (1986) *Arable Cultivation in Roman Italy c. 200 BC–c. AD 200*, London: Society for the Promotion of Roman Studies.

Temkin, O. (1973) *Galenism: Rise and Decline of a Medical Philosophy*, Ithaca: Cornell University Press.

—— (1991) *Hippocrates in a World of Pagans and Christians*, Baltimore: Johns Hopkins University Press.

Tieleman, T. (1996) *Galen and Chrysippus On the Soul: Argument and Refutation in the* De Placitis *II–III*, Leiden: Brill.

Touwaide, A. (1997) 'Une note sur la thériaque attribuée à Galien', *Byzantion* 67: 439–79.

van der Eijk, P. J. (ed.) (1999) *Ancient Histories of Medicine: Essays in Medical Doxography and Historiography in Classical Antiquity*, Leiden: Brill.

van der Eijk, P. J., Horstmanshoff, H. F. J. and Schrijvers, P. H. (eds) (1995) *Ancient Medicine in its Socio-Economic Context*, Amsterdam: Rodopi.

von Staden, H. (1975) 'Experiment and experience in Hellenistic medicine', *Bulletin of the Institute of Classical Studies* 22: 178–99.

—— (1992) 'Spiderwoman and the chaste tree: the semantics of matter', *Configurations* 1: 23–56.

Walzer, R. and Frede, M. (1985) *Galen: Three Treatises On the Nature of Science*, Indianapolis: Hackett.

Wasserstein, A. (1982) *Galen's Commentary on the Hippocratic Treatise* Airs, Waters, Places *in the Hebrew Translation of Solomon ha-Me'ati*, Jerusalem: Israel Academy of Sciences and Humanities.

Weidemann, T. (1992) *Emperors and Gladiators*, London: Routledge.

Wilkins, J., Harvey D., and Dobson M. (eds) (1995), *Food in Antiquity*, Exeter: University of Exeter Press.

Yuge, T. and Doi, M. (eds) (1988) *Forms of Control and Subordination in Antiquity*, Leiden: Brill.

INDEX